The Japanese American Cases

LANDMARK LAW CASES
&
AMERICAN SOCIETY
Peter Charles Hoffer
N. E. H. Hull
Series Editors

For a complete list of titles in the series go to www.kansaspress.ku.edu

ROGER DANIELS

The Japanese American Cases

The Rule of Law in Time of War

UNIVERSITY PRESS OF KANSAS

Published by the University Press of Kansas (Lawrence, Kansas 66045),
which was organized by the Kansas Board of Regents and is operated
and funded by Emporia State University, Fort Hays State University,
Kansas State University, Pittsburg State University, the University of Kansas,
and Wichita State University

Library of Congress Cataloging-in-Publication Data
Daniels, Roger, author.
The Japanese American cases : the rule of law in time of war / Roger Daniels.
pages cm.—(Landmark law cases and American society)
Includes bibliographical references and index.
ISBN 978-0-7006-1925-2 (hardback)—ISBN 978-0-7006-1926-9 (paper)
1. Japanese Americans—Legal status, laws, etc.—History—20th century.
2. Japanese Americans—Evacuation and relocation, 1942–1945.
3. World War, 1939–1945—Law and legislation—United States. I. Title.
KF7224.5.D36 2013
341.6'7—dc23
2013032144

British Library Cataloguing-in-Publication Data is available.

Printed in the United States of America

10 9 8 7 6 5 4 3 2 1

The paper used in this publication is recycled and contains 30 percent
postconsumer waste. It is acid free and meets the minimum requirements
of the American National Standard for Permanence of Paper for
Printed Library Materials z39.48-1992.

FOR MY GRANDSON, NOLAN ARTHUR ARMSTRONG DANIELS

B. AUGUST 23, 2005   WITH LOVE AND HIGH HOPES

IN MEMORY OF

HENRY R. WINKLER, 1916–2012

SCHOLAR, CITIZEN, FRIEND

CONTENTS

Are the laws silent in time of war? The federal Constitution does not die when the United States goes to war. In fact, the Constitution provides for wartime exigency, for example, allowing Congress to suspend the writ of habeas corpus in time of war or civil insurrection. But nothing in the Constitution itself permits the wholesale denial of civil rights and liberties associated with citizenship simply on the basis of the ancestry of a group. The Fourteenth Amendment defined citizenship in simple terms—birth in the United States or naturalization. Despite these solemn and celebrated texts, at the beginning of World War II, Congress, the president, the departments of state and war, and the US Army agreed that native-born Japanese men, women, and children residing on the West Coast could be forcibly removed from their homes and "relocated" to prison camps in the desert and the mountains of the West. Relocation itself was not unprecedented—the removal of Indians from their ancestral lands to "reservations" in Oklahoma and elsewhere during the nineteenth century was a national disgrace. Then, the Supreme Court rejected the dispossession of the Indians, to no avail. In the Japanese internment cases described here in movingly frank detail, the Supreme Court dodged its duty to interpret the Constitution, allowing racism and irrational fears to perpetrate another national tragedy.

Roger Daniels is one of the country's foremost historians of immigration and ethnicity. The tale he tells here is not just one of law. It is the story of a people who sought the American dream in a new land, built businesses, and started families, who truly loved their adopted country, and found how unmerited prejudice can turn a democracy into an engine of injustice. Men of goodwill in the federal government set aside their qualms or remained quiet as the injustice spread across the West Coast. When a relative handful of the internees brought lawsuits to protest their treatment, federal judges found claims of national security outweighed constitutional rights. From the bench a few judges and justices spoke out against the relocation, but they were the minority. Daniels tracks the cases from the decisions of individual counsel who had the courage to buck the White House all the way to the high court. He takes us behind the scenes at the Marble Palace in the District of Columbia, where the justices deliberated. He uncovers the machinations of those who concealed information that would have shown the relocation was never a military necessity. He compares the fate of the continental Japanese Americans with those who lived, and were never interned, on the Hawaiian Islands.

Daniels does not close his account with the outcome of the constitutional cases. He follows the story to reparations for those wrongly interned and reminds us that not all the internees were docile or obedient. What is even more important, he brings the story of the camps to life, adding vital human context to the legal challenges. There are other accounts of these cases, but none any more essential reading than this. For Daniels understands that the law is about people, and that is a lesson we must never forget.

ACKNOWLEDGMENTS

Although it does not take a village to make a book, scholarship in the Internet age has become more collaborative. My chief intellectual debts incurred in writing this book are to Barbara Takei, who modified my views about the camp at Tule Lake, and to Peter Irons's trailblazing scholarship since 1983, as noted in the text. I profited greatly from critical readings of the first two chapters by Eric Muller and of single chapters by Eileen Tamura and by Anna Tamura, who are not related.

Harry and Jane Scheiber were gracious hosts when I put forth the nucleus of this book in a Constitution Day lecture at Berkeley in 2010. Although I am now separated from my home university by two-thirds of a continent, University of Cincinnati librarians Sally Moffitt and Dan Gottlieb, and James Hart of the university's law library, each provided key assistance. Another continuing source of information and consistently good advice is Art Hansen. A great advantage of being in the Pacific Northwest, apart from the presence of my grandsons and their parents, is the ability to draw upon the wisdom, assets, and friendship of Tom Ikeda, whose Densho team is creating the outstanding online archive of Japanese American history and culture. Among those who have assisted me in the creation of the book in hand are Jasmine Alinder, Margo Anderson, Allan W. Austin, Lori Bannai, Tom Crouch, Stan Falk, Art Hansen, Don Hata, Lane Hirabayashi, John Howard, Kris Lindenmeyer, Karen Korematsu, Dale Minami, Brian Niiya, Dwight Pitcaithley, Greg Robinson, Linda Tamura, Tetsuden Kashima, and Allan Winkler.

At the University Press of Kansas, Mike Briggs commissioned what became this book in 2003 and waited, patiently, until I cleared my desk of prior commitments. Once the actual writing began, in 2012, he provided counsel and encouragement. Peter Hoffer was a supportive series editor. In the production process Production Editor Kelly Chrisman Jacques guided the flow with clarity, dispatch, and occasional humor; Susan Ecklund edited the copy and Mary Brooks read proof without unnecessary fuss; and Kathleen Rocheleau provided a useful index. I was particularly pleased with Art Director Karl Janssen's choice of the Lange image for the cover, and I hope that

Publicity Manager Rebecca Murray Schuler and Marketing Director Mike Kehoe persuade lots of folks to buy the book.

Finally, and most important, I attest that for more than half a century, Judith, on an almost daily basis, and in crisis times almost hourly, has interrupted her own work and leisure to listen, read, react, mark up, and counsel. She has been an integral part of whatever bears my name.

AUTHOR'S PREFACE

This account of the Japanese American cases of 1942–1944 and 1983–1987 is also a partial account of the ordeal of the Japanese American community and its partially successful struggle to obtain a kind of justice from the government that had grievously inflicted unearned punishments upon it. The book is thus also a history of the public reputation of Japanese Americans, a task I began with the publication of *The Politics of Prejudice* in 1962. In that half century a civil and human rights revolution took place that has largely removed statutory discriminations based on race. While the current celebratory recognition of its accomplishments focuses, understandably, on its effects—or lack of them—on and by African Americans, the revolution affected and improved the legal status of all persons of color, while leaving the socioeconomic status of most such persons largely unchanged.

PROLOGUE

As World War II was coming to an end, Eugene V. Rostow (1913–2002), an assistant professor in the Yale Law School, published two articles, one in his school's law review, the other in *Harper's* magazine, in which he coined the term the "Japanese American cases." He addressed only the four Supreme Court cases stemming from President Franklin Delano Roosevelt's Executive Order 9066 of February 19, 1942, which, with other edicts and statutes, enabled the now infamous wartime incarceration of 120,000 Japanese Americans, more than two-thirds of them American citizens.

In this book I use Rostow's phrase, which has become part of our common language, to analyze not only those cases but also a much wider range of cases in federal courts involving military service, citizenship, loyalty, damages, and redress, as well as statutes and other political actions stemming from those cases in the sixty-eight years since Rostow wrote. As Rostow hoped to influence public opinion—and clearly did so—I also will consider how all the cases shaped and were shaped by public opinion. This is, in the final analysis, the story of the encounters of one American ethnic group with American racism as reflected in legal activities by all three branches of the federal government. The cases have been so essential in the evolution of the Japanese American community that the following account is, in part, a pocket history of Japanese Americans.

I can think of no more appropriate way to begin than to quote the forward-looking concluding paragraphs of Rostow's "Our Worst Wartime Mistake," published in *Harper's* for September 1945:

> Three chief forms of reparation are available, and should be pursued. The first is the inescapable obligation of the federal government to protect the civil rights of Japanese-Americans against organized and unorganized hooliganism. If local law enforcement fails, federal prosecutions under the nation's Civil Rights Act should be undertaken.
>
> Secondly, generous financial indemnity should be sought. Apart from the sufferings of their imprisonment, the Japanese-Americans have sustained heavy property losses from their evacuation.

Finally, the basic issues should be presented to the Supreme Court again, in an effort to obtain a prompt reversal of these wartime cases. The Supreme Court has often corrected its own errors in the past, especially when that error was occasioned by the excitement of a tense moment. After the end of the Civil War, several earlier decisions were reversed by *Ex Parte Milligan*. The famous flag-salute case of 1940 has recently been overruled in the decision of *West Virginia v. Barnett*. Similar public expiation in the case of the Japanese-Americans would be good for the court, and for the country.

CHAPTER ONE

The Facts behind the Cases

In the spring of 1942, four young Nisei, second-generation Japanese Americans, acted to institute the lawsuits that became the Japanese American Cases. The litigants, Minoru Yasui (1916–1986), Gordon K. Hirabayashi (1918–2012), Fred T. Korematsu (1919–2005), and Mitsuye Endo (1920–2006), chose to resist government oppression in test cases. They challenged the constitutionality of federal government actions, which, as an alleged matter of "military necessity," deprived them and some 70,000 other American citizens of their liberty solely on the basis of their ancestry. All in their twenties, these four were not initially aware of one another and received little support from the institutions of their own ethnic community or from those of the larger society that should have been sympathetic to their cause. The American Civil Liberties Union (ACLU) initially promised support for one of the cases but quickly withdrew it; a number of individual attorneys associated with the ACLU's West Coast chapters did provide counsel. In 1943, when the cases began to reach the Supreme Court, the national body did file amicus briefs in favor of the litigants, but during the crucial ten weeks after Pearl Harbor it made no public attack on government actions or rhetoric directed against Japanese Americans. As this volume went to press in 2013, the ACLU was still lying about its shameful role in the Japanese American Cases; its official website claimed:

> The ACLU, led by its California affiliates, stood alone in speaking out about this atrocity. Arrayed against the four protesting Nisei in the spring of 1942 were not only the power of the United States Government but the all but unanimous force of public opinion outraged by a "dastardly attack" by "naval and air forces of the Empire of Japan" on American naval and military bases in and around Honolulu on December 7, 1941. The one significant orga-

nization of the Nisei generation, whose leaders were appalled that their government refused to recognize their constitutional rights to liberty and equal protection under the law, nevertheless chose not to protest and went on to attack the Nisei litigants and others who urged protest if not resistance.

Although the Pearl Harbor attack was a surprise, war with Japan had long been anticipated. Even before World War I, American military authorities had identified Japan as the most probable Pacific enemy. The Soviet dictator V. I. Lenin had noted in 1920 that Japan and America "cannot live in peace on the shores of the Pacific although those shores are three thousand versts apart. . . . That war is brewing, that war is inevitable, is beyond doubt."

Before that, Japan's stunning defeat of czarist Russia in 1904–1905 had served notice that it was a force to be reckoned with, and three successive American presidents—Theodore Roosevelt, William Howard Taft, and Woodrow Wilson—made serious efforts to lessen trans-Pacific tensions. But significant and persistent issues remained between Tokyo and Washington.

American expansion across the Pacific as a result of the Spanish American War of 1898 created an overseas American empire whose western Pacific outposts, particularly Guam and the Philippines, were places that Tokyo felt ought to be within its own sphere of influence. Washington soon discovered that defending the Philippines from a possible Japanese attack would require a large permanent military presence in the islands that was far beyond what American politics would permit. The Filipinos were thus promised eventual independence; legislation passed by Congress in 1934 provided that the Philippines would become independent on July 4, 1945.

Another bone of contention between the Pacific rivals was the American Open Door policy which held that all modern nations should have equal rights in exploiting China; Japan insisted that it, as the most powerful East Asian nation, should have special rights there. When World War I broke out, Japan, long allied with Britain, quickly declared war on Germany and seized its territories in China and its small island possessions in the South Pacific. It also issued the Twenty-One Demands on China for further concessions. One of Japan's rationales for its policies was that it merely wished to exercise the same kind of oversight in East and Southeast Asia that the United States exercised in the Western Hemisphere. At the 1919 Versailles Peace Conference, President Wilson and Japan's delegates clashed over Japan's demands on China.

A further issue was created by American immigration and naturalization policies. Until 1882 there were no restrictions on the immigration of free persons to the United States; in that year Congress passed the Chinese Exclusion Act, initiating a seventy-year period of explicit racial discrimination in American immigration law. By the turn of the century there was an increasing call for a similar prohibition against Japanese immigrants. This created one of Tokyo's worst nightmares: it was convinced that a Japanese Exclusion Act would be detrimental to its aspirations for great power status. During a quarter century Japanese and American diplomats made arrangements such as the Gentlemen's Agreement of 1907–1908 under which the Japanese government regulated and diminished immigration from Japan, and the United States refrained from measures directed specifically against Japanese. In 1924 Congress, against the wishes of the State Department, abrogated the agreement unilaterally by banning any further immigration by aliens ineligible for citizenship, which included Japanese.

None of the Japanese who immigrated to the United States in that era could become naturalized citizens because naturalization was limited by statute to "white persons" and those of African birth or origin until 1952. An acculturated Japanese immigrant, Takeo Ozawa (b. 1875), filed a suit contesting the naturalization statute's color bar, which a unanimous Supreme Court rejected in *Ozawa v. US* (1922). But because the Fourteenth Amendment to the Constitution, in creating a national citizenship in 1868, had specified that "all persons born . . . in the United States . . . are citizens of the United States and the state in which they reside," the children of immigrants, including our Nisei litigants, were birthright citizens and entitled to all the rights and protections granted by the Constitution.

Passage of the 1924 immigration act with its provision barring the immigration of "aliens ineligible to citizenship" took anti-Japanese actions in the United States off the boil but triggered massive anti-American demonstrations in Tokyo and created deep-seated and long-lasting resentment in Japan. Writing in 1950, the diplomat-historian George F. Kennan noted in his provocative *American Diplomacy, 1900–1950* that the "long and unhappy story" of US-Japanese relationships in the twentieth century was constantly worsened by the fact that "we would repeatedly irritate and offend the sensitive Japanese by our immigration policies and the treatment of people of Japanese lineage . . . in this country."

Although a sizable number of Japanese immigrants, discouraged by worsening trans-Pacific relationships, returned to Japan after 1924, many taking US citizen children with them, the Japanese American population continued to grow. The number of Japanese persons in the continental United States grew from 24,000 in 1900 to 127,000 in 1940, and in the territory of Hawaii from 59,000 to 158,000 in the same period. In each place, by 1940 about two-thirds were native-born American citizens, and within the United States all but 15,000 lived in the three West Coast states.

Japanese of both generations represented only 0.09 percent of the American population in 1940, that, is 9 persons in 10,000; in the three Pacific states where their incidence was highest, they were 1.2 percent of the total, 12 persons in 1,000, with a slightly larger reckoning, 14 persons in 1,000, in California. In the multicultural territory of Hawaii, not then generally included in American population data, Japanese were the largest ethnic group, amounting to 37.5 percent of the population, more than 1 person in 3.

Trans-Pacific tensions, which had slackened somewhat in the later 1920s, increased sharply after Japan seized China's rich northeastern province of Manchuria in 1931, renamed it Manchukuo, and installed a member of China's former imperial family as its puppet ruler. In 1936 Tokyo allied itself with Berlin and Rome in a treaty nominally directed against the Soviet Union, and the following year Japan began an undeclared war with China that continued until Japan surrendered to the United States in 1945. The United States verbally opposed Japanese expansion, granted minimal aid and credits to China, and continued to sell much larger amounts of war materials to resource-poor Japan.

After World War II broke out in September 1939, Japan, as it had done in World War I, sought to gain advantages from European distress. Even before France fell in June 1940, Japan pressured French colonial officials in Vietnam—then called French Indochina by Westerners—to cut off rail shipments from Hanoi to China. By September 1940 several thousand Japanese troops had taken up positions in northern Vietnam, and in July 1941, 125,000 Japanese troops took over southern Vietnam. The United States only then cut off all military supplies to Japan and began the long, fruitless negotiations in Washington that ended only on Sunday, December 7, 1941.

While many Japanese Americans were oblivious to world affairs, the two generations reacted differently. The immigrant generation got most of its news from Japanese-language newspapers and radio broadcasts whose major source was Domei, a news service controlled by the Japanese government, and tended to support Japan's expansionist policies. All the institutions of the immigrant community— the associational groups based on place of birth in Japan, the business and professional groups of the *nihonmachi* (Japantowns)—were Japan and Japanese language oriented. Like most other American immigrants, the Issei (first-generation immigrants) continued to support institutions of their native land. Most kept their savings in American branches of Japanese banks. Denied the right of naturalization, the Issei could not become voters. Most trade unions and trade associations of the larger society barred them from membership. If they attended a Buddhist temple, it had been nurtured and supervised by religious organizations in Japan; if they attended a Christian church, the celebrant was likely to be a former missionary and the congregation a segregated one.

Most Nisei, who could neither read Japanese nor understand complex discourse in that language, got their news from American sources. More than most other children of immigrants, they were urged to persist and excel in the public schools, and most acquired American ideals. Japanese American students received academic honors to a much greater degree than their incidence in the school population would have suggested. In Seattle's nine public high schools in 1937, three of the valedictorians and two of the salutatorians were Nisei. Their parents and the ethnic community exulted in their success.

That academic success, which a relatively large percentage of Japanese American students continued in colleges and universities, rarely resulted in the kinds of economic success that white graduates achieved. No public school on the West Coast hired a Nisei teacher until well after World War II. A relatively few Nisei won public employment in civil service jobs, but the vast majority of college graduates either provided professional services for the ethnic community or had to find jobs within the ethnic economy for which they were overqualified. One of the all too accurate stereotypes of Nisei life in the 1930s was the college graduate who managed a fruit stand, often marketing produce grown by members of his family.

By the later 1930s, increasing numbers of Japanese Americans had become anxious about their fate should there be a war with Japan. As one Nisei student at the University of California wrote in a Berkeley magazine in 1937: "What are we going to do if war does break out between the United States and Japan? . . . In common language we can say 'we're sunk.' Even if the Nisei wanted to fight for America, what chances? Not a chance! . . . our properties would be confiscated and most likely [we would be] herded into prison camps—perhaps we would be slaughtered on the spot."

Such extreme fears were not common then, but they were clearly more prevalent in 1941, when a Nisei spoke to a *Los Angeles Times* columnist. After telling him that many if not most of the older generation were pro-Japan, he spoke of his own generation's fears: "We talk of almost nothing but this great crisis. We don't know what's going to happen. Sometimes we only look for a concentration camp."

At the beginning of World War II the United States Government began to make concrete plans appropriate to its neutral status and contingency plans in case it should become involved in the conflict. The immediate task was providing internment facilities for German seamen—and, after Mussolini entered the war in mid-1940, Italian seamen—from vessels whose captains chose to enter or stay in American ports rather than risk almost certain capture by the British navy if they put to sea. More than 1,600 German and Italian seamen plus a few other persons without immigrant status were the only peacetime internees in the United States. They were eventually housed in three existing military facilities under Immigration and Naturalization Service (INS) supervision. In addition, the State Department, which had activated its Special War Problems Division on September 1, 1939, kept a watching brief to make sure that the conditions of confinement comported with the Geneva Convention. After the fall of France in June 1940, amid widely believed false reports that "fifth columnists" had been largely responsible, President Franklin D. Roosevelt publicly transferred the INS from the protective Department of Labor to the prosecutorial Department of Justice (DoJ), signed the Alien Registration Act, and in early September secretly empowered the FBI to investigate foreign espionage and gave it unprecedented authority to wiretap.

The Alien Registration Act for the first time required all resident aliens to register, be fingerprinted, and inform the government of any change of address. Each was issued an identity card, essentially an internal passport that, unlike the draft cards required for all men of military age later that year, they did not have to carry. The alien registration, accomplished at post offices at Roosevelt's insistence, revealed that there were almost 5 million aliens; the INS had anticipated 3.6 million. More than a million—almost 700,000 Italians, more than 300,000 Germans, and 91,000 Japanese—would become enemy aliens after Pearl Harbor. Under existing American law all enemy aliens fourteen years of age and older would be liable to internment at the discretion of the government as "alien enemies."

American security officials, civilian and military, never intended to seize any sizable percentage of the alien enemy population. Their efforts, overseen by a Justice Department and War Department joint committee but largely done within the DoJ, focused on Japanese and Germans. It produced a sizable Custodial Detention List of likely candidates for internment. The list was divided into three categories labeled A, B, and C to indicate presumed importance. The committee's plan was that arrested aliens would eventually be brought before a local Alien Enemy Hearing Board—there were some ninety of them—to tell their stories without counsel; board recommendations were advisory. A final decision in each case would be made by the attorney general. At no time in the period before war came to the United States was there any formal discussion of the incarceration of American citizens.

The attack on Pearl Harbor triggered the planned response. Late that Sunday the first roundups began, and within twenty-four hours the FBI, often aided by local law enforcement, had arrested 1,717 enemy aliens, 1,212 of them Japanese. The authority for this action was contained in three separate presidential proclamations dated December 7 and 8, 1941, as provided for in Title 50 of the US Code. The first stated that "an invasion has been perpetrated upon the territory of the United States by the empire of Japan," while the second and third stated that "an invasion or predatory incursion is threatened" by Germany and Italy. All three went on to describe the conduct required of alien enemies and warned that those "deemed dangerous to the public peace and safety of the United States" were subject to "summary apprehension."

Summary apprehension did not mean automatic internment; perhaps most of the thousands initially arrested were quickly released. The best estimate, by Louis Fiset, is that fewer than 11,000 resident enemy aliens—8,000 Japanese, 2,300 Germans, and 200 Italians—were actually interned. In addition, some 3,100 Japanese nationals, initially rounded up by the army and held by the War Relocation Authority (WRA), were subsequently transferred to the DoJ camps. (The WRA is discussed later in this chapter.) About a thousand enemy diplomats were interned and housed at resort hotels operated by the government until they could be exchanged for American diplomats.

A very different secret State Department program resulted in the rendition of 4,088 Germans, 2,264 Japanese, and 288 Italians from a number of South and Central American nations with Pacific coastlines, to the United States and internment in DoJ camps. Of the Japanese, it is estimated that 80 percent came from Peru. The conditions of confinement in the DoJ camps, for both domestic enemy aliens and those imported, generally met or exceeded the standards called for in the Geneva Convention, although there were instances of brutality, including three homicides committed by guards. There were four homicides committed by soldier's guarding WRA camps.

Except for the harebrained State Department rendition scheme, the government's actions had been within the limits of the law. It is clear that the overwhelming majority of those seized posed no threat to the United States. Unfortunately, superimposed upon these generally not unreasonable restraints was a program of mass incarceration of the entire ethnic Japanese population of the West Coast, citizen and alien alike. It was thrown together by military bureaucrats, all lawyers, partly in response to an inflamed public opinion, and called for by increasing numbers of elected and appointed public officials. Eventually it was supported by Secretary of War Henry L. Stimson, who, in a telephone conversation on February 11, persuaded the president to agree to sign an executive order, which the War Department would present to him eight days later.

We have no transcript, but shortly afterward Stimson's right-hand man, Assistant Secretary of War John J. McCloy, told a colleague in San Francisco: "The President, in substance, says go ahead and do anything you think necessary . . . if it involves citizens, we will take care of them too. He says there will probably be some repercussions, but it has got to be dictated by military necessity, but as he puts it, 'Be as reasonable as you can.'"

McCloy went on to say that he thought the president would sign an executive order giving the army authority to evacuate the entire West Coast, although he noted that Stimson wanted to start by evacuating areas around two large bomber plants in Los Angeles. McCloy indicated that he thought he could bring the secretary around to a total as opposed to a partial evacuation.

Originally, neither Stimson nor McCloy, both lawyers, favored acting against citizens. The night before Stimson got his "carte blanche" from the president, the war secretary had written in his diary: "The racial characteristics [of Japanese, often described by Westerners as "inscrutable"] are such that we cannot understand or trust even the citizen Japanese. This latter is the fact but I am afraid it will make a tremendous hole in our constitutional system to apply it."

McCloy, in arguing with his Justice Department colleagues, on February 1, had put the case more crudely. After Attorney General Francis Biddle insisted that the Justice Department could not support any interference with the rights of citizens, McCloy responded: "You are putting a Wall Street lawyer in a helluva box, but if it is a question of the safety of the country [and] the Constitution . . . why the Constitution is just a scrap of paper to me."

Why did the president agree? There is no easy answer to that question. Roosevelt himself never discussed or even mentioned his reasons in a public discourse, nor has any one of his associates claimed to have heard him do so privately.

When Roosevelt looked at his war maps on the morning of February 11, he could see that the Japanese drive south had achieved landings on various islands of what is now Indonesia—Borneo, Celebes, and Amboina—and on New Guinea; that its drive east was approaching Rangoon in Burma; and that the invested British bastion at Singapore seemed doomed, as were the besieged and outnumbered American forces on the Bataan Peninsula in the Philippines, which he knew he could not meaningfully reinforce. Mid-Pacific Wake Island, with its small Marine Corps garrison, had been overcome just before Christmas. American naval vessels in Southeast Asian waters in collaboration with British and Dutch warships were outnumbered by Japanese naval forces, which had command of the air.

He had no reason to fear a Japanese invasion of the West Coast. The president had told Stimson that "military necessity" must be the rationale, but they both knew from the briefings they regularly received from the Chiefs of Staff and their subordinates that although Hawaii was surely still at risk and that one or more hit-and-run raids on the West Coast were an outside possibility, there was no likelihood of an invasion of the United States.

The president also knew from his own scanning of eleven newspapers each day, as well as from reports on the West Coast press and public opinion from his Office of Government Reports, that there was growing agitation on the West Coast to do something about the presence of thousands of Japanese persons in the region. He was aware that West Coast members of Congress, Democrats as well as Republicans, were united in their demands that something be done to ease the fears of their constituents, which many of them shared, about the presumed dangers from the Japanese in their midst.

Although Roosevelt apparently never doubted eventual American victory, and despite the stunning successes of the Japanese forces, he remained committed to a Germany-first strategy established almost a year before Pearl Harbor. His final objective, beyond victory, was a new international order. He had bitter memories of how President Wilson's similar dreams had come to naught after the Democrats had lost control of Congress in the off-year election of 1918. The next off-year election was less than nine months away. It seems to me likely that the president's fear of the political consequences of not taking steps against the West Coast Japanese was more significant than any fears he might have had of invasion or sabotage.

It is also significant that he received support from his cabinet, once its members became aware of what Stimson and his men were planning. Although Attorney General Biddle and most of his subordinates struggled with Stimson's men in trying to maintain the rights of Japanese Americans, they regularly deferred to their demands. Biddle, the junior member of the cabinet both in age and in service—he had been appointed in September 1941—provided this rationalization in his 1962 memoir: "If, instead of dealing almost exclusively with McCloy . . . I had urged the Secretary to resist the pressure of his subordinates, the result might have been different. But I was new to the Cabinet, and disinclined to insist on my view to an elder statesman, whose wisdom and integrity I greatly respected."

What Biddle does not say is that he failed utterly in one of his chief duties as attorney general: to give legal advice to the president. He gave none on the subject except to suggest that the president explain his actions to the people.

If the president needed further reinforcement for his decision, it was provided on February 13, when he received a resolution signed by every member of Congress from the West Coast, which had been given to the press, calling for "the immediate evacuation of all persons of Japanese lineage and all others, aliens and citizens alike from the states of California, Oregon, and Washington, and the territory of Alaska."

On February 19, 1942, a day of infamy as far as the Constitution is concerned, the president signed Executive Order 9066 (EO 9066), sent over from the War Department. A mere reading of the text of fewer than 800 words gives no indication of its intent. No ethnic group or specific location is mentioned. Its key passage was a sweeping transfer of presumed presidential power:

> I hereby authorize and direct the Secretary of War, and the Military Commanders whom he may from time to time designate, whenever he or any designated Commander deems such action necessary or desirable, to prescribe military areas in such places and of such extent as he or the appropriate Military Commander may determine, from which any or all persons may be excluded, and with respect to which, the right of any person to enter, remain in, or leave shall be subject to whatever restrictions the Secretary of War or the appropriate Military Commander may impose in his discretion. The Secretary of War is hereby authorized to provide for residents of any such area who are excluded therefrom, such

transportation, food, shelter, and other accommodations as may be necessary, in the judgment of the Secretary of War or the said Military Commander, and until other arrangements are made, to accomplish the purpose of this order.

Attorney General Biddle, not the secretary of war, explained it to the press in Washington on February 20 when the news broke, and as is often the case with official explanations of unpleasant actions, some of what he said was simply untrue. Biddle announced accurately that the president had issued the order at the request of Secretary Stimson, stressed that it was not "martial law," so habeas corpus was not suspended, and said that in his opinion "the courts would say 'This is a military matter and we will not go beyond it.'" He granted that the primary targets were the West Coast Japanese, both citizen and alien, but falsely added that the move "was taken largely for the protection of the Japanese themselves." He knew from his conversations with Stimson and others that the War Department's chief concern was the aircraft plants of Southern California and Seattle. In any event, Lewis Wood of the *New York Times* learned enough to report accurately: "President Roosevelt in a drastic move authorized the Secretary of War . . . to eject any or all citizens or aliens from designated military control areas. Primarily aimed at Japanese residents on the Pacific Coast, the order could assure a mass evacuation from the Western seaboard to the inland States, and could be applied as well to regions all over the country."

Three days later, in his fireside chat of February 23, 1942, in which he discussed the war, Roosevelt had an ideal opportunity to explain his action, but he did not take it or any of the other innumerable opportunities he had to do so. The all but universal level of approval that decision received from the press, politicians, and the general public made it easy for him to evade explanation. As stated earlier, he never attempted to make an explanation in public, and if he made one in private, to Eleanor or anyone else, there is no known record of it.

Before we turn from the perpetrators to the victims, there is a glaring incongruity that needs to be addressed. How was it that the small, and by mid-February largely terrorized, Japanese American minority in West Coast states (which had been essentially untouched by war) had to be exiled and eventually locked up in ten improvised concentration camps stretching from eastern California to the Arkansas Delta, whereas in war-torn Hawaii, where every third person was of Japanese ancestry, fewer than 700 Japanese persons, just over 10 percent of them citizens, were incarcerated in several small facilities, and only 1,875 Hawaiian residents of Japanese ancestry, mostly citizens, were ever sent to the mainland for internment in DoJ camps or incarceration in the camps operated by the WRA to house the evicted Japanese? By April 1943 such movement ceased. And rather than persons judged dangerous, many were individuals of low income who were more of a drain than a benefit to the Hawaiian economy and war effort.

The incongruity of this was not lost on Washington's civilian policy makers. They, with navy secretary Frank Knox (1874–1944) in the lead, often backed up by the president, persistently pushed for mass incarceration of all Japanese in Hawaii, on an island other than Oahu, where the vast majority of them lived. Because martial law had immediately been declared after the attack, there were no legal impediments to this. By December 10 the army in Hawaii had in custody 482 Japanese persons, 43 of them American citizens. Strict censorship of all communications between Hawaii and the mainland was established so that information generally known in Hawaii was unknown on the mainland. Two companies of the federalized Hawaiian National Guard, which were entrenched on Hawaiian beaches waiting for the enemy that never came, had large numbers of Nisei officers and enlisted men. In the weeks after Pearl Harbor they continued to bear arms in the territory's defense.

On December 17 the new Hawaiian army commander Lieutenant General Delos C. Emmons replaced the disgraced Major General Walter C. Short. Four days later Emmons announced publicly that there had been no sabotage during or after the Pearl Harbor attack and renewed a pledge made by his predecessor the previous summer that if the Japanese population remained loyal to the United States in a war with Japan, it would receive fair treatment. This was published in Honolulu newspapers but not transmitted to the mainland press. Emmons was not then aware that two days before, in response to arguments from navy secretary Knox, supported by the president, the cabinet had endorsed the incarceration of the entire Japanese population of Oahu—an estimated 118,000 persons, all but 20,000 of them citizens—in a camp or camps somewhere else in the islands.

During the next six months, with the eventual support of the two top American commanders, Emmons spent a good bit of his time fending off this and other attempts to incarcerate all or most of the Hawaiian Japanese. His reasons were real, as opposed to hypothetical, military necessity. When, on January 10, the War Department, at the specific request of Knox, asked Emmons whether it was practical to move Oahu's Japanese to some other island, he replied that it would be very dangerous and impractical. He had lots of reasons: it would require a large number of troops to guard them, and he currently had only half the number of troops necessary for current missions; it would require large amounts of construction materials, which were in very short supply; it would cripple the Oahu economy as Japanese provided the bulk of skilled laborers, many of whom worked for the army. They were indispensable and would have to be replaced by equivalent numbers from the mainland. And if, despite all that, it was still considered necessary to move them, Emmons insisted, they must be sent to the mainland. Emmons's conditions, as he well knew, could not possibly be met until after the war because of manpower and matériel shortages and the lack of shipping space. When Washington planners called for transfer of significant numbers of Japanese—as many as 15,000—Emmons said that his first priority was the shipment to the mainland of 20,000 Caucasian women and children who were a drain on the economy.

Roosevelt was told of the reasons for inaction, but perhaps he did not understand their implications: on February 26 he wrote to Knox, the most ardent advocate of mass incarceration in Hawaii:

Like you, I have long felt that most of the Japanese should be removed from Oahu to one of the other Islands. This involves much planning, much temporary construction and careful supervision of them when they get to the new location.

I do not worry about the constitutional question—first, because of my recent order and, second, because Hawaii is under martial law. The whole matter is one of immediate and present war emergency.

In mid-March, before the forced exile of Issei and Nisei from the West Coast had begun, Assistant Secretary McCloy, the point man in the War Department's Japanese American policy, made an inspection trip to Hawaii. After learning that military officials in Hawaii were opposed to mass evacuation, he made statements that were printed in Honolulu newspapers—but not revealed to the mainland press— saying that a mass evacuation of Japanese in Hawaii was impractical and not contemplated. Perhaps at McCloy's suggestion, Emmons informed the War Department as a "present estimate" that there were 1,500 dangerous Japanese aliens and citizens who should be sent to the mainland for some kind of captivity. Knox, with continuing support from the president, continued to push for mass incarceration of the Hawaiian Japanese. Eventually, in a joint memo to the president that seems to exist only in Roosevelt's papers at Hyde Park, his two top military advisers, General George C. Marshall and Admiral Ernest J. King, told him that decisions about whom to send to the mainland should be left in the hands of the Hawaiian commander, who should be authorized to send up to 15,000 Japanese American citizens, in family groups, to camps on the mainland. In the final analysis, the nonincarceration of the Japanese Americans of Hawaii was governed by a real military necessity rather than a fictive one. Had everything that was generally known in Hawaii been known on the mainland, the whole wartime history of Japanese Americans might have been quite different.

———

For the West Coast Japanese Americans the eleven months following Pearl Harbor were an extended waking nightmare as their illusions about their place in wartime American society were inexorably destroyed. On December 6, 1941, they were free persons living largely segregated lives in a free if somewhat restricted society. By mid-November 1942 the communities that had been theirs were being populated by westward-heading internal migrants, and all but a few thousand of them were in some kind of federal confinement, mostly in one of the ten large, jerry-built facilities that their custodian, the WRA, refused to call concentration camps. A few thousand, able and willing to take advantage of a brief window of opportunity before the army denied them permission to leave, were able to migrate east and lived out the rest of the war in nervous liberty. Except for the fact that two of the WRA camps were in desolate parts of eastern California, a contemporary German might have pronounced the West Coast *Japanerfrei*, that is, free of Japanese.

During much of December 1941, most of the West Coast Nisei continued to believe that they, as opposed to their parents' generation, the Issei, who were Japanese nationals and thus "alien enemies," had little to fear. Some, like the Los Angeles journalist Togo Tanaka (1916–2009), warned about treacherous Issei in a broadcast on the night of Pearl Harbor: "As Americans we now function as counterespionage. Any act or word prejudicial to the United States committed by any [Japanese] must be warned and reported to the F.B.I., Naval Intelligence, Sheriff's office, and local police. Any menace to the security of our country must be wiped out."

Although federal officials initially assured Nisei that they were not targets, the attorney general announced on December 8 that all border crossings were closed "to all persons of Japanese ancestry whether citizen or alien," and a few handfuls of Nisei were briefly placed in custodial detention but soon released. By early January, Justice Department officials, responding to pressure from their colleagues in the War Department, agreed that "all of the alien enemy premises in a given area can be searched at the same time." Because most Japanese American households contained members of both generations, being ethnically Japanese had become probable cause. Thus, before the army had taken over, most Japanese Americans had been deprived of the protection of the Fourth Amendment, which provides that the right of the people to be secure in their persons, houses, papers, and effects, against unreasonable searches and seizures, shall not be violated, and no warrants shall issue, but upon probable cause, supported by oath or affirmation, and particularly describing the place to be searched, and the persons and things to be seized. A teenage Nisei girl from San Jose later described what happened at her house in a letter to a friend written from an Arizona concentration camp:

One day I came home to find two F.B.I. men at our front door. They asked permission to search the house. . . . Trembling with

fright, I followed and watched each of the men look around. . . .
Since I was the only one at home [they] questioned me, but did
not produce sufficient evidence of Fifth Columnists in our family.
This made me very happy, even if they did mess up the house.

Other searches yielded tangible results, which the searchers and the
press sensationalized to produce headlines in both the regional and
the national press such as "F.B.I. Finds Ammunition and Other Contraband in Raids on Monterey Bay Japanese" and "Contraband Cam-
eras, Radio Sets Are Seized in First Sweep of the Vallejo District."
Attorney General Biddle explained in a May report to the president
that most of the 60,000 rounds of ammunition seized came from the
stock of two stores owned by Japanese, and that "We have not found
a camera that we have reason to believe was for use in espionage." But
the widely distributed press reports in early 1942 helped to create a
climate of opinion that dangerous Japanese must be removed from the
putative West Coast "war zone," which the most respected American
newspaper columnist Walter Lippmann insisted was "a battlefield."

Japanese living in rural areas—both established farmers and agricultural laborers—sometimes suffered from a kind of terrorism all
too familiar in much of the American South. Federal officials concerned with farming in California reported to Secretary of Agriculture Claude Wickard in early January that although violence against
Japanese farmers was an isolated phenomenon, greatly exaggerated
by the press, it was quite clear that the Japanese rural population was
"terrified." "They will not leave their homes at night. . . . The police
authorities are probably not sympathetic to the Japanese and are giving them only minimum protection. Investigation of actual attacks
have [sic] been merely perfunctory and no prosecutions have been
initiated."

Although a few of the federal agricultural officials in the West
showed real concern for their Japanese clients, their mission—the
department's slogan was "Food can win the war"—was to keep them
producing and tending their crops even though they might not be
there to harvest, market, and profit from their labor. Later, when the
forced removal had been announced, military officials threatened to
charge any farmers who plowed their crops under or otherwise failed
to tend them properly with sabotage.

A very few western state officials did help Japanese American farmers retain their property. Perhaps the outstanding example was Bob Fletcher. In mid-1942 he quit his state job and arranged to manage three vineyards belonging to his Florin, California, Japanese American neighbors, paid the taxes and mortgages, and harvested and marketed the 1942 crop. He did the same in 1943 and 1944, splitting the profits and putting half into the family bank accounts. When the neighbors returned in 1945, they found their property intact and resumed their tenure. Few were that fortunate. Fletcher, aged 101 at his 2013 death, was revered as a community hero.

In urban areas, unemployment of Japanese workers increased as ethnic enterprises collapsed for lack of capital and credit—all bank accounts of "alien enemies" were frozen, as were all accounts in the American branches of Japanese banks—and many Caucasian employers fired Japanese employees. The largest single group of Japanese American public employees in the Pacific Northwest—twenty-three young Nisei women employed as clerks in the Seattle public schools—had civil service status and could not by law be dismissed without cause. The superintendent of schools, under fire from angry parents, appealed for assistance at the end of February from the local Nisei leadership. In an action that epitomizes the mind-set of the all-male Nisei leaders, the women were summoned to a meeting with the superintendent in the office of a male Nisei editor and bullied into agreeing to a mass resignation. School board members later issued a statement commending the clerks' "high regard for their responsibility as American citizens."

In California an even more sweeping attempt by the state personnel board to purge the state's civil service not just of Nisei but also of naturalized American citizens of German and Italian ancestry and their citizen children was voided by state attorney general Earl Warren, himself a child of Scandinavian immigrants, who denounced it as an attempt at "cleansing" and a violation of the American and California constitutions as well as the state's civil service law. Yet he would testify late in February, with a kind of paranoid logic, in support of the removal of all the state's Japanese, both alien and citizen:

Unfortunately [many] are of the opinion that because we have had no sabotage and no fifth column activities in this state . . . that means that none has been planned for us. But . . . this is the most ominous sign in our whole situation. . . . The fifth column activities that we are to get are timed, just like the invasion of France and of Norway. . . . I believe that we are just being lulled into a false sense of security. . . . Our day of reckoning is bound to come.

By mid-February the man sent to represent the Justice Department on the West Coast, Tom C. Clark (1899–1977), with a concurrent appointment as coordinator of alien enemy control in the Western Defense Command (WDC) under Lieutenant General John L. DeWitt, was taking positions identical with those of the military. In Clark's oral history for the Truman Library in 1972–1973, he paints himself as opposed to moving citizens, but in mid-February 1942 he briefed reporters in both California and Washington about some of the various plans to move large numbers of Japanese aliens and citizens out of strategic areas that he was recommending.

By the time the president's executive order had been signed and publicized, the combination of increasing federal legal restrictions, punitive actions by state and local governments, and increasing discrimination by private bodies and individuals had largely demoralized many if not most of the adult Nisei. Leaders of the Japanese American Citizens League (JACL), a Nisei organization that would not admit aliens and claimed a membership of 20,000 in sixty chapters in 300 communities, immediately announced that it was instructing its members "to continue cooperating with our government in whatever action it may deem necessary," but they went on to say that it "is difficult to conceive that our government . . . would break down the equality that has always existed between its citizens and discriminate against one bloc of them."

By the end of February, JACL leaders, including its president Saburo Kido (1902–1977), an attorney, Mike Masaoka (1915–1991), its executive secretary, and Fred Tayama (b. 1905), one of its Los Angeles officials, after being summoned to get instructions from army and Justice Department officials, told the well-informed West Coast correspondent for the *New York Times* that all should be treated equally and that in the best interests of both the nation and the citizen Japanese, they should be sent to what would be "practically concentration camps," where they would be protected by the army and fed by the government. They also suggested that there be a moratorium for "the duration" on their mortgages and long-term leases. They got the camps but not the moratoria or other financial easements.

Between February 21 and March 7, a House select committee—the so-called Tolan Committee, which had been established in 1941 to investigate "national defense migration"—held hearings in major West Coast cities on the "Evacuation of Enemy Aliens and Others" from military areas. All but two of the fifteen Japanese American witnesses repeated the JACL line, essentially, "We are loyal so we will cooperate and not protest this injustice." In Portland, JACL national treasurer Hito Okada (1907–1984), perhaps thinking of the founding fathers, said, "We are willing to sacrifice our homes, our money, and our lives" to help win the war.

JACL president Kido, speaking to reporters prior to a closed three-day meeting in San Francisco on March 8, said that evacuating American-born Japanese was a "travesty on our good name and rights," but that he and his organization representing 80,000 (!) citizens of Japanese ancestry all over the country were determined to cooperate with whatever the government told them to do. Reporters learned that proposals at the conference to form a united front with other Japanese groups were rejected because the JACL "represented most of the Japanese anyway [and that the organization] should play a lone hand."

General DeWitt, whose WDC, including Alaska, had been designated a theater of operations four days after the attacks on Pearl Harbor, had asserted in an early February telephone conversation with War Department officials: "I haven't gone into details of it, but Hell, it would be no job as far as the evacuation was concerned to move 100,000 people."

But when, under the provisions of EO 9066, war secretary Stimson redelegated presidential authority to General DeWitt on February 20, the often befuddled West Coast commander discovered that the real problem was not how to "move 100,000 people" but where to put them and how to house, feed, and provide for public health, sanitation, and even recreation and education for what were largely American citizens, none of whom was charged with any crime.

Although the general and his staff were not at all clear as to what they were going to order, his headquarters began to issue proclama-

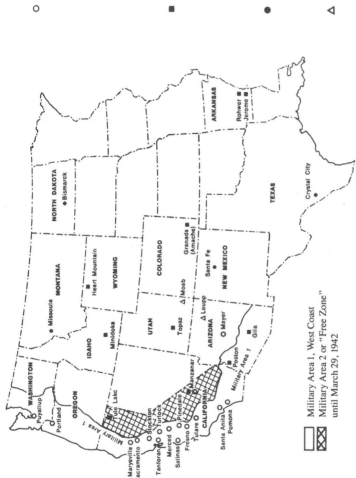

KEY

○ ASSEMBLY CENTERS
Puyallup, Wash.
Portland, Ore.
Marysville, Calif.
Sacramento, Calif.
Tanforan, Calif.
Stockton, Calif.
Turlock, Calif.
Merced, Calif.
Pinedale, Calif.
Salinas, Calif.
Fresno, Calif.
Tulare, Calif.
Santa Anita, Calif.
Pomona, Calif.
Mayer, Ariz.

■ RELOCATION CENTERS
Manzanar, Calif.
Tule Lake, Calif.
Poston, Ariz.
Gila, Ariz.
Minidoka, Ida.
Heart Mountain, Wyo.
Granada, Colo.
Topaz, Utah
Rohwer, Ark.
Jerome, Ark.

● JUSTICE DEPARTMENT
INTERNMENT CAMPS
Santa Fe, N. Mex.
Bismarck, N. Dak.
Crystal City, Tex.
Missoula, Mont.

△ CITIZEN ISOLATION CAMPS
Moab, Utah
Leupp, Ariz.

☐ Military Area 1, West Coast
▨ Military Area 2 or "Free Zone"
until March 29, 1942

Map showing Western Defense Command zones and all Japanese American incarceration sites. The assembly centers were administered by the US Army; the relocation centers and the citizen isolation camps by the War Relocation Authority; and the Justice Department camps by the Immigration and Naturalization Service. All but the INS-run sites were concentration camps established outside of normal US law. Source: Commission on Wartime Relocation and Internment of Civilians, *Personal Justice Denied* (Washington, DC, 1983), reprinted from Michi Weglyn, *Years of Infamy* (1976).

tions on March 2, ten days after he had been granted extraordinary powers over the civilian population of the West Coast: all were entered in the *Federal Register*. Proclamation 1 of that date, over General DeWitt's signature, was directed at "any Japanese, German, or Italian alien, or any person of Japanese Ancestry," making it clear that, for the government, the distinctions between alien and citizen were no longer significant as far as those of Japanese ancestry were concerned. It also divided the states of Arizona, California, Oregon, and Washington into two "military areas." The map on page 21 shows the zones established by General DeWitt, as well as the various sites in which Japanese Americans were imprisoned throughout the United States between 1942 and 1946. Military Area No. 1 was divided into two zones: a "prohibited" coastal and Mexican border zone about a hundred miles deep, which took in most major cities, including San Diego, Los Angeles, San Francisco, Portland, and Seattle; and a restricted zone so configured that it included almost all of the places where significant numbers of Japanese resided. It amounted to roughly two-thirds of Washington, more than half of California, two-fifths of Oregon, and a third of Arizona. The remainder of those states constituted Military Area No. 2. The order stated that "designation of Military Area No. 2 as such does not contemplate any prohibition or regulation or restriction except with respect to the zones [around specific military or other sensitive facilities] established therein." It also required regulated persons living in Military Area No. 1 to file a change of address with their local post office before moving. Enemy aliens needed permission from the DoJ to move, but citizens retained the right to travel. Most found it difficult to exercise that right.

Most Japanese Americans simply did not have the assets necessary for a move; much of their money was in bank accounts blocked by the government. Those traveling by train met no special barriers, but those who chose to load a car or truck with family and possessions and head east encountered a variety of difficulties. Even within their own states many filling stations refused to sell them gas. If they crossed a border, that state's police often turned them back or otherwise discouraged their further progress. Many of the relatively few who started returned, and their experience discouraged others.

Seattle JACLers reported to the Tolan Committee that while De-Witt's proclamation left Japanese free to leave Military Area No. 1, "this was no solution . . . for immediately from Yakima, Idaho, Montana, Colorado and elsewhere authoritative voices shouted: 'No Japs Wanted Here!' The Japanese feared with reason that . . . they would be kicked from town to town in the interior like the 'Okies' of John Steinbeck's novel."

On March 10 a General Staff officer back from a West Coast inspection trip reported on his return to army headquarters that "there was no definite organization for handling . . . the evacuation of enemy aliens." The following day, perhaps in response to this criticism, DeWitt signed an order creating the Wartime Civil Control Administration (WCCA). The order regulated the initial incarceration sites in the West Coast states "to provide for the evacuation of all persons of Japanese ancestry from Military Area No. 1 and the California portion of Military Area No. 2 . . . with a minimum of economic and social dislocation, a minimum use of military personnel and maximum speed; and initially to employ all appropriate means to encourage voluntary migration."

This secret order demonstrates the duplicity with which the military leadership treated some of its citizens; for weeks after this policy document was signed, DeWitt's headquarters continued to urge Japanese Americans to move into California's Military Area No. 2. The WCCA, housed in a downtown San Francisco hotel commandeered by the army, was largely staffed by civilians borrowed from a wide variety of federal organizations, including most significantly the Census Bureau and the Department of Agriculture. (The president had directed "all Executive Departments, independent establishments and other Federal Agencies, to assist the Secretary of War or the said Military Commanders in carrying out" EO 9066.) To head the WCCA, DeWitt chose Colonel Karl R. Bendetsen, one of the group of military bureaucrats in the War Department who had originally pushed for mass incarceration of Japanese Americans regardless of citizenship.

On March 18 President Roosevelt issued EO 9102, drafted in the White House, creating the WRA (1942–1946), whose director reported directly to the president and was instructed to design "a program for the removal, from the areas designated from time to time by the Secretary of War or appropriate military commander under the authority of Executive Order 9066 of February 19, 1942, of the persons or classes of persons designated under such Executive Order, and for their relocation, maintenance, and supervision."

To head the new agency, which reported directly to him, Roosevelt named Milton S. Eisenhower, a civil servant who had joined the Department of Agriculture in 1928 managing its public relations and serving as Secretary Henry Wallace's liaison officer to Roosevelt's White House, and much better known in 1942 Washington than his older brother Dwight, then a brigadier general on General Marshall's staff. Milton, disillusioned after it became clear to him that General DeWitt's man Bendetsen could block his less restrictive plans for the exiled Japanese Americans, submitted his resignation. Told to find a replacement, he recruited a colleague in the Agriculture Department, Dillon S. Myer, an administrator overseeing soil conservation. Myer remembered, years later, that after "a couple of hours" of discussion, "I said to Milton 'Do you think I should take this job?' He said 'Dillon, if you can sleep and still carry on the job my answer would be yes. I can't sleep and do this job. I had to get out of it.' So I told him that I would take on the job."

Myer took over in mid-June 1942 and ran the agency until it was dissolved in 1946. This new civilian agency would take over from the military as soon as appropriate facilities could be constructed and the inmates assigned to it delivered. Although Bendetsen and his immediate superiors in the military originally planned to keep the imprisoned Japanese under military control, after Chief of Staff Marshall learned what they and Stimson and McCloy were planning, he insisted that a bare minimum of military manpower be utilized.

One final legal step was necessary. The military planners understood that there were likely to be court challenges to their program, and realized, in late February, that there was nothing on the statute books providing penalties for a civilian who disobeyed a military order unless martial law had been declared. A statute, drafted in the War Department, making such disobedience a misdemeanor, punishable by imprisonment of not more than a year or a $5,000 fine, or both, upon conviction, was sent to Congress on March 9 and passed both houses without a dissenting vote on March 19; two days later the president made it Public Law 503.

There was a lone dissenting voice, however. Senator Robert A. Taft (R-OH) complained in the Senate that it was "the sloppiest criminal law I have ever read or seen anywhere . . . the Senate should not pass it." But because he understood "the pressing character of this kind of legislation," he did not make the formal objection that would have delayed approval.

While the congressional process was going on, DeWitt issued Public Proclamation 2 on March 16, which established Military Areas Nos. 3 through 6 covering the states of Nevada, Utah, Idaho, and Montana. This proclamation had, in the event, little significance except as an indication of the general's ambition to spread restrictions throughout the WDC. Once Public Law 503 was on the books, DeWitt was free to issue orders with teeth, orders that immediately affected people's lives. On March 24 he issued Public Proclamation 3, which ordered that in three days' time "all alien Japanese, all alien Germans, all alien Italians, and all persons of Japanese ancestry" living in "Military Area No. 1 . . . shall be within their place of residence between the hours of 8:00 P.M. and 6:00 A.M., which period is hereinafter referred to as the hours of curfew." In addition, "All such persons shall be only at their place of residence or employment or traveling between those places or within a distance of not more than five miles from their place of residence."

The day the curfew went into effect, March 27, DeWitt issued Proclamation 4 ordering that at midnight, March 29, "all alien Japanese and persons of Japanese ancestry, who are within the limits of Military Area No. 1 [where the vast majority of Japanese Americans lived] be and they are hereby prohibited from leaving that area for any purpose until and to the extent that a future proclamation or order of this headquarters shall so permit or direct."

Japanese Americans present in Military Area No. 2, almost 5,000 of whom had registered their intention to move there from Zone 1 after March 12, could believe for five days that they had escaped the fate of their fellows in Zone 1. General DeWitt's Public Proclamation 6, issued on June 2, and effective at noon that day, froze those in the large California portion of Zone 2 in language identical to that of the Zone 1 proclamation. Those living in the Arizona, Oregon, and

Washington areas of Zone 2 were not mentioned. They were never frozen and, if citizens, were free to move anywhere in the nation except the excluded zones.

None of the various WDC directives discussed so far forced any citizens to move. Independently the US Navy had evicted the roughly 500 families of Japanese, mostly involved in deep-sea fishing, from Terminal Island, San Pedro, part of the Port of Los Angeles. Like the army, it was inconsistent. On February 14 the navy posted notices that all Japanese must be off the Island by March 14; but, without warning, it put up new notices on the afternoon of February 25 saying that all Japanese must be gone by midnight February 27. It did not care where they went and made no offers of moving assistance.

The first persons to enter army custody in what it called an "assembly center" were actually 1,000 volunteers, organized by the JACL in Los Angeles, who made the 230-mile trip to Manzanar in their own motor vehicles with army and police escorts and by special train on March 21–23 and were described as the "vanguard of 112,000" who would be forced to leave their homes. An Associated Press photo of the train and some of its passengers leaving Los Angeles was captioned "Concentration Camp Special."

But what would become the regular process of rounding up the future inmates was tested at the other end of DeWitt's zone on tiny Bainbridge Island, in Puget Sound facing Seattle. On March 24 the WCCA placarded the island with Civilian Exclusion Order 1 ordering that "all persons of Japanese ancestry, both alien and nonalien [!], be excluded from Bainbridge Island" by March 30. It established a Civil Control Center "at or near the ferryboat landing," and specified that a "responsible member of each family . . . will report to the Civil Control Office . . . between 8 a.m. and 5 p.m. on . . . March 25" to register all family members and be assigned a family number. Everyone was ordered to report to the ferryboat landing on March 30, where armed soldiers waited to escort them on the ferry to Seattle and on the train that took the 257 Bainbridge Islanders—the WCCA had anticipated 225—to the Manzanar camp deep in California, where they arrived on April 1. The process was repeated 106 times as the WCCA statistical section headed by Calvert L. Dedrick, a ranking Census Bureau official on long-term loan to the army who became a key member of Colonel Bendetsen's staff, divided California and the Zone 1 parts of Arizona, Oregon, and Washington into 106 districts, which held, on average, about a thousand Japanese each. Eventually the WDC processed more than 92,000 persons through its assembly centers and by mid-November had passed almost all of them on to the WRA. That story has often been told, and, important as the incarceration story is, it is not germane here. Instead, we will return to the Nisei litigants and their causes.

CHAPTER TWO

Challenging the Government

The four litigants' paths to the Supreme Court, including their deci-
sion-making processes, were as varied as their backgrounds. The first
to act was twenty-five-year-old Minoru Yasui. The oldest and best
educated, he was born and grew up in Hood River, Oregon, where
his father ran a general store and was a leader of its sizable Nikkei community, that is, persons of Japanese ancestry wherever born.
Min attended a Methodist church and as a teenager became a char-
ter member of the local JACL chapter. He earned degrees from the
University of Oregon and its law school in 1937 and 1939, as well as
a second lieutenant's commission through its ROTC program. When
he passed the bar exam in 1939, he became the only Japanese American lawyer in Oregon—aliens could not practice law—but no firm
would hire him. His own practice was unsatisfactory, and in 1940 he
left for Chicago, where he went to work in the Japanese Consulate
General abstracting items from the American press; he resigned on
Monday morning, December 8, 1941. Perhaps a week later he got a
telegram ordering him to report for active duty at Camp Vancouver,
Washington, just across the river from Portland, but when, after returning to the West Coast, he checked in, a colonel told him that he
would not be activated then but would be contacted later. That never
happened.

Min's father, Masao, had been picked up for internment on December 12, 1941. In early February, Min traveled to Fort Missoula,
Montana, to observe his father's unsuccessful hearing before the local
Alien Enemy Review Board; internees were allowed neither counsel
nor the right to call witnesses. On his return to Portland, Min reestablished a law practice in downtown Portland and kept busy; many
Japanese of both generations had serious new legal problems.

On March 28, 1942, the day after General DeWitt's curfew went
into effect, Yasui, after consulting other attorneys, deliberately sought
to make himself a test case. As he described it in a 1983 interview:

I was in my office [in a small Japanese-run hotel in downtown Portland] on the 28th day of March, which is a Saturday evening. Waited 'til 8 o'clock, Rei Shimojima was my secretary [and she called] the police, the FBI, to notify them that there was a Japanese person in violation of curfew walking up and down Third Avenue. . . . I've told this story many a time, but I walked and walked from eight o'clock, and the record will show that I was not actually arrested until 11:20 p.m. I walked for over three hours, and during that period, I got tired of walking up and down Third Avenue. So I did approach a police officer, and being a smart aleck and being an attorney, I pulled out the proclamation pointing out that [I] was in violation of a military proclamation, I had my birth certificate with me, and I proved that I was a person of Japanese ancestry. [I] asked the officer to arrest me, and the officer says, "Look, you'll get in trouble. Go on, run along home." And that certainly didn't serve my purposes, so I went down to the Second Avenue police station and talked to the sergeant and explain[ed] what I wanted done. And the sergeant obliged me and he threw me into the drunk tank. So that's how the case began.

Only after being bailed out on Monday morning by his attorney, Earl Bernard, did Yasui phone his mother in Hood River to tell her what he had done. He expected her to protest. Instead she told him, "I will support you." Although he enjoyed the support of family and friends, including some Portland attorneys, there was no community support group for him. In addition, when news of his intention to challenge the constitutionality of the curfew and other measures reached JACL leaders, they denounced him and other unnamed protesters.

In JACL Bulletin 142, "Re: Test Cases," on April 7, 1942, national secretary Mike Masaoka denounced resisters as "self-styled martyrs" and reported that "National Headquarters is unalterably opposed to test cases." Among the eleven numbered reasons given for this policy in the bulletin were that "as good Americans" we should do what our government tells us; public opinion is opposed to any resistance; a "challenge" might "irritate" the military into "treating us worse. . . . We do not intend to attempt to win a case and lose a cause"; and the ACLU had decided not to challenge the government and "we are not disposed to question its wisdom." Finally, the Bulletin predicted that after victory "our rights and privileges will be returned because we cooperated."

Initially Min had not planned to be the test case himself, but rather to plan it and help defend it in court. As he put it:

> What we were looking for, really, was an ideal case. A young ex-GI who had been honorably discharged, married with a couple of kids, because we wanted to create sympathy. But at that time, knowing the uncertainties, I could scarcely blame anyone for refusing to go ahead and deliberately violate the law. And it seemed to me that someone had to do it, and the ultimate choice became, since nobody else would do it, I did.

Min, his attorney Bernard, a pillar of the Oregon bar, and other lawyers, including the federal prosecutor, planned to waive trial by jury and have the case decided by the local federal district judge, James Alger Fee, who had been appointed by President Herbert Hoover in 1931 and would be promoted to a seat on the Ninth Circuit Court by President Eisenhower in 1954.

In mid-May, when Portland Nikkei were ordered to report for incarceration, Min's month and a half of freedom ended. At the beginning of the five days allowed for preparation, he drove home to Hood River, informing the army that he would return to Portland under protest, but that it would have to come and get him. Accordingly, a lieutenant in a sedan, accompanied by four armed soldiers in a jeep, came to his home in Hood River and escorted him to Portland's International Livestock Exposition Center, a huge cattle barn. With the addition of a barbed wire fence, guard towers, and soldiers carrying rifles and manning machine guns, the building became the Portland Assembly Center. Min dubbed the concentration camp, which held a maximum of nearly 3,700 prisoners, the North Portland Pigpen. Since he had chosen not to resist DeWitt's order to report, he would be charged only with curfew violation.

A month later, on June 12, 1942, Min's trial before Judge Fee took place, with the federal prosecutor seconded by War Relocation Authority attorneys from Washington, DC. It lasted only one day and ended with an interrogation of Yasui by the judge. Although the defendant had previously testified that he was raised by parents who had been Christians in Japan and was himself a Methodist, Fee persisted in asking him about Shinto religious practices and other aspects of Japanese culture despite Min's continued denials of either knowledge of or interest in such matters. After the trial ended, for reasons that are not clear, Judge Fee would not reveal his verdict for five months. Min was sent back to the Portland camp and in September was shipped with other Portlanders to the purpose-built WRA camp called Minidoka in Idaho, where he arrived on September 6, 1942. Before he was returned to Portland to hear Judge Fee's verdict, two of the other resisters had been arrested, tried, convicted, and sentenced, and the fourth had challenged the government in a different way.

The other litigant to turn himself in, Gordon Kiyoshi Hirabayashi, was a twenty-four-year-old whose parents had each converted to the Mukyokai sect of Japanese Christianity before immigrating to America. They settled south of Seattle, where his father farmed and ran a roadside market, and raised their five children in that tradition, which Gordon, the eldest, found "too rigid and restrictive." By late 1941 he had become a Quaker and been granted conscientious objector status by the Selective Service System.

When war came he was a senior at the University of Washington living in the YMCA adjacent to campus, where he tended the boilers in exchange for a free room. He soon received an order to report to a work camp for conscientious objectors, but that was canceled after the draft status of all Nisei was changed to IV-C, formerly reserved for aliens. When General DeWitt's curfew went into effect, Gordon obeyed it for a week or so; his friends would warn him when the 8:00 p.m. hour approached and he would hurry back to his room at the Y. Then, as he put it years later, "I stopped and I thought, Why the hell am I running back? Am I an American? And if I am, why am I running back and nobody else is? . . . So I stopped and turned around and went back. . . . And it became a kind of expression of freedom for me to make sure that I was out after eight."

For the better part of a month Gordon violated the curfew regulations with impunity and, assuming that he would soon be sent somewhere by the government, did not register for the spring quarter. After the announcements for the piecemeal exodus of the Seattle Nikkei, he joined other volunteers in driving groups of them to the state fairgrounds in Puyallup, where the army was throwing together a temporary concentration camp that would house most of them until late summer. As Gordon tells the story: "I fully expected that when the University district deadline came up I would join [the families I had driven to Puyallup. But] about two weeks before my time came up, I said to myself, If I am defying the curfew, how can I accept this thing?"

Gordon discussed the matter with his parents, who admired his principles, but he had to deal with his mother, Mitsuko, who had always urged her children to become educated professionals. Now she pressed him to go to camp with the family. He remembered her saying: "I know you're right and I admire this stand of yours, but we don't know if we'll ever see each other again. It's a matter of life and death. Why stick to a principle? Stick with us."

Gordon comments: "She used everything—tears *and everything*. But I couldn't do it." Months later, when he was in jail awaiting trial, he received a letter from his mother describing her arrival at the concentration camp at Tule Lake, California:

> She said when she arrived . . . and was unpacking at Tule Lake, a knock came. And she opened the door, and there were two ladies, dusty, shoes dusty and so on. They had walked from the other end of camp. . . . They said, "We heard that the family of the boy that's in jail is arriving today. So we came out to welcome you and to say thank you for your son."

Gordon told an interviewer decades later that he realized only when he read that letter that a burden of guilt about not being a faithful son, which he had not been fully aware of, was suddenly lifted from his shoulders.

In spite of his mother's pleas, he had typed a four-page statement of his beliefs and showed it to some people within the local Friends meeting. This brought about a visit from Mary U. Farquharson, who had been the state senator representing the university district and a founder of the local chapter of the ACLU, asking him about his still inchoate plans. She encouraged Gordon to make himself a test case. After he had done so, she became the key figure in organizing the Gordon Hirabayashi Defense Committee, the only local committee created to support an individual resister.

On May 17, the day after the last Seattle Nikkei had been bused to camp, Gordon and his Quaker lawyer, Arthur G. Barnett, went to the local FBI office so he could turn himself in. Since he had not registered, no one was looking for him: the government had no master list, only numbers from the 1940 census, then more than two years old. The FBI agents, under instructions to avoid any legal difficulties if possible, spent the better part of the day trying, without success, to get Gordon to go to camp, but he refused. Gordon, in his 1990 statement, says that at first he was "charged" only with failing to register, but that during his initial interrogation he was asked if he had obeyed curfew: "And I said, Well, what were *you* doing the past few nights? Were you out after eight o'clock? He said, Yeah. And I said, So was I."

After finding evidence of his curfew violation recorded in Gordon's confiscated notebook, which he had brought with him, a count of curfew violation was added to the charge against him. At the end of the day he was taken to the King County jail and locked up in the "federal tank." At the ensuing brief arraignment, after accepting Gordon's not-guilty plea on both counts, federal district judge Lloyd L. Black, a Roosevelt appointee of 1939, agreed to set bail at $500, which the defense committee was prepared to pay. But when Gordon asked what would happen to him after he was bailed, Judge Black ruled that he would be taken to the Puyallup camp. Although Gordon realized that he would be more comfortable there behind barbed wire than in the jail, which he described as "cockroachy" and serving "greasy food," Gordon felt that as a resister he should not accept bail, which involved consenting to injustice. He remained in the cramped jail for five months until his trial opened on October 20, 1942, in Seattle's federal courthouse.

The trial took but a single day. In the afternoon Judge Black charged the jurors that the curfew and removal orders were valid and that their only responsibility was to determine whether Gordon was of Japanese ancestry, and if he was, whether he had complied with the regulations that applied to him, facts the defense did not deny. The jury retired for ten minutes and returned the guilty verdict demanded.

The following day Judge Black passed sentence. Taking into account the five months already served of a twelve-month maximum sentence, he ruled that Gordon should serve an additional thirty days on each count, served consecutively, for a total of seven months, and then asked if the prisoner had anything to say. Gordon, primed by jailhouse lawyers, asked if Black would add fifteen days to each count to total ninety days, so that he might serve his time in a work camp where he could be outdoors. Smiling, the judge agreed and sentenced him to three months on each count to be served concurrently. Two days later, after an appeal had been filed, as Gordon tells the story, there was again a disagreement about the terms of bail; with the Puyallup camp closed, Judge Black said that, if bailed, Gordon would have to go to one of the WRA camps; Gordon again chose to stay in the Seattle jail.

The third litigant, twenty-three-year-old Fred Toyosaburo Korematsu, was born in Oakland, the third of four sons of parents who had been born in Japan. When Fred was growing up, his parents operated a flower nursery in San Leandro, near Oakland, whose 1940 population was almost 66,000. As Fred told his story in 1983, his folks, like most Nikkei, favored the eldest son. That son and the second son, whom Fred called the "smartest," were both sent to college. Fred graduated from San Leandro's Castlemont High School, but when he was ready to plan for college, he was told that there was "no more money" and that he would have to fend for himself. He went to Los Angeles, to try, but nothing worked out and he soon returned home. Fred did not use the terms "outlier" or "misfit," but they match his self-description in his oral narrative. All the friends and the only girlfriend he mentions were Caucasians; his references to family members are never by name but by relationship—parents, brother, father.

After World War II broke out in Europe and the American defense program began to grow, Fred took welder's training in Oakland, passed the test, and was hired by an East Bay shipyard. When the draft was instituted, he and a group of high school friends decided to join the National Guard or the Coast Guard as an alternative to possible army service. His friends were all accepted, but recruiters "wouldn't even speak to me" except to say, "'I'm sorry, we can't accept you.'"

Sometime after Pearl Harbor, as security precautions increased at the shipyard, Fred stopped working there and got a welder's job at a small plant in Berkeley that had no security apparatus. (In a prepared statement he read in a later part of the same 1983 interview, Fred says, "I participated in defense work until the union forced me out without a reason.") He continued to live at home until May 4, when copies of Civilian Exclusion Order 34 were posted in San Leandro announcing the coming expulsion of "all Japanese persons, both alien and non-alien," in five days. He told his family that he was leaving and might go to Nevada. He went to San Francisco and had incompetent plastic surgery—afterward "everyone recognized me"—and then moved into an Oakland rooming house, assuming the identity of Clyde Sarah, a Spanish Hawaiian.

On Memorial Day he committed a classic fugitive error by returning to a place where he was known. Waiting on a street corner in San Leandro for his girlfriend, he was picked up by local police, who took him to their station, where a young woman who worked there, probably a high school classmate, recognized him. Fred admitted who and what he was and spoke freely to various FBI interrogators, both at the time of his arrest and after he had decided to bring a test case. Because San Leandro had no long-term custodial facilities, Fred was soon taken to the federal tank of the San Francisco jail. There, Ernest Besig, director of the Northern California Branch of the ACLU (NCACLU), trolling in San Francisco's jail for someone willing to be a test case, found Fred and two other Nisei who had been apprehended in places they were no longer allowed to be. Press and FBI reports indicate that by mid-June at least fifteen other Nisei had been apprehended in Northern California. Besig introduced himself, said something about the ACLU—Fred initially thought that it was a religious group—handed out cigarettes, and said that he would come back. The next day, only Fred said that he was willing to be a test case. Besig filed the necessary papers, Fred was arraigned after a perfunctory hearing, and Besig posted bail. But when they tried to leave, MPs were waiting to take Fred into custody. Besig objected, insisting that the MPs had no authority over a civilian, but eventually told Fred to go with them. For some reason they had been ordered to deliver him to San Francisco's Presidio, where he was held for several days. Fred "really enjoyed it" at the Presidio because "the meals were terrific and they treated me real good."

Eventually he was taken to the camp at the Tanforan Racetrack, near Oakland, which the army called an assembly center. Fred was assigned to a horse stable with a single bare lightbulb suspended from the ceiling and neither heat nor running water: "The front door . . . had a gap . . . about six to eight inches from the ground, [a] dirt floor [with just] a cot and a straw mattress [with] gaping holes [in] the walls, and the wind [and] dust blew in."

Fred sat and lay on the cot for perhaps forty-five minutes and said to himself, "Boy, this is really a miserable place." An elder brother (Hiroshi) soon came and took him to a different part of the camp to see the other family members. Later the brother, who had been chair of the San Francisco YMCA's Committee on Alien Resettlement before he had been incarcerated, arranged for a meeting with about thirty young Nisei to counsel Fred on whether he should continue his case. As Fred described it: "They were discussing it to themselves or in little groups. And I stood around . . . but no one actually came up to speak to me. Finally one did, and he said, 'Fred, we're all in camp,' . . . they're undecided on if I should fight the case or not . . . there's no way that they can help me. So therefore it was up to me to decide on what to do."

Fred persisted. He accepted Besig's colleague Wayne M. Collins as his attorney. Collins would become the most important single attorney in the second set of Japanese American cases. He and Fred agreed, as Bernard and Yasui had done, to forgo trial by jury. These decisions made legal sense but were poor public relations. The purposes of the government were served by its secrecy about what was really happening in Hawaii and by having the outrageous nature of its claims ignored. Besig continued to visit Fred in Tanforan and counseled him about all sorts of matters by mail after he had been sent to the Topaz camp in Utah and later when he temporarily settled in Detroit.

After a hearing before one federal judge who set a trial date but was on vacation when it came, Fred's day in court was September 8, 1942, before Judge Adolphus F. St. Sure, a Coolidge appointee of 1925. The trial was perfunctory, with only one witness for the prosecution, an FBI agent, and only Fred for the defense. He avowed what he had done. Judge St. Sure found Fred guilty but sentenced him only to five years of probation. In a normal situation Fred would not have had to go to jail, but an MP was there to take him back to Tanforan. Collins filed the planned appeal.

Mitsuye Endo, the fourth and youngest resister, took a very different path from the others. Twenty-two years old in 1942, she was a civil servant of the state of California employed as a typist at the headquarters of its Department of Motor Vehicles in Sacramento. Her first resistance was connected with a protest against the continuing efforts of the California State Personnel Board to remove Japanese American civil servants even after their efforts against citizens of German and Italian origin had been dropped and California attorney general Earl Warren had taken action against their efforts. There were said to be 314 Japanese American civil servants statewide, with 465 others on the eligible list. JACL president Kido had approached a fellow attorney, San Franciscan James Purcell, who began looking into the matter on a pro bono basis.

When the removal of the Nikkei made the matter moot, Purcell decided, as Min Yasui had done previously, to try to find an ideal person for a test case from among the civil servants he was aware of. Unlike Yasui, he found one, Mitsuye Endo. As a woman she was less threatening, she had never been in Japan, did not speak Japanese, was a practicing Methodist, and had a brother serving in the US Army. Purcell interviewed Endo in her horse stall accommodation at the Walerga Assembly Center outside Sacramento, where she had been sent by DeWitt's Civilian Exclusion Order 52 of May 7, 1942, and she authorized him to file a petition for a writ of habeas corpus— "you may have the body," in lawyer Latin—which he would not apply for until she was settled in a WRA camp. Shortly after Endo told him that she had been shipped to the Tule Lake, California, camp, he filed for a writ on July 12, 1942, from US district court judge Michael J. Roche, an Irish immigrant who, after a quarter century of service as a judge in California, had been appointed to the federal bench by Franklin Roosevelt in 1935.

To the surprise of both Purcell and the local deputy federal attorney Alfonso J. Zirpoli, Judge Roche immediately began what turned out to be an all-day hearing. Although such writs are supposed to be handled expeditiously, Judge Roche then held it without acting for almost an entire year, until July 3, 1943, twelve days after the Supreme Court had acted on the *Hirabayashi* and *Yasui* cases. He then denied the writ but gave no reasons for either the denial or the unconscionable delay. Purcell, of course, appealed.

Why the delay? I know of no evidence connecting Judge Roche with Justice Department, WRA, and army lawyers, but we do know that such lawyers did come to the West Coast to discuss Japanese American cases with other judges, and that those lawyers were very much concerned that the Supreme Court might look askance at the holding of an exemplary citizen by a civilian agency. As Justice Holmes once remarked, there is such a thing as "presumptive evidence, like finding a trout in the milk." And it is quite clear that many federal lawyers were less concerned with "justice" than with protecting programs in which their department chiefs had a stake.

Endo, who became Mrs. Tsutsumi as a result of a marriage with a fellow prisoner at the Topaz camp, never commented publicly about the way the government lawyers abused her rights. She was a very private person who refused almost all interviews, as I know from personal experience not only during and immediately after her captivity but throughout her long life. Her 2006 obituary in a Japanese American newspaper reported that her daughter did not learn that her mother was a hero of the wartime incarceration until she was a young adult. What we do know is that Mitsuye was steadfast and refused to accept the offered "leave clearance" from the WRA unless the rules were changed so that she could depart by right, instead of by permission of her captors, and return to California.

Finally, on November 16, 1942, Minoru Yasui, who had been brought back to Portland from the Minidoka camp for the occasion, heard Judge Fee announce the result of his five months of deliberation. In a curious decision Fee ruled that the statute of March 21, 1942, which made it a criminal offense to disobey General DeWitt's orders, was unconstitutional as applied to American citizens, but held that Min, because of his employment by the Japanese government, must be deemed to have renounced his American citizenship and thus, as an alien enemy, was subject to the curfew, which he had deliberately violated.

We have to imagine Judge Fee's thought processes because he never explained them. He obviously believed, as most Americans now do, that the March 21 statute and other aspects of the government's project to remove Japanese American citizens from the West Coast were unconstitutional. He knew, by the time he issued his decision, of Judge Black's actions in Gordon Hirabayashi's case the month before. He probably also knew that by the time of his decision, all the Japanese American citizens subject to General DeWitt's orders were safely in WRA custody, so his declaration of unconstitutionality was not likely to interfere with the American war effort. I believe, but cannot demonstrate, that a judge of his experience knew well that revocation of the citizenship of a native-born citizen was then limited to a few specific acts, such as bearing arms against the United States or voting in a foreign election.

Two days later Judge Fee sentenced Min to a year in prison and fined him $5,000, the maxima under the statute. Bernard quickly filed an appeal. Min was immediately taken back to the Multnomah County jail to begin serving his sentence. He tells us that "the decision of James Alger Fee stating that the military orders were unconstitutional and could not be enforced against citizens of the United States . . . gave me a tremendous boost." He hoped that the Supreme Court would agree with that part of Judge Fee's decision, and he was confident that the ruling on his citizenship would not survive.

As for his time in jail, he said: "I will frankly say, I think the jailers were being solicitous of my welfare, because they . . . were concerned that someone might do me harm, so I languished in solitary confinement [in a cell] approximately 6 feet by 8 feet."

But, as he explains, it was not traditional solitary confinement because he had books and rudimentary writing materials and was allowed to have visitors, including one Caucasian couple who came about every other week bringing in Chinese takeout.

The appeals process was a slow one, and as it began all four litigants remained in custody, Korematsu and Endo in WRA camps, Hirabayashi and Yasui in county jails. They no longer had an active role to play. The appellate process went on without their physical presence in court. During that period, which lasted until June 1943 for Min and Gordon, and until December 1944 for Mitsuye and Fred, there were some changes. Mitsuye's place of captivity changed in the early fall of 1943 as she, along with others classified by the WRA as "loyal," were shipped out of Tule Lake to other camps as those regarded as "disloyal" were imported there. The last thirteen months of her thirty-month confinement were in the central Utah camp called Topaz. Gordon remained locked up in Seattle for four months after sentencing, which was nine months into his sentence, when Judge Black relented and said that he could be bailed to Spokane in eastern Washington and outside the forbidden zone. There, pending the result of his appeal, he worked with the American Friends Service Committee (AFSC) assisting the resettlement of Nikkei released from their confinement. Gordon sometimes traveled to a point close to the zone from which he was barred, and was met there by an AFSC volunteer who had driven a stored automobile of a family that was preparing to leave the Minidoka camp, which Gordon would then drive to Spokane or Minidoka.

While lawyers on both sides planned their strategies, changes in the situation of the incarcerated people took place. Problems stemming largely from mismanagement by the WRA officials at Manzanar led to peaceful protests and physical attacks on and beatings of inmates, mostly JACLers, by other inmates who claimed that the victims were *inu*, literally dogs, but in this usage informers or stool pigeons. On the evening of December 6, 1942, camp authorities called in troops to maintain order. Out-of-control, untrained troops fired into an unarmed, unruly crowd that refused to disperse, killing two young men and wounding at least ten inmates and one fellow soldier. No soldiers were ever disciplined for the homicides. The tragedy was falsely described in much of the press and by a number of members of Congress as a pro-Japan riot, appearing in newspapers on the first anniversary of Pearl Harbor. The original protest had been about conditions in camp.

In the aftermath of the riot, WRA officials removed two groups of inmates from Manzanar. A number of the targets of the dissidents and their families were removed for their own safety. Most were soon given what the WRA called "leave clearance" and set at liberty to resettle in Chicago and elsewhere. Many of those thought to be the ringleaders of the disorder were sent to a small, tightly restricted desert penal facility without indictment, trial, or even a hearing. This was the beginning of what became a small archipelago of restrictive confinement sites maintained by the WRA, which led to the eventual transformation of one "ordinary" concentration camp, the Tule Lake Relocation Center, into the Tule Lake Segregation Center in the summer of 1943.

In February 1943 the War Department announced that Japanese American males aged eighteen to thirty-seven would again be eligible to volunteer to enter the army. A few days later, in a public letter to war secretary Stimson, President Roosevelt gave his "full approval" to the army's plan to form an "all-Japanese" unit of volunteers. In support of this, Roosevelt made a strong egalitarian statement: "No loyal citizen of the United States should be denied the democratic right to exercise the responsibilities of his citizenship regardless of his ancestry. . . . Americanism is not, and never was, a matter of race or ancestry."

At that moment there were some 70,000 Japanese American citizens in the concentration camps he had established to confine them and Japanese American aliens. Many of the incarcerated Japanese Americans, while pleased by the president's statement, raised an interesting question: "If what the president said is true, why are we in concentration camps?"

As an anonymous federal historian of the Selective Service System remarked, it was recognized that the army's new venture represented a "step in the gradual relaxation of restrictions against the use of Japanese Americans in the armed forces." From the inception of the draft in late 1940 until shortly after the Pearl Harbor attack, more than a thousand Japanese American young men had been drafted without any official discrimination and assigned to units throughout the army. The original Selective Service Act had contained a statutory prohibition against discrimination because of "race, creed or color" or political opinion. In the months immediately after Pearl Harbor, some army commanders discharged Nisei soldiers by transferring them to the enlisted reserve; others were given menial assignments, while still others remained in training or on active service. In a few cases, to be discussed later, serving Nisei soldiers were treated outrageously by their immediate commanders.

Most West Coast draft boards simply reclassified all Nisei registrants as IV-F, physically unfit for duty. On March 20, 1942, the Selective Service System ordered all registrants of Japanese ancestry classified as IV-C, a category reserved for aliens. For almost a year afterward, while the draft status of mainland Japanese Americans remained unchanged, they could again enlist in the army. Almost all were assigned to a segregated unit that would be heavily involved in combat, the vaunted 442nd Regimental Combat Team. By January 1944 nearly 3,000 mainland Japanese Americans had voluntarily enlisted in the army, as did several thousand others in the territory of Hawaii.

The public phase of the appellate process began, ironically, on February 19, 1943, the first anniversary of FDR's EO 9066, when all three cases came before the seven-judge Ninth Circuit Court of Appeals in San Francisco. That court had not yet acquired the reputation for liberalism it now has; in 1944, for example, it sustained the deportation of labor leader Harry Bridges, which the Supreme Court would reverse. Its chief judge, Curtis D. Wilbur, was an Annapolis graduate without formal legal education who, as Calvin Coolidge's secretary of the navy in the mid-1920s, had spoken publicly of Japanese civilization as "hostile." He was a Hoover appointee to the Ninth Circuit in 1929 and had been a judge in California courts for twenty-one years, rising to chief justice before his cabinet appointment.

In charge for the government was Edward J. Ennis, who had joined the Justice Department in 1932 after earning a law degree from Columbia and became general counsel of its Immigration and Naturalization Service in 1941. When war came, Attorney General Biddle made Ennis head of the Justice Department's Alien Enemy Control Unit so that he was the main person within the department dealing with the questions of the treatment of enemy aliens and, very quickly, Japanese American citizens. He tells us in a 1972 interview that he drafted the initial proclamations declaring resident Axis nationals enemy aliens on the night of Pearl Harbor, and that in mid-December he had flown out to meet with General DeWitt, who wanted many more Japanese nationals rounded up than Ennis was then willing to authorize but said nothing about rounding up citizens. When those demands came, Ennis, more than any other ranking member of the Justice Department, resisted them. But when Roosevelt signed Executive Order 9066, drafted by army lawyers, Ennis, although convinced that it and the actions flowing from it were unconstitutional, defended them vigorously: "My office prepared the briefs for the government in *Korematsu, Yasui* and *Endo*, which, as I say, is a curious commentary on the responsibility of the Department of Justice, in defending policies which it, in fact, opposed."

Whether his omission of *Hirabayashi* was intentional is not clear from the context. Later, as he explained:

I represented the War Department, and impressed upon the courts this argument of military necessity, because the Department of Justice as the attorneys in court for other branches of the government, defended the action which, as a matter of policy, we opposed. We defended its constitutionality on the theory that the military in time of war apparently has the constitutional authority to make mistakes.

During the proceedings, the Ninth Circuit first disposed of a suit brought by the most persistent opponents of Japanese Americans, the Native Sons of the Golden West, which sought to nullify the citizenship of Japanese Americans, something it had been agitating for since the Progressive Era. Its counsel, Ulysses S. Webb, who had served nine terms as state attorney general, asked the court to overturn the Supreme Court's *Wong Kim Ark* decision of 1898 that had reaffirmed the citizenship of native-born Chinese Americans. The judges, without even hearing from opposing counsel, dismissed the case out of hand.

The hearing for the three Japanese American cases took a day and a half. The three plaintiffs had not agreed on a joint strategy; each lead attorney chose a somewhat different tack, and all three made their presentations before the government's response. Wayne Collins led off for Fred Korematsu, basing much of his argument on a presumed analogy between martial law and DeWitt's orders and citing the famous *Milligan* decision of 1866 and the lesser-known 1932 case of *Sterling v. Constantin*, each of which affirmed judicial oversight of actions taken under martial law. He was followed by Frank L. Walters, the Seattle attorney who had appeared for Hirabayashi at his trial but who had no appellate experience. His appeal stressed the violation of the Constitution's equal protection clause, but in the eyes of some observers he was inadequate or worse in his responses to questions from the bench. Finally, Bernard for Yasui made what the same observers felt was a competent argument, which included a demolition of Judge Fee's denial of Yasui's American citizenship. A query from the bench produced the response from Ennis that the government would not defend that contention.

The government's case was first presented by the local federal prosecutor, Andrew J. Zirpoli, and then by Ennis. The former led off in the late afternoon and stressed arguments that had been developed earlier by WRA attorneys that the alleged inability of white persons to distinguish between different "orientals" would somehow facilitate any hypothetical invasion by Japanese troops and that the WRA was, in essence, providing protective custody for Japanese Americans from mob and individual violence. Ennis, whose presentation of the government's case took place the following morning, eschewed such arguments, stressing, as Franklin Roosevelt had done to Stimson, "military necessity." However, when challenged from the bench about the hypothetical danger, he admitted that there had not been a single documented subversive activity but speculated that Japanese Americans might have inflicted "incalculable damage" to the American cause "even if only a few hundred" had tried to abet an invasion of Imperial Japanese forces, which, of course never took place. Even this kind of what we have learned to call "Homeland Security logic" should not have been enough to justify the incarceration of some 70,000 American citizens—men, women, and children—who, as he spoke, were confined in the various WRA camps.

Ennis's presentation ended the hearing; the seven judges retired to consider, discuss, and decide. There was to have been one further case. Abraham Lincoln Wirin, the most effective speaker among the West Coast civil liberties lawyers, had expected to argue for the reinstatement of a habeas corpus petition he had presented for a Los Angeles Nisei couple to Judge Harry A. Hollzer, a Hoover appointee of 1931. Hollzer had denied and forwarded it in a timely manner, but Wirin's clients, shocked by their treatment in Santa Anita and Manzanar, withdrew. Thus the habeas corpus approach was not yet in play at the appellate level.

Just over five weeks later, Judge Wilbur announced the decisions of his court; he did not say that those decisions had been shaped, according to Ennis, by his telling Wilbur that this was what Attorney General Biddle wanted done, although it seems likely that Ennis was the originator of the government's strategy. Ennis was also making suggestions to the ACLU's Roger Baldwin, who, in turn, was now seeking to manage the cases he had originally spurned. Ennis let it be known that he felt that the *Endo* case, still pending before Judge Roche, was the one that the government might well lose. Ennis's basic strategy was to get a quick ruling from the Supreme Court on the curfew cases, and have the other two come up later.

Judge Wilbur and five of his colleagues went along with Ennis's suggestions. Instead of deciding the three criminal cases that had been appealed to them, they agreed to ask the Supreme Court, using language supplied by Ennis, to accept the *Hirabayashi* and *Yasui* cases directly, and in a separate procedure asked whether it was appropriate to rule on the *Korematsu* appeal, since Judge St. Sure's sentence was probation, not technically a final judgment, and normally only final judgments may be appealed.

The seventh Ninth Circuit judge, William Denman, objected strenuously. A Harvard Law School graduate of 1897, he practiced law in San Francisco, with time out to chair Wilson's US Shipping Board in 1917, until President Roosevelt appointed him to the Ninth Circuit bench in 1935. A committed New Dealer, he was the rare circuit court judge who publicly supported Roosevelt's 1937 court-packing plan and had, by 1943, written important opinions approving the second Agriculture Adjustment Act and the powers of the National Labor Relations Board.

He thought that his colleagues had failed to perform their allotted task—to decide the three criminal cases appealed to them—and that West Coast judges were best qualified to decide the cases. As soon as Judge Wilbur released the news of the court's actions, Denman sent a short statement to San Francisco papers whose key sentence was "I dissent from the war-haste with which the question involving the deportation of 70,000 of our citizens, without hearing, is hurried out of the court." The next day, March 28, Denman filed a vigorous and discursive dissent, which, amazingly, his colleagues refused to publish or forward to the Supreme Court.

In Washington, Harlan Fiske Stone, a Coolidge appointee to the Supreme Court in 1925 whom Roosevelt appointed chief justice in 1941, moved quickly. On April 3, a Saturday, the justices voted to hear Gordon's and Min's cases immediately. This came as a shock to lawyers involved in the cases, who had assumed that it might be a year before the high court took up the cases. Ennis said that he secretly wrote the certificate that Judge Wilbur forwarded to the Supreme Court, having been told that it was Attorney General Biddle's wish. The latter may have been advised to do so by Ennis.

On Monday, April 5, 1943, Stone told Judge Wilbur to send the records of the three cases to Washington. One result of this strategy was that the *Korematsu* case was separated from the other two, which were finally decided much more quickly than the attorneys involved had anticipated. The separate process that delayed Endo's final result may or may not have been part of the larger government strategy.

The purpose of the severing strategy adopted by the Department of Justice is not as clear as its results. Why did the department, which in practice may well have meant Ennis with Biddle's approval, endeavor successfully to separate the cases? I know of no way to answer that question. One can only speculate. If one believes the axiom "Justice delayed is justice denied," then surely the separation of the cases must be viewed as justice denied. But is that appropriate here? Would the result have been the same if all four cases had been heard at the end of the spring 1943 term? Was the delay an attempt to get *Endo* as far in the future as possible? If that were the case, was it done to delay the presumed result—the release of Nisei from captivity—or was it done in the hope that further progress in the war (or perhaps its successful conclusion) would have created a climate of opinion on a court fearful of inhibiting the war effort? There are, of course, other possibilities, but the question seems unanswerable. The inability to answer certain kinds of questions is one of the factors that makes history, in the words of the great Dutch historian Pieter Geyl, "a debate without end."

CHAPTER THREE

The Supreme Court Decides

As the prosecution of the Japanese American cases was largely controlled by Edward Ennis, Roger N. Baldwin attempted a similar kind of domination of the defense. Baldwin was a founder of the ACLU and, as its only director, dominated it until 1950. After earning a master's degree at Harvard, he taught sociology briefly at Washington University in St. Louis and then achieved a national reputation as that city's chief juvenile court probation officer. During World War I, influenced by radicals such as Emma Goldman, he joined the American Union Against Militarism, which opposed American entry into the war, and went to jail for refusing even to register for the draft. By the World War II era he had become an establishment civil libertarian who delighted in associating with movers and shakers in the New Deal, including the president. During the two wartime years that the Japanese American cases were before the courts, Baldwin spent a good deal of time planning joint legal strategy with Ennis, other Justice Department lawyers, and those from the War Relocation Authority. It is difficult to improve on Dwight Macdonald's characterization of Baldwin's actions in the Japanese American cases as "feeble and confused."

The onset of World War II in September 1939, on the heels of the infamous August pact between Hitler and Stalin, caused Baldwin and others in the ACLU, established in 1920 as a successor to the three-year-old National Civil Liberties Bureau, to reconsider one of their founding principles. He and most of the ACLU's board members were opponents of Hitler and had been willing to work with members of the American Communist Party during most of the 1920s and 1930s. Two members of the ACLU's board had been open officials of the Communist Party (CP), and several others were fellow travelers. After the pact was signed and until Hitler invaded the USSR on June 22, 1941, the CP, which had vigorously opposed Hitler and all his works and been in the forefront of Americans who had sup-ported anti-fascist activities in a united front, switched overnight to opposing most vigorously the increasing efforts of Roosevelt's admin-istration to aid the Western democracies and China. Thus, pushed by long-standing anticommunist members, a majority of the ACLU board supported a February 1940 resolution that barred from board membership anyone who supported totalitarianism in any form. It did not bar such persons from ACLU membership. (The board was self-perpetuating; neither the general membership nor affiliated groups had a vote, which was restricted to about 100 of 6,000 dues-paying members.) The board then privately asked for the resignation of the unmentioned target of the resolution, Elizabeth Gurley Flynn, a legendary figure in the American labor movement who had publicly joined the CP in 1936 and had been reelected to the board in early 1939. She refused to resign and protested in the pages of the *Daily Worker* and elsewhere.

The board then conducted a formal hearing—what some critics called a heresy trial—in a private New York City club. After a bit-ter six-hour debate ending at 2:20 a.m. on May 8, 1940, the board split evenly, 9–9, on the expulsion resolution. Its chair, John Haynes Holmes, broke the tie by voting against Flynn. The expulsion was an embarrassment for the ACLU for decades. In 1968 the board re-scinded the resolution; eight years later it restored Flynn to the board posthumously.

The significance of this change for the Japanese American cases was that the somewhat reconstituted board was less likely to oppose the government in general and President Roosevelt in particular. A month and a day after the issuance of Executive Order 9066, the ACLU board, which had been silent about the public campaign to do something about the West Coast Japanese Americans, sent a mild protest to Roosevelt suggesting that his order and some actions authorized by it might be unconstitutional, but gave its protest no publicity. A referendum sent to members of the ACLU board and its larger National Committee asked them to choose between two resolutions on "Removals from Military Areas." One resolution, never published, held that "any order investing civil or military au-thorities with power to remove citizens from any zone constitutes a violation of civil liberties." The other, chosen by an overwhelming majority—"52 favoring, 26 opposed, 5 undecided, and 9 not voting"—argued in its main paragraph that the "government in our judgment has the constitutional right in the present war to establish military zones and to remove persons, either citizens or aliens from such zones." Its three other paragraphs were largely minor caveats.

The majority resolution's hidden strategy was to prevent ACLU lawyers from arguing that Roosevelt had committed an unconstitutional act but allowing them to argue in court that it was General DeWitt whose orders overstepped what Roosevelt had authorized. Thus, in letters to the West Coast affiliates on June 24, 1942, Baldwin instructed that they were not "free to sponsor cases in which the position is taken that the government has no constitutional right to remove citizens from military areas." He added that the board would permit cases that objected on grounds of racial discrimination.

The West Coast lawyers and activists responded according to their circumstances. A. L. Wirin, in Los Angeles, raised no objections, but the habeas corpus case that he still hoped to present did not require that kind of argument. Mary Farquharson in Seattle, who was not an attorney, following a path suggested by Baldwin, formed a separate committee to support Gordon Hirabayashi's case. Baldwin, who had agreed to support the Seattle case before the board's decision, eventually supplied the Hirabayashi defense committee with $1,000, which covered most of its expenses. In Portland, Earl Bernard, who was not associated with the ACLU, which had no presence in Oregon, presented a brief for Yasui that did not challenge the legality of DeWitt's curfew order; its basic claim was that the order could not be enforced against an American citizen.

But in San Francisco, Ernest Besig responded that in any new cases "we must consider ourselves bound by the change in policy," a concession that cost him nothing as the likelihood of even one new case seemed all but impossible. But he insisted that he would continue his commitment to his client Fred Korematsu. Strongly urged to comply with the current policy in subsequent communications from the New York board, Besig responded: "We don't intend to trim our sails to suit the Board's vacillating policy." His defiance of the board would be reflected in the brief that Collins presented to the Ninth Circuit, which was in violation of the board's order. The board actually threatened to expel the very active Northern California chapter (NCACLU), which Besig managed, for its disregard of ACLU board directives; if it had done so, the ACLU would have forfeited its opportunity to participate in the Japanese American cases.

The hurried preparation of the briefs on relatively short notice because of the expedited handling managed by Ennis created problems for both the appellants and the government. The conflicts among lawyers for the appellants are apparent in their several briefs and arguments. The conflicts for the defense were most acute in those for Hirabayashi and were apparent to anyone who read them. The conflicts within the government remained secret for decades.

Roger Baldwin was able to pressure the Hirabayashi Committee and its counsel to allow the more experienced ACLU lawyers to rewrite its brief. In addition, it would accept, as cocounsel, Harold Evans, a Philadelphia lawyer and prominent Quaker with appellate experience, who would get half of the time allotted to present the case to the Court. Frank Walters, who defended Gordon in Seattle and presented the appeal, was limited to providing a history of the case, while Evans made the constitutional arguments. The brief for Hirabayashi and the amicus brief for the ACLU were written by ACLU counsel Osmond K. Fraenkel and eight other lawyers in its New York office. None of them even suggested that President Roosevelt had done anything unconstitutional. They focused on Public Law 503 and DeWitt's order, arguing that both exceeded the presidential prescription to prevent "sabotage and espionage," and that DeWitt's exclusive focus on expelling and seizing citizens of Japanese ancestry was unlawful racial discrimination. The defendant himself knew nothing about this "fancy dancing," and when he learned of it, years later, was disturbed that it had been done in his name.

Two amicus briefs for Hirabayashi, each written by West Coast lawyers, were not shackled by the limits imposed by Baldwin. The NCACLU's brief, written by Wayne M. Collins, was impolitic and blunt—Peter Irons calls it "billingsgate"—but it went to the heart of the matter, asserting that Roosevelt's executive order imposed conditions "in excess of any constitutional power reposed in the President" and claiming that General DeWitt's orders constituted a "military dictatorship" imposed on Japanese American citizens.

The JACL's brief, signed by the aggressive and industrious Wirin, who had recently acquired that organization as a client, had a secret coauthor. The anthropologist Morris E. Opler, at the time a community analyst for the WRA at the Manzanar concentration camp, had been disturbed by the blunders of its local administrators and the WRA Washington leadership generally and volunteered to help Wirin. The Opler-Wirin brief, largely a positive analysis of Japanese American culture and character in the tradition of Franz Boas, also contained a direct attack on General DeWitt, citing his now notorious statement to Congress in April 1943 that "a Jap is a Jap," wherever born. The amicus briefs had no discernible effect on the result but did reveal some of the divisions between those who were defending, more or less, the civil liberties of Americans. The JACL brief in May 1943 marks that organization's first public support for the Nisei litigants it had previously denounced. Many, perhaps most, of the Japanese Americans actually incarcerated had long supported the Nisei resisters. Stories in the camp newspapers had kept them informed. The visit of Issei women, who are all but invisible in nonfamily accounts of life in the camps, to thank Gordon Hirabayashi's mother for what her son was doing, noted in the previous chapter, is evidence of this largely ignored solidarity.

A different kind of lawyerly conflict arose during the construction of the government's briefs. During the course of helping to prepare the government's briefs for Solicitor General Charles H. Fahy to present to the Supreme Court, Ennis learned of advice given to General DeWitt by US naval intelligence that was at variance with what DeWitt reported to Washington. Ennis and his assistant John Burling suggested to Fahy that the Court should be made aware of this discrepancy. Fahy refused. This and other more serious refusals by the solicitor general in the *Korematsu* brief the following year were suppressions of evidence not made public until the publication of Peter Irons's book *Justice at War* (1983), the impact of which will be discussed in chapter 7. We know that John Burling, Ennis's deputy, who also signed the briefs, was aware of the suppression and remained silent. We do not know if other lawyers in the department knew, or whether it came to the attention of Attorney General Biddle.

Ennis, some have argued, should have gone public: he was a sworn officer of the court, and suppression of evidence is a crime. But being what we now call a "whistle-blower" (who is often celebrated) was not then part of the culture. Ennis had other options: he could have resigned or, at the very least, refused to allow his name to go on the brief. Although he claimed later that he had considered resigning, Ennis endorsed views he did not believe and signed all the government briefs in the Japanese American cases.

Ennis's notions about the obligations of a government lawyer are nicely put in his 1972 oral history in which he commented on his handling of the case involving the declaration of martial law in Hawaii and its duration through the war:

> I thought martial law was entirely wrong in Hawaii after the first year. I went out and defended General Richardson and Admiral Nimitz, and took those cases up to the U.S. Supreme Court [*Duncan v. Kahanamoku*, 327 US 304 (1946)] and argued them, and lost them, I am glad to say. I thought they were wrong at the time. I made no secret of my views and despite that the military had enough confidence in me that I would give all the arguments that were on the government's side.

By 1981, when he revealed some of what he had done to the federal redress commission, history had given him a new excuse for his acquiescence: "Watergate hadn't happened yet."

"No secret" had a special meaning for Ennis. He did not mean that he told the Supreme Court justices that he did not believe what he was telling them. He meant that he did not keep his beliefs secret from his colleagues and superiors in the Justice Department. That, and not his duty to the court, the Constitution, and his profession, seems to have been his highest loyalty.

Another government lawyer involved with the cases took a different view. Maurice Walk, assistant solicitor for the WRA, resigned in protest in September 1943 when asked to write a brief justifying the agency's detention policy and standards of release. He told his boss, "I am unable to collaborate in defense of a policy of which I so strongly disapprove." He went on to predict: "The notion of 'segregation' and 'disloyalty' around which the [WRA's] program has been conceived would, if allowed by the Courts, become the juristic formulation in terms of which future Fascist persecution of racial and political minorities will be justified." But Walk did not go public with his criticism and silently stepped aside.

Oral argument on the three cases before the Supreme Court took place over May 11–12, 1943. Frank Walters, whom the Hirabayashi Committee insisted on retaining despite protests from the ACLU, led off for the plaintiff. However, his brief had been rewritten by the ACLU's New York lawyers, who deleted his claim that General DeWitt's order to report was a "bill of attainder," specifically forbidden by the Constitution (Art. I, Sec. 9), and made other changes, restricting him to an essentially factual account of the case's history. He was surprised when Justice Robert H. Jackson interrupted him to ask whether DeWitt's orders were "bills of attainder." But when Walters affirmed this, Jackson, an upstate New Yorker who had long been a confidant of Franklin Roosevelt, posed several questions suggesting serious doubts about the soundness of Walters's positive answer.

Walters was followed by Harold Evans, who, keeping within the guidelines imposed by the ACLU, focused on the inadequate nature of Public Law 503, the post–Civil War *Milligan* decision, and the fact that actual combat had occurred only at great distances from DeWitt's headquarters. Interrupted repeatedly by questions and comments from several justices, Evans did not have enough time to articulate the claims of lack of due process and presence of racial discrimination in the brief he had been given.

The next morning Bernard opened for Yasui. Even though the government continued its disavowal of Judge Fee's nullification of Yasui's citizenship, Bernard carefully demolished the Oregon jurist's justifications for voiding Yasui's citizenship and spelled out the damages wrought by that voiding. Wirin, inserted into the case by the ACLU and speaking rapidly and well, made the due process and racial discrimination arguments Evans had been forced to omit, attacked DeWitt's various arguments as issued in bad faith, called the general a "puppet" of false patriots and greedy exploiters, and insisted that "race prejudice, not military necessity," was DeWitt's motivation. He also attacked Justice Roberts, who was seated before him, for his public remarks about Japanese American sabotage and espionage during the Pearl Harbor attack, and noted that both Secretary Stimson and Attorney General Biddle had described such comments as "false and misleading."

Justice Hugo L. Black asked Wirin, "To what extent can we review the decision of a general selected to make these decisions?" Wirin replied that in the 1932 case of *Sterling v. Constantin*, "the Court had laid down the three principles: the existence of an emergency, action in good faith, and appropriate steps to meet the emergency." He claimed that DeWitt met none of them. Black questioned whether such criteria could not be applied "to almost every order of a general even in time of actual invasion." Wirin replied, "In case of an invasion, martial law would prevail, and other standards would govern the situation."

Justice Jackson then intervened to say that while DeWitt "might have made an error," nothing before the court demonstrated bad faith, which Wirin made no attempt to counter. But when Justice William O. Douglas, conceding that "some individuals among those evacuated are loyal Americans," claimed that even this did not call into question the military judgment, Wirin disputed him. He argued that the time elapsed between Pearl Harbor and DeWitt's order could have been used to establish loyalty. He concluded that "neither color nor race has any military significance."

Solicitor General Charles Fahy then presented the government's case. He dismissed the charges of defense counsel that the legal basis of General DeWitt's order was vague and without congressional sanction as "secondary constitutional issues," and that the key issue was the power of the president and Congress to wage war. That power, he argued, overrode the due process rights of citizens. He went on to defend Public Law 503—the same law that Senator Taft described as "the sloppiest criminal law I have ever read or seen anywhere"—as clear in its essential purpose, while dismissing defense charges against it as "grasping at a straw." Justice Jackson, himself a former solicitor general, put the case to the Roman Catholic Fahy that "we all agree that in peacetime" a law that criminalized an action of "a descendant of an Irishman" that was permissible "by the descendant of another national" would be struck down. Fahy had to agree. "What makes it treasonable now," he claimed, "is the war power and the circumstances of war." Fahy quickly added, "We do not admit however that there is any discrimination involved." The obvious incongruity of those two statements is further emphasized by the fact that earlier in his presentation Fahy had relied on what he called "racial characteristics" of the Japanese immigrants and their children, such as resistance to assimilation, as if they were genetic factors rather than learned behavior. Throughout his presentation, and especially in his peroration, Fahy, understanding the internal inconsistencies in his argument, stressed the war powers and waved the flag shamelessly. He insisted that the war in the Pacific represented the greatest threat to the United States in its history even though President Roosevelt and his top military advisers always insisted on a Germany-first policy. Time and again the president raised the specter of Nazi world domination and never suggested that such a threat could be mounted by Japan. In words Fahy would repeat in his final argument in Fred Korematsu's case seventeen months later, he suggested that in wartime duties were more important than rights. "During time of war especially, it is not enough to say, 'I am a citizen and I have rights.' One must also say, 'I am a citizen, and I have obligations.'"

The final piece of Japanese American business to be discussed that day was the question of whether Korematsu's suspended sentence was appealable. Since there was unanimity about this on the defense side, and given the difficulties of wartime travel, there was no objection to having Wirin handle this too. For the government, Fahy delegated the argument to John L. Burling, the assistant director of the Justice Department Enemy Alien Control Unit, who helped Ennis prepare all the government briefs in the Japanese American cases. Both sides argued that a suspended sentence was reviewable, with only Justice Felix Frankfurter suggesting from the bench that it might not be. In the immediate aftermath of the pleadings, lawyers on both sides expressed the view that the justices would affirm the convictions.

Chief Justice Stone, still in a hurry-up mode and wanting the matter settled before the Court's summer recess, scheduled the conference for May 17, 1943. We have no direct account of the conference deliberations. The nine men who met to discuss and decide the first two Japanese American cases were truly a Roosevelt court. After having had no opportunity to appoint a justice in his first term, by early 1943 Roosevelt had appointed eight men to the court and promoted Stone to chief justice. Only Owen J. Roberts of the 1943 justices did not owe his present seat to FDR; six of them had been New Dealers personally known to Roosevelt. The court had already, in a July 1942 case, demonstrated its willingness to allow the president great latitude in his war powers by refusing to assert any jurisdiction for the court to review the judgment of a military tribunal established by Roosevelt to try and execute eight Nazi would-be saboteurs, two of them American citizens (*Ex parte Quirin*, 317 US 1).

Chief Justice Stone assigned the opinion to himself and made sure that it was decided on the narrowest possible grounds. That opinion and three concurring opinions with it, plus comments from the conference on *Korematsu* and Black's opinion in that case and the three dissents from it, make it clear that only four justices, Stone, Black, Frankfurter, and Reed, were fully comfortable with the court's abysmal performance in the Japanese American cases. It is possible to imagine that with the right kind of intellectual and moral leadership, a five-man majority could have been forged to declare that the actions taken by the government to incarcerate Japanese Americans were unconstitutional. But that kind of leadership did not exist in the Stone court or in the short-lived Vinson court that followed it. Only after Earl Warren became chief justice a decade after the Japanese American cases were decided did what was still very much a Roosevelt court find its true voice in matters of civil rights.

In the conference Stone strove for unanimity, and Black, in support, insisted that the decision should be approved on the narrowest grounds possible. In agreement Stone said that the justices should consider only the curfew violation and ignore the count of failure to report for incarceration. While this is usually described as a lawyerly decision, and is sometimes ascribed to Gordon's "error" in asking for a sentence that would get him out of the grubby King County jail, it was a legal fiction, as Justice Roberts would note in his dissent in *Korematsu* more than a year later. Then he wrote that the totality of DeWitt's orders were "a cleverly designed trap to accomplish the real purpose of the military authority, which was to lock him up in a concentration camp." At the end of the conference, as the justices announced their decisions in reverse order of seniority, all but Murphy voted to accept the chief justice's views; Murphy reserved his vote. As Justice Jackson described the process of getting unanimity in his *Korematsu* dissent, "We yielded, and the Chief Justice guarded the opinion [in *Hirabayashi*] as carefully as language will do."

On June 1, 1943, the court issued its answer to the procedural question raised about whether Korematsu's suspended sentence could be appealed in the affirmative, remarking, in a unanimous decision, that it was a "final and appealable" sentence and sending the case back to the Ninth Circuit for trial.

On the final day of the court's term, June 23, 1943, which could be called "a date which will live in infamy," as far as the Constitution is concerned, the Stone Court announced its unanimous decision affirming Gordon Hirabayashi's conviction for curfew violation, while turning a blind eye to his conviction for failing to report for incarceration in the so-called assembly center at Puyallup, Washington. Chief Justice Stone's opinion is not one of his better efforts. Some two-thirds of his nearly 7,000-word text was devoted to demonstrating that the president's executive orders and the various actions stemming from them had been supported by acts of Congress as well as by such congressional bodies as the Tolan Committee. It also retraced the history of the Pearl Harbor attack and aspects of the larger war. It included the canard, which the War Department had long since denied publicly, that sabotage had been a factor in the disaster at Pearl Harbor. And even though government lawyers had stipulated in court that there had been no documented acts of sabotage by any Japanese person in the United States, Stone used the word eighteen times, usually paired with "espionage," throughout his opinion. Much of the rest of it focused on the history of racist discrimination in California and the nation against resident Japanese nationals and American citizens of Japanese ancestry. He wrote, "Viewing these data in all their aspects, Congress and the Executive could reasonably have concluded that these conditions have encouraged the continued attachment of members of this group to Japan and Japanese institutions."

Aware that this was a form of racism, Stone went on to justify some forms of legislative and judicial racism:

Distinctions between citizens solely because of their ancestry are by their very nature odious to a free people whose institutions are founded upon the doctrine of equality. . . . Because racial discriminations are in most circumstances irrelevant, and therefore prohibited, it by no means follows that, in dealing with the perils of war, Congress and the Executive are wholly precluded from taking into account those facts and circumstances which are relevant to measures for our national defense and for the successful prosecution of the war, and which may, in fact, place citizens of one ancestry in a different category from others. . . . The adoption by Government, in the crisis of war and of threatened invasion, of measures for the public safety, based upon the recognition of facts and circumstances which indicate that a group of one national extraction may menace that safety more than others, is not wholly beyond the limits of the Constitution, and is not to be condemned merely because, in other and in most circumstances, racial distinctions are irrelevant.

Although his argument would seem to be capable of justifying everything the government had done and was doing to Japanese Americans and a good deal more, Stone, who had reacted to imagined dangers, was determined in this instance to ignore the fact that "curfew," which was all he would rule upon, was but the first step in a three-part process—limitation of movement, removal from homes, and incarceration without term behind barbed wire. Stone ruled that

the conviction under the second count [curfew violation] is without constitutional infirmity. Hence we have no occasion to review the conviction on the first count since, as already stated, the sentences on the two counts are to run concurrently and conviction on the second is sufficient to sustain the sentence. For this reason also it is unnecessary to consider the Government's argument that compliance with the order to report at the Civilian Control Station did not necessarily entail confinement in a relocation center.

Three separate concurring opinions, all by justices appointed by Roosevelt, indicated significant uneasiness about what they were agreeing to. Justice Wiley B. Rutledge, in a one-paragraph comment, insisted that although granted wide powers

a person in the position of General DeWitt . . . of course must have wide discretion and room [to act]. But it does not follow there may not be bounds beyond which he cannot go and, if he oversteps them, that the courts may not have power to protect the civilian citizen. But in this case that question need not be faced and I merely add my reservation without indication of opinion concerning it.

Since, in *Korematsu* a year and a half later, Rutledge did not join the three dissenters and silently concurred, it is not clear where he would draw the line. In the court's conference on that case he observed: "I had to swallow *Hirabayashi*. I didn't like it. At that time I knew that if I went along with that order then I had to go along with detention for a reasonably necessary time. Nothing but necessity would justify it because of *Hirabayashi*, and so I vote to affirm tentatively. I think that the authorities could hold him to determine loyalty." Rutledge appears to be saying that his vote was based on a desire to be consistent rather than his judgment of the case then at hand. If so, it seems a foolish consistency.

Justice Douglas had protested in a private note to Stone that the chief justice's opinion "implies or is susceptible to the inference that the Japs who are citizens cannot be trusted because we have treated them so badly." But no trace of that concern was reflected in the concurrence Douglas filed, which claimed, in passing, that "loyalty is a matter of mind and of heart not of race . . . in the history of America."

The crux of Douglas's opinion stressed having faith in the judgment of soldiers. "We must credit the military with as much good faith . . . as we would any other public official. . . . The point is that we cannot sit in judgment on the military requirements of that hour. . . . the military [should not] be required to wait until espionage or sabotage becomes effective before it moves."

If one substitutes, in Douglas's opinion "the police" for his "the military," and "murder or rape" for his "espionage or sabotage," the fatuity of his argument becomes apparent. Douglas went on to deny the racism that Stone had avowed. In language more appropriate to a dissent, he insisted, "We are dealing here with a problem of loyalty not assimilation. . . . Detention for reasonable cause is one thing. Detention on account of ancestry is another."

After a feeble and feckless analogy between what Gordon did and a conscientious objector who, without waiting for a hearing on his plea for status simply refuses to serve, Douglas ended his opinion: "We need go no further here than to deny the individual the right to defy the law. It is sufficient to say that he cannot test in that way the validity of the orders as applied to him."

The "in that way" suggests that, even then, Douglas, like Ennis before him, may have been anticipating an *Endo* case with a different result. But for a self-proclaimed civil libertarian like Douglas to transmute a general's edict into a law and describe turning oneself in to challenge the constitutionality of a three-step procedure whose certain end was exile and incarceration without term as defiance, was casuistry.

The final concurrence by Justice Frank Murphy was, we now know, originally written as a dissent. Under pressure from some of his colleagues, particularly Felix Frankfurter, who stressed the need for national unity, he modified his opinion. Originally Murphy found the statute "unconstitutional in its broad aspects" and the action taken under it "defective." Murphy removed those words but preserved his criticisms about the decision, writing:

> Today is the first time, so far as I am aware, that we have sustained a substantial restriction of the personal liberty of citizens of the United States based upon the accident of race or ancestry. Under the curfew order here challenged no less than 70,000 American citizens have been placed under a special ban and deprived of their liberty because of their particular racial inheritance. In this sense it bears a melancholy resemblance to the treatment accorded to members of the Jewish race in Germany and in other parts of Europe. The result is the creation in this country of two classes of citizens for the purposes of a critical and perilous hour—to sanction discrimination between groups of United States citizens on the basis of ancestry. In my opinion this goes to the very brink of constitutional power.

Murphy had originally written "over the brink of constitutional power." Had Murphy's opinion been submitted as a dissent, it would have focused a little more public light on the sweeping nature of the *Hirabayashi* decision; the *New York Times* report of the case, in a page six story, did not mention Stone's reference to permissible racial prejudice and ignored the other opinions. Justice Jackson, a former US attorney general who, after voting "yes" in conference, had doubts, wrote a substantial dissent but never circulated or submitted it. Had he done so, that too would have been news.

On July 5, 1944, just short of a year after it had been filed, Judge Roche finally denied Mitsuye Endo's petition for habeas corpus without giving reasons for his denial or the delay. The next month James

Purcell filed an appeal with the Ninth Circuit. Thus by August 1943 the first two Japanese American cases had been settled initially in favor of the government; the other two were on their way back to the Ninth Circuit. The fate of the first pair of defendants was settled while the final outcome of the war was still in doubt; that of the other two would be judged in the last months of 1944 with victory in sight.

The Ninth Circuit finally ruled on Fred Korematsu's appeal six months after the Supreme Court returned it. On December 2, 1943, Judge Wilbur ruled that no further oral argument was necessary and in a cursory opinion, writing for himself and five silent colleagues, noted that the Supreme Court in *Hirabayashi* had ruled that DeWitt's curfew order was valid. He stated that although the "Supreme Court did not expressly pass upon the validity of the evacuation . . . [w]e are of the opinion that this principle, thus decided, so clearly sustains the validity of the proclamation for evacuation, which is here involved, that it is not necessary to labor the point." In a footnote Wilbur denied any judicial authority over the military in war power cases: "It is not for any court to sit in review of the wisdom of their action or substitute its judgment for theirs." If, as a Stone biographer wrote, the chief justice had reduced the high court's review powers almost to the vanishing point, Wilbur went on to reach that point.

Judge Denman, as had been the case when the Ninth Circuit had ruled in *Hirabayashi*, seemed to dwell in a different universe than his colleagues. In the nativist atmosphere of the Ninth Circuit—its dockets listed defendants as "Kiyoshi Hirabayashi" and "Toyosaburo Korematsu," suppressing each man's legal first name—Judge Denman in his dissent "in part" embraced Korematsu as "a fellow citizen who, because happening to have a common ancestry with the people under the domination of the Japanese Government with which we are at war after decades of peaceful intercourse, was required to report for imprisonment in a military assembly stockade to await deportation for further such imprisonment."

Denman, as he had done in his unpublished dissent at the February trial, drew a parallel with the German treatment of Jews and called attention to Justice Murphy's similar reference in his dissent in *Hirabayashi*. In a long and discursive opinion, he criticized his colleagues for resolving all questions "in favor of an uncontrolled military autocracy." He concluded: "General DeWitt's orders exceed the area of discretionary powers legally to be exercised by him in Military Area No. 1."

Wayne Collins had filed a petition for certiorari in *Korematsu* with the court in February, and its oral argument was slated for late April. Since Wilbur had scheduled the hearing on Endo's petition for May 16, too late for a hearing on it until the fall, it seemed that *Korematsu* would be decided before *Endo* had been heard by its final arbiters.

For whatever reason, Judge Denman decided to intervene. He phoned Endo's lawyer, James Purcell, sometime on or before April 14 asking him if he would object to certification directly to the Supreme Court, the same device Ennis had persuaded Wilbur to adopt in *Hirabayashi* in 1943. Purcell was delighted and filed a motion in Denman's court on April 14, 1944, asking for certification. Denman then told Frank Hennessey, the federal attorney in San Francisco, that he would hear arguments on Purcell's motion on April 24. The federal attorney's office passed this on to the Justice Department, where Fahy had word sent back to tell Denman that, given his timetable, *Korematsu* could not be heard by the court in its current term. Denman's reaction was to send his request for certification to the court on April 22, two days before his now-canceled hearing. His request was accompanied by four questions, all phrased, as Fahy had noted, with hostility toward the government's argument. The first and most important was:

Has the War Relocation Authority the power to hold in custody . . . an American citizen, now more than twenty months after such citizen has been evacuated from her residence in California, without any right in such citizen to seek a release from such custody in a hearing by the authority with the substantial elements of due process for the determination of facts warranting her further detention because such citizen is of Japanese ancestry?

The Supreme Court accepted the case on May 8, 1944, and ordered the entire record certified to it. Ennis, who had long assumed that the second pair of Japanese American cases would be decided together, suggested to Fahy that it might be well for the *Korematsu* case to be further delayed so that it and Endo's petition could be heard at the same time. Fahy agreed, and asked the court to do so. As it happened Wayne Collins—who was in the capital to appear at the Endo hearing for Purcell, also wanted the two heard together. In April and May 1944, the Supreme Court agreed, in related actions, to accept the Endo case and scheduled it for the fall 1944 term; it rescheduled *Korematsu* for the same term. The court would hear both in a two-day proceeding on October 11–12, 1944.

That delay extended Mitsuye Endo's imprisonment to at least twenty-nine months as she remained in the camp called Topaz in southern Utah. Fred Korematsu, who had been released on what the WRA called "leave" in March 1944, was in Detroit working in a war plant.

Government and ACLU lawyers tried to control the *Endo* case as they had tried to control the other three. Ennis, using the San Francisco federal attorney Zirpoli as an intermediary, tried to set up a meeting with Endo's lawyer James Purcell, who responded that it would be a waste of time. Baldwin's assistant, New York ACLU lawyer Clifford Forster, urged Purcell, who had no formal connection with the ACLU, through Besig, to drop the *Endo* appeal. The San Francisco director relayed Purcell's reply: "You can tell your New York office to go to hell!"

The scheduling of *Endo* activated WRA attorneys, who had been hovering around the cases since early 1943 and now had an active role to play. They were led by WRA solicitor Philip M. Glick, who had invented a theory of "precautionary detention," which asserted that the WRA was holding citizens against their will in order to protect them from hostility they might encounter outside of camp. Fearing that a successful result of Endo's case would interfere with the WRA's ability to detain citizens, he personally went out to the desolate Topaz camp in southern Utah. He told Peter Irons in 1981 that he had said to her: "Miss Endo you're clearly a person who has been loyal to the United States . . . all you need do is ask for the right to leave the center and you can go. Any leave we grant you will expressly exclude return to the restricted area, but we will help you relocate anywhere else in the United States."

Understanding that accepting what the WRA called "leave clearance" would abort her petition for habeas corpus, Mitsuye Endo remained steadfast. Although she had applied for leave clearance on the first anniversary of Executive Order 9066 (February 19, 1943), she refused to apply for "indefinite leave," which WRA regulations required to complete the process, unless the restriction on return to her home in Sacramento was removed. The WRA did have plans to release persons certified as loyal, but it opposed Endo's petition because, if granted, it could prevent the retention of those it regarded as disloyal.

If WRA lawyers were discomforted by the delay in *Endo*, it came to suit army lawyers, including John McCloy. Their desire for delay had nothing to do with the war, or military necessity, or national security, but with national politics. On May 8, 1944, seeking support for the view he had developed that it was no longer necessary to keep "loyal" Japanese Americans from returning to their West Coast homes, McCloy asked the army's chief of staff, General George C. Marshall, for his views. Marshall, who had never advocated mass exile and incarceration of Japanese Americans or claimed a military justification for it, responded that, except for the possibility that, if the return of Japanese Americans to the West Coast set off anti-Japanese riots in the region it might trigger reprisals against American prisoners of war in Japanese captivity, there were no military reasons for continuing exclusion from the West Coast. However, he went on to tell McCloy that there were "strong political reasons why the Japanese should not be returned to the West Coast before November."

If McCloy had any doubts about this, they were erased on June 13, when he went to the White House to discuss with the president plans that he and General Delos Emmons were developing to end mass exclusion and allow large numbers of loyal Japanese Americans to return to their homes. (Emmons had been brought from Hawaii to replace General DeWitt after the latter was relieved as western defense commander in September 1943.) In a recorded telephone conversation McCloy told Emmons:

I just came from the President a little while ago—keep this to yourself—and he put thumbs down on [allowing large numbers to return]. He wants to reinvigorate the distribution in the rest of the country and it is all right, he said, to introduce some very gradually as a relaxation of the general program into California but to do it on a very gradual basis and nothing like the scheme we have in mind. He was surrounded at that moment by his political advisors and they were harping hard that this would stir up the boys in California and California, I guess, is an important state.

From another quarter of the administration, Interior secretary Harold L. Ickes also began to press for relaxing the controls on Japanese Americans. He had long been critical of the entire process. An early supporter of Japanese Americans, he criticized those who opposed their reentry into American society. In April 1943 he had sponsored the resettlement of seven Japanese Americans—four men and three women—to live and work on his chicken farm and that of a neighbor in Olney, Maryland, and arranged for it to be publicized. This was not a case of getting someone to do chores; the men were college-trained poultry specialists.

After mid-February 1944, when Roosevelt transferred the formerly independent WRA into the Interior Department after increasing congressional criticisms of the agency for "pampering" its prisoners, Ickes and his undersecretary, Abe Fortas, began to reshape WRA policies but left director Myer, solicitor Glick, and other top officials in place. In addition, Ickes began to pepper the president with suggestions for liberalizing the terms of confinement and abandoning the restrictions on resettlement. The president continued to resist advice for an immediate change of policy, but his answer was "not yet" rather than "no."

On June 12, 1944, Roosevelt sent Ickes and the State Department a memo laying down lines of policy:

> The more I think of this problem of suddenly ending the orders excluding Japanese Americans from the West Coast the more I think it would be a mistake to do anything drastic or sudden. . . . I am thinking of two methods:
>
>> Seeing, with great discretion, how many Japanese families would be acceptable to public opinion on the West Coast.
>> Seeking to extend greatly the distribution of other families in many parts of the United States, and they are all in agreement that the Coast would be willing to receive back a portion of the Japanese who were formerly there—nothing sudden and not in too great quantities at any one time.

Also, in talking to people from the Middle West, the East and the South, I am sure that there would be no bitterness if they were distributed—one or two families to each county as a start. Dissemination and distribution constitute a great method of avoiding public outcry.

Why not proceed seriously along the above line—for a while at least.

F.D.R.

In early September, in response to a presidential inquiry about the distribution of released Japanese Americans, Abe Fortas had a map prepared for the president showing the number of released Japanese Americans in each state. There were some shown for every state except South Carolina, but more than half of the nearly 26,000 were in the seven states abutting the Great Lakes, with more than half of the latter group in Illinois. And, although Fortas did not say so, the overwhelming majority—like the overwhelming majority of other American migrants during World War II—moved to large cities, especially Chicago.

In a Columbus Day speech broadcast to the nation less than a month before the November 1944 presidential election, Roosevelt made his first and only mention of Japanese Americans in talking to the American people. In a passage listing the variety of forces fighting to liberate Italy that began with "men from forty eight United States, . . . Great Britain, and . . . France" and ended with "South Africa, and India," the president added: "There are combat teams composed of Americans of Japanese ancestry who came from Hawaii—all providing an effective answer to the false Nazi claims of 'Nordic superiority.'" It is not possible to say whether the omission of Nikkei from the mainland was a deliberate slur—Hawaiians did constitute a majority of the 442nd—or the kind of error that occurred during a hectic campaign that apparently cannot now be determined.

More than two months later, after the election had been won and the *Korematsu* and *Endo* cases had been argued and decided but not yet announced, Roosevelt said in public some of what he had been saying to his advisers for some months. His November 21, 1944, press conference response to a reporter's question was the only substantial explanation he ever made about the resettlement of Japanese Americans. He never even tried to explain why he had ordered that they be rounded up and imprisoned.

> THE PRESIDENT: . . . A good deal of progress has been made in scattering [Japanese Americans] around the country, and that is going on almost every day. . . . There are about . . . a hundred thousand Japanese-origin citizens in this country. And it is felt by a great many lawyers that under the Constitution they can't be kept locked up in concentration camps. And a good number of them . . . you had better check with the Secretary of the Interior on this—somewhere around 20 to 25 percent of all those citizens have replaced themselves, and in a great many parts of the country.

The president went on to speak about "scattering" the released Japanese Americans in rural counties—typically he spoke of places he was familiar with—"the Hudson River valley" and "western 'Joe-gia' (Georgia)"—but that was a fairy tale. Sizable urban areas from Salt Lake City to New York City drew the vast majority of these twice-relocated people. He never mentioned resettlement on the Pacific coast, to which more than half of the exiles eventually returned.

In his press conference Roosevelt did say, "After all they are American citizens, and we all know that American citizens have certain privileges," and added, giving his second and last public kudos to Japanese American soldiers: "And, of course we are actuated . . . in part by the very wonderful record that the Japanese in that battalion in Italy have been making in the war. It is one of the outstanding battalions we have."

When a reporter followed up by asking whether the restrictions on Japanese returning to their former homes would be changed, the president ignored him and answered a question on another topic. Every aspect of Roosevelt's wartime treatment of Japanese Americans is an indelible stain on his reputation.

In the preparation of the government brief for the *Korematsu* appeal, Ennis and Burling had further conflicts with Solicitor General Fahy. The publication of General DeWitt's *Final Report: Japanese Evacuation from the West Coast, 1942*, which is dated July 1943 but was not publicly released until January 1944, revealed that the West Coast commander had relied upon spurious evidence that had been invalidated by subsequent reports made to him by the Federal Communications Commission and the FBI. They had placed a footnote in the brief they drafted, calling attention to these matters and disavowing them. Had it been retained, it surely would have caught the eye of some of the justices as calling into question the alleged "military necessity" that was held to be justification for the army's actions against Japanese Americans. When army lawyers showed the footnote to John McCloy, the assistant war secretary complained directly to Fahy. This reignited the dispute among the Justice Department lawyers when the solicitor general drafted a replacement footnote that Ennis and Burling thought gave away too much.

The dispute was resolved by Assistant Attorney General Herbert Wechsler, who drafted an even weaker footnote, which both parties reluctantly accepted but which satisfied neither. As submitted to the court, the footnote cited none of the crucial documents the two dissidents had discovered and merely read: "We have specifically recited in this brief the facts relating to the justification for the evacuation, of which we ask the court to take judicial notice; and we rely on the final report only to the extent that it relates to such facts."

Ennis and Burling, who had threatened to withhold their signatures from the brief, nevertheless signed it. These seemingly minor bureaucratic squabbles would have grave consequences some four decades later.

The Supreme Court hearing on Korematsu's appeal of his September 1943 conviction for refusing to obey General DeWitt's order to report for removal to the assembly center at the Tanforan Racetrack in May 1942 began on October 11, 1944. The two lawyers who opened for the defense were not a matched pair, and their oral arguments headed in different directions.

The blunt Collins, the West Coast maverick, essentially made a stump speech. His approach can be likened to that of a latter-day Clarence Darrow, but Darrow's rhetoric was directed at lay jurors. Collins, who had never even seen a Supreme Court hearing until a few days before he had to appear as Korematsu's advocate, spoke as if he were addressing a jury rather than an appellate panel. His verbal weapon was more like a sawed-off shotgun than a sniper's rifle and caused even his supporter Ernest Besig to despair. We do not have a copy of his speech to the court, but those attuned to the nuances of appellate rhetoric would wring their hands and roll their eyes when discussing his performance. His brief ended with: "General DeWitt let Terror out to plague these citizens but closed the lid on the Pandora box and left Hope to smother. It is your duty to raise the lid and revive Hope for these, our people, who have suffered at the hands of one of our servants. Do this speedily as the law commands you. History will not forget your opinion herein."

Paired with Collins was the urbane Charles A. Horsky, a member of the elite Washington law firm of Covington and Burling who did pro bono work for the ACLU. He had been an attorney in the solicitor general's office and would later serve as a prosecutor in the Nuremburg war crimes trials. Like many appellate lawyers, he tended to shape his argument to appeal to the known beliefs of particular justices. He concentrated on demonstrating to the justices who had refused to admit in *Hirabayashi* that reporting to go to an assembly center led inexorably to imprisonment without definite term that this was, in fact, the case. It was clear to him that Justice Murphy, despite his failure to vote no, essentially agreed with him, so his task was to get four more votes.

Horsky received some guidance from his former colleagues Ennis and Burling, with whom he met to discuss strategy while drafting his appeal. (Burling was doubly his colleague as he had been employed by Burling's father's law firm.) This coziness is all too common among Washington lawyers who glide back and forth between government service and private and public practice. In this instance it raises serious ethical questions about the Justice Department lawyers. There is no evidence known to me that they showed Horsky any of the documents that they had vainly tried to get into the government brief, but it seems likely that they at least pointed Horsky to passages in General DeWitt's *Final Report*. Describing his purposes to a *Washington Post* reporter in 1988, Horsky said that in his *Korematsu* brief: "I was trying to persuade the Court that there was no legitimate crisis for the Army to arrest citizens [but] I couldn't get enough evidence."

He also, as he explained to Peter Irons, criticized both DeWitt's report and the solicitor general's reliance upon it. This dispelled some of the coziness among the lawyers; Horsky remarked that what he had said to the court about Fahy's argument "so irritated him that we were not on speaking terms for about a decade."

In oral argument Horsky was able to make the point he wanted, when, during his presentation, Chief Justice Stone asked him, "Is [the] question of confinement as distinct from exclusion present in this case?" Horsky affirmed this, pointing to the admission in the government brief that if Korematsu had reported as ordered, he "would have found himself, for a period of time . . . in a place of detention." Horsky then argued that Public Law 503 did not authorize detention. He also called the court's attention to the "extraordinary footnote" in the government's brief.

Fahy's argument rested on the claim in the government's brief that detention was not at issue in the case. We have no clear notion of what Fahy said, but the twenty pages of notes he took with him to the podium included the palpably false statement that Korematsu "was never detained in an Assembly Center."

The proceedings in what was termed *Ex parte Endo* began immediately after Fahy ended his remarks. The Justice Department's brief never claimed that the long-term detention of loyal citizens was constitutional, and there seems no reason to doubt Ennis's postwar claim that he had always thought that *Endo* was a case the government was bound to lose. The government brief that he and Burling gladly signed all but gave the game away. It quoted James F. Byrnes, a former Supreme Court justice who, as the head of the Office of War Mobilization, was, after Roosevelt, the most authoritative voice on home front affairs, in recent testimony before Congress:

The detention or internment of citizens of the United States against whom no charges of disloyalty or subversiveness have been made or can be made, for longer than the limited period necessary to screen the loyal from the disloyal, and provide the necessary guidance for relocation, is beyond the power of the War Relocation Authority. In the first place, neither the Congress nor the President has directed the War Relocation Authority to carry out such detention or internment. Secondly lawyers will readily agree that an attempt to authorize such confinement would be very difficult to reconcile with the constitutional rights of citizens.

That statement, so convenient for the defense, does raise the question of where the WRA got its power to continue to hold tens of thousands of American citizens of unchallenged loyalty in uncomfortable captivity. The answer, of course, was from the president, who directed it through verbal and written instructions sent through the Bureau of the Budget and Harold Ickes.

Some legal scholars have derided Wayne Collins for refusing to accept the government's surrender in the *Endo* case and insisting on attacking the president and General DeWitt in a long and vituperative brief. Clearly Collins's briefs and pleadings lacked the learned constitutional sophistication that scholars properly admire and praise. But he, unlike many of the advocates on both sides, never forgot that the Japanese American cases were about securing "the Blessings of Liberty" to tens of thousands of American citizens who had been denied them for more than two years by a whole host of officials, high and low, even after the government had admitted that the putative causes of their incarceration, "espionage" and "sabotage," could not be attributed to them. That was, as Fred Korematsu put it years later, "a great wrong."

Collins had made the necessary legal points that Endo's continuing confinement lacked both executive and legislative sanction. Roger Baldwin told Besig that ACLU lawyers were "shocked" that Collins had signed both his own brief and the NCACLU's amicus brief. But Baldwin did have his office, which failed to enter a brief in *Korematsu*, prepare one for *Endo* written by Osmond Frankel, and signed by seven other attorneys, including Charles Horsky. Its basic argument was that "no power had been granted by the Congress or can constitutionally be granted to any agency of government to detain citizens indefinitely without the formulation against them of any charges whatever." Suiting his argument to the case at hand, he conceded that there might be justification for the prolonged detention of "American citizens of Japanese ancestry who have been found disloyal and therefore dangerous" but noted that Endo's loyalty had been vouchsafed by the government. He went on to insist, echoing Denman and Murphy: "This is the outrageous doctrine of 'protective custody' invented by the Nazis in their persecution of the Jews. . . . It has no place in American life."

The justices met in conference on October 16, 1944, to decide both *Korematsu* and *Endo*, one day short of seventeen months after they had decided *Hirabayashi* and *Yasui*, and three weeks and a day before the presidential election. The war had changed greatly in those months; by mid-1942 the United States had destroyed the attacking power of the Japanese navy; by the end of that year it had commenced offensive operations in the southwest Pacific and North Africa; and in mid-1944 it had begun the invasion that would end the war in Europe. By October the justices knew that victory was just a matter of time and that any fears of espionage that they may have entertained in the spring of 1943 had been chimerical. The comments on their conference are based on notes by Justices Douglas, Jackson, and Murphy.

Stone again did most of the talking, indicating that he would prefer not to have to consider evacuation, but since Korematsu had not been indicted for curfew violation, it proved impossible to avoid. Stone persisted in laying great emphasis on sabotage despite the government's continued assertions that there had been none. Black, Douglas, Frankfurter, Reed, and Rutledge all supported Stone's view; Rutledge, as noted, "swallowed it" to be consistent.

Douglas's caveat was that "there was no constitutional authority to arrest without probable cause." But on December 6 he informed Stone that he would silently approve. His 1980 autobiography says, "I wrote a concurring opinion, which I never published, agreeing to the evacuation but not *via* the concentration camp" and goes on to claim, "I have always regretted that I bowed to my elders and withdrew my opinion."

The other three justices said that they would dissent. In his dissent Jackson explained, "I don't accept military orders as something we have to accept without inquiry into their reasonableness." Stone responded that "if you can do it for curfew," as Jackson had done, "you can do it for exclusion." Murphy, like Douglas, had regrets, but his were that he had voted with the other eight while expressing a view more appropriate to a dissent. This time his dissent made a similar argument. In some ways Roberts's views evinced the widest swing. Upon his return from Pearl Harbor in 1942, he had cut a wide swath through the upper echelons of official Washington, retailing the canards about Japanese American subversion on Oahu that were not in the report he signed, and had concurred, warily, in *Hirabayashi*. Now he found that Korematsu was wrongfully convicted. Stone assigned the opinion to Black.

Stone led off in the discussion of *Endo* as well, but here he was preaching to the choir, even if some of his statements were inaccurate. The whole basis of the military orders, according to Stone, was "the presence of disloyal people among the mass of Jap citizens. . . . Once loyalty is shown, the basis for the military decision disappears. On the merits, this woman is entitled to summary release." No one disagreed with him, and he assigned the opinion to Douglas.

Justice Black, writing for a 6–3 majority, upheld Korematsu's conviction, arguing, in the first instance, "In the light of the principles we announced in the *Hirabayashi* case, we are unable to conclude that it was beyond the war power . . . to exclude those of Japanese ancestry from the west coast war area at the time they did." Stung by the objections of three of his colleagues, Black denied that exclusion and detention were the same thing:

> It is said that we are dealing here with the case of imprisonment of a citizen in a concentration camp solely because of his ancestry. . . . Our task would be simple, our duty clear, were this a case involving the imprisonment of a citizen in a concentration camp because of racial prejudice. Regardless of the true nature of the assembly and relocation centers—and we deem it unjustifiable to call them concentration camps with all the ugly connotations that term implies—we are dealing specifically with nothing but an exclusion order. To cast this case into outlines of racial prejudice . . . merely confuses the issue.

To help take the curse off his views, Black made a point of citing the concurrent opinion in *Endo*, which would be presented immediately after the opinions in *Korematsu* had been delivered: "The *Endo* case . . . graphically illustrates the difference between the validity of an order to exclude and the validity of a detention order after exclusion has been effected."

In a long interview with the *New York Times* in 1967, given with the understanding that it remain unpublished until his death, the aging Justice Black spoke bluntly about many issues and had this to say about his *Korematsu* opinion:

I would do precisely the same thing today, in any part of the country. I would probably issue the same order were I President. We had a situation where we were at war. People were rightly fearful of the Japanese in Los Angeles, many loyal to the United States, many undoubtedly not, having dual citizenship—lots of them. They all look alike to a person not a Jap. Had they attacked our shores you'd have a large number fighting with the Japanese troops. And a lot of innocent Japanese Americans would have been shot in the panic. I saw nothing wrong in moving them away from the danger area.

Justice Frankfurter added a two-paragraph concurrence aimed at the three dissenters. He added to Charles Evans Hughes's rhetorical definition of the war power as "the power to wage war successfully" a codicil: "The validity of action under the war power must be judged wholly in the context of war." He went on to a virtual demolition of any restraint on the military in wartime. "If a military order does not transcend the means appropriate for conducting war," he argued, it is constitutional. Having said that, he verbally washed his hands: "To find that the Constitution does not forbid the military measures now complained of does not carry with it the approval of that which Congress and the Executive did. That is their business, not ours."

The three dissenters defended their common conclusion in different ways. Justice Roberts described the case as one "convicting a citizen as a punishment for not submitting to imprisonment in a concentration camp, based on his ancestry, and solely because of his ancestry, without evidence or inquiry concerning his loyalty and good disposition towards the United States." Roberts argued that Korematsu was faced with

> two conflicting orders, one which commanded him to stay and the other which commanded him to go, [which] were nothing but a cleverly designed trap to accomplish the real purpose of the military authority, which was to lock him up in a concentration camp. The only course by which the petitioner could avoid arrest and prosecution was to go to that camp according to instructions to be given to him when he reported at a Civil Control Center.

Rather than admit that his concurrence in *Hirabayashi* had been in error, Roberts sloughed it off by saying that *Korematsu* was "not a case of keeping people off the streets at night," as if the right to use the public streets were not constitutionally protected.

Justice Murphy's dissent begins with a revision of the final sentence of his concurrence in *Hirabayashi*: "This exclusion of 'all persons of Japanese ancestry, both alien and non-alien' from the Pacific Coast area on a plea of military necessity ought not to be approved. Such exclusion goes over 'the very brink of constitutional power' and falls into the ugly abyss of racism." He went on to argue:

> The judicial test of whether the Government on a plea of military necessity can validly deprive any individual of any of his constitutional rights is whether the deprivation is reasonably related to a public danger that is so "immediate, imminent and impending" as not to admit of delay and not permit the intervention of ordinary constitutional purposes to alleviate the danger. Civilian Exclusion Order No. 34, banishing from a prescribed area of the Pacific Coast "all persons of Japanese ancestry, both alien and nonalien" clearly does not meet that test.

Murphy went on to argue that the decision was largely justified by the "erroneous assumption of racial guilt," which he demonstrated with quotations from General DeWitt's *Final Report*. He accepted a major undemonstrated assumption of DeWitt's document—"No one denies . . . that there were some disloyal persons of Japanese descent who did all in their power to aid their ancestral land"—but insisted that "to infer that examples of individual disloyalty prove group disloyalty" was to deny the basic principle that guilt was individual, not collective. He also pointed to the nearly four months between Pearl Harbor and the issuance of DeWitt's order and claimed that there had been time to make individual determinations of loyalty or its absence. He specifically rejected the concessions to the admissibility of racial distinction explicitly present in Stone's *Hirabayashi* opinion and covert in Black's opinion in *Korematsu* as "a legalization of racism." Murphy's opinion was thus an explicit denial of the constitutional acceptability of racism. "Racial discrimination in any form and in any degree has no justifiable part whatever in our democratic way of life."

The footnotes of Murphy's opinion show that he had consulted a considerable proportion of the small body of journalistic and legal literature critical of the government's policies toward Japanese Americans then available. He might also have cited Gunnar Myrdal's now classic study *An American Dilemma: The Negro Problem and Modern Democracy*, which had been published to great acclaim that January, but he did not; nor did he address that aspect of American racism. The Swedish scholar's work would not find a place in the court's footnotes for another decade.

The final dissenter, Justice Jackson, who had been solicitor general, penned a somewhat paradoxical dissent. Like Denman, his words embraced "Korematsu . . . born on our soil . . . has been convicted of an act not commonly a crime [consisting of] merely being present . . . near the place where he was born." A "series of military orders forbid [him] to remain, [and] they also forbid him to leave. . . . the only way Korematsu could avoid violation was to give himself up to the military authority. This meant submission to custody, examination [and] indeterminate confinement in detention camps."

Jackson went on to argue that, as a justice, he had no way of determining whether a military order was reasonable, even though he had done just that in *Hirabayashi*, a decision he apparently now regretted. But, unlike Rutledge, he did not feel bound by that vote. Instead, he concluded:

> My duties as a justice as I see them do not require me to make a military judgment as to whether General DeWitt's evacuation and detention program was a reasonable military necessity. I do not suggest that the courts should have attempted to interfere with the Army in carrying out its task. But I do not think they may be asked to execute a military expedient that has no place in law under the Constitution. I would reverse the judgment and discharge the prisoner.

The opinions in the unanimous *Endo* decision were less complex. Douglas, who had suggested in *Hirabayashi* that there was an appropriate way to challenge a military order, felt that Ms. Endo had found it. His opinion carefully began by treating in some detail the government's actions affecting Japanese Americans. Until he began to speak of the WRA, there was no suggestion that anything untoward had been done by the president, the Congress, or the military. Instead, it was the WRA that he went on to blame as responsible for holding an American citizen in a detention camp against her will.

This palpable fairy tale was too much for Justice Roberts, who, in his concurrence insisted that

> the court endeavors to avoid constitutional issues which are necessarily involved. The opinion, at great length, attempts to show that neither the executive nor the legislative arm of the Government authorized the detention of the relator. . . . This seems to me to ignore patent facts. As the opinion discloses, I think it inadmissible to suggest that some inferior public servant exceeded the authority granted by executive order in this case. . . . It is to hide one's head in the sand to assert that the detention of relator resulted from an excess of authority by subordinate officials.

Justice Murphy's two-paragraph concurrence accepted some of Douglas's fairy tale, but his version had a different villain:

> I join in the opinion of the Court, but I am of the view that detention in Relocation Centers of persons of Japanese ancestry regardless of loyalty is not only unauthorized by Congress or the Executive but is another example of the unconstitutional resort to racism inherent in the entire evacuation program. As stated more fully in my dissenting opinion in *Fred Toyosaburo Korematsu v. United States* . . . racial discrimination of this nature bears no reasonable relation to military necessity and is utterly foreign to the ideals and traditions of the American people. Moreover, the Court holds that Mitsuye Endo is entitled to an unconditional release by the War Relocation Authority. It appears that Miss Endo desires to return to Sacramento, California, from which Public Proclamations Nos. 7 and 11, as well as Civilian Exclusion Order No. 52, still exclude her. And it would seem to me that the "unconditional release" to be given Miss Endo necessarily implies "the right to pass freely from state to state," including the right to move freely into California. . . . If, as I believe, the military orders excluding her from California were invalid at the time they were issued, they are increasingly objectionable at this late date, when the threat of invasion of the Pacific Coast and the fears of sabotage and es-

pionage have greatly diminished. For the Government to suggest under these circumstances that the presence of Japanese blood in a loyal American citizen might be enough to warrant her exclusion from a place where she would otherwise have a right to go is a position I cannot sanction.

The political reason for delaying both decisions was dissolved by the November 7 election, as did any judicial reason for delaying *Korematsu* after Douglas withdrew his concurrence on December 6. No such reason existed for delay in *Endo*. After Stone again failed to announce it on November 27, Douglas had written a note urging that the decision be released on December 4, the subsequent decision Monday, "unless prior to that time Mitsuye Endo either has been released or promised her immediate and unqualified release." He noted that "the Court is unanimous in the view that she is unlawfully detained" in his opinion, which had been printed and distributed on November 8. "Everything is at a standstill," he complained, "because officers of the government have indicated that some change[s] in detention plans are under consideration." Two more decision Mondays would pass before both *Korematsu* and *Endo* were released in tandem on December 18 as Black's *Korematsu* opinion had suggested.

Before that there was a great deal of maneuvering as Stone and Frankfurter kept the White House and the War Department informed and the chief justice deliberately delayed justice to accommodate them. The army wished, above all, to save face and make it seem that it was in full control. Pacific coast congressmen continued to express concern, lest the West Coast exiles, or some of them, would be allowed to return to their homes. On December 11 the army's John McCloy sent a letter to Clarence F. Lea, a fourteen-term congressman from Northern California, who chaired an informal committee of West Coast members of the House opposing any return of Japanese Americans, maintaining the fiction that mass exclusion would continue only as long as the West Coast commanding general considered it a military necessity. In that instance, he informed them, "these are problems for which civilian agencies are responsible and there is no reason to believe that they are incapable of handling them."

On Sunday, December 17, Major General Henry C. Pratt, the third western defense commander since DeWitt's relief in September 1943, called an extraordinary press interview at San Francisco's Presidio to announced that, effective January 2, 1945, the ban on Japanese Americans returning to their former homes would be rescinded because "existing military necessity does not justify control over citizens who have been determined not to be potentially dangerous." He promised that all those allowed to return would be "either loyal or harmless." The details of that return and other legal and political consequences of the wartime incarceration will be treated in subsequent chapters.

The next morning, on Capitol Hill, the court finally announced its *Korematsu* and *Endo* decisions, which were noted in major newspapers along with some comments on the various dissents. The front-page story in the *New York Times* quoted from both decisions and all the dissents but managed to avoid using the words "concentration camp," although they appeared in several of the opinions. This would be typical of the general denial that soon came to characterize what Americans were likely to read about the camps for the next quarter of a century.

CHAPTER FOUR

Closing the Camps

As soon as the court decisions had been announced, on December 18, 1944, Secretary of the Interior Harold L. Ickes declared in a statement that he did not foresee a "hasty mass movement" from the camps to the West Coast. He made it clear that his War Relocation Authority would "intensify its efforts" to relocate loyal Japanese Americans in regions other than the West Coast but would also assist those who "prefer to exercise their legal and moral right of return" to their former homes. He added that the WRA would work toward closing its nine relocation centers—the camp at Rohwer, Arkansas, had already been closed on June 30, 1944—but none would be closed in less than six months. He hoped that all the centers would be closed within a year. Actually, none of the other camps was closed during the war. Eight camps were shut down in October and November 1945. The last WRA camp, Tule Lake in Northern California, would not close until March 20, 1946. Its special, separate history will be discussed later.

Fears about turmoil and violence that might result from the return of the Japanese American exiles were widespread throughout California and western Washington and Oregon. Such fears were most intense in California, and, not surprisingly, within the state the most extreme reactions of officials were in Los Angeles, which had been home to some 36,000 Japanese Americans in 1940.

In mid-December 1944 its district attorney Fred N. Howser used a Bill of Rights Week speech to denounce the impending return of Japanese as "a second attack on Pearl Harbor." The *Los Angeles Times* labeled the decision allowing return "a grave mistake" and argued that the real way for Japanese Americans to show their loyalty was "by seeking homes elsewhere than on the Pacific Coast." The city's mayor, Fletcher Bowron, who had been a strong advocate of mass incarceration before it became federal policy, warned of impending "race riots" because Negro war workers had moved in to housing in what had been Little Tokyo, and called for troops to be sent in to protect white citizens. More positively, the mayor staged a symbolic welcome for some of the first returners at city hall in mid-January, telling them, "We want you and all other citizens of Japanese ancestry who have relocated here to feel secure in your home." Earl Warren, California's governor since 1943, had publicly called for any return to be delayed until the war was over, but with the official announcement and the court's decision, he ceased his public opposition. Public officials in the Pacific Northwest, including Washington's governor and Portland's mayor, regretted that the ban had not been continued until the end of the war. An exception was San Francisco's mayor, Roger D. Lapham, who called for returning Japanese Americans to be given "the same treatment and consideration" as "residents of any other extraction." The California department of the American Legion, which had opposed any wartime return, told its members that any who denied any citizen his rights would forfeit their right to be considered a "good legionnaire." Perhaps it was reacting to the national scandal that had occurred when the Legion post in Hood River, Oregon, had removed the names of serving Nisei soldiers from the city's honor roll billboard.

In the event there was nothing even approaching a race riot in reaction to the Japanese American return, although there was some violence and threats of violence against some returning Nisei in California's Central Valley, including warning gunshots fired in some instances by renegade law enforcement officers. More common was vandalism against the property of Japanese Americans and their supporters. In Pasadena, California, for example, Linus Pauling, not yet a Nobel Prize winner, who had been one of the earliest there to speak out for the returning exiles and employ them, had his garage "decorated" by vandals with a rising sun and the words "Americans Die But We Love Japs—Japs Work Here—Pauling." More serious were economic boycotts such as the one in Seattle enforced by the Teamsters Union, whose members were instructed not to transport to market produce from farms owned or leased by Nisei. And even a decorated veteran such as the future senator Captain Daniel K. Inouye, in San Francisco awaiting a ship to take him home to Hawaii, would be told by a barber that "we don't cut Jap hair." It was difficult for returners to find admittedly scarce housing or to get jobs, even at a time when vacancies still outnumbered job seekers. There was no longer a viable ethnic economy to employ them.

Despite a good deal of hand-wringing and posturing up and down the coast, including protests from organized farm groups, by the end of 1944 the region seemed largely to accept the fact that some of the Nisei would be returning. The West Coast correspondent of the *New York Times* in a year-end story summarized the region's mood as a kind of resignation, partly because the local WRA resettlement officials were publicly discouraging the exiles from returning.

After a visit to the camp at Manzanar, most of whose inmates came from the nearby Los Angeles area, he reported that fewer than twenty of the thousands of families there planned an immediate return. At Manzanar and other camps officials encouraged resettlement east of California but were less willing to assist actively those who were determined to return to their former homes, even though they could no longer forbid them to do so. A familiar pattern developed in which one adult in a family, usually male, would take temporary leave and scout the intended destination before the whole family moved. WRA officials anticipated correctly that few families would immediately exercise their newly restored right to return to the forbidden zone. At first only a trickle came back to Los Angeles.

For those who decided to resettle east of California, there were already established WRA resettlement offices in urban centers from Spokane, Washington, to Boston able to give personalized assistance and where hostels for temporary accommodation had been in operation for some time. Resettlers were entitled to train or bus tickets to their destinations, with a cash supplement of $25 for individuals and up to $100 for a family.

Data from the WRA show that on January 1, 1945, there were still 80,878 Japanese Americans confined in its camps, only about 7,000 fewer than in July 1944. The pace quickened as the totals dropped to 73,559 by April 1, 1945, and to 63,857 by July 1, 1945. In the next five months the pace of release accelerated, and eight relocation centers, as noted, closed between October 15 and November 30, 1945.

The saddest aspect of the camps' closing was that there were large numbers of persons in them who so feared what their fate as freed persons in wartime America might entail that they refused to fill out the forms saying where they wanted go; they wanted to stay in camp, where their basic needs were attended to and they felt safe. These were, more often than not, older Issei who were still enemy aliens. The WRA eventually sent such persons back to the area from which they came, providing transportation and the $25 to $100 subsistence funds.

Others, who went willingly, continued to find that community institutions were not yet in a position to lend meaningful support. One Los Angeles official contrasted Depression and postwar public assistance rates for Japanese Americans. In the 1930s the rates were very low—he remembered that just before Pearl Harbor there had been only 25 receiving relief, but in January 1946 some 4,000 Japanese Americans in Los Angeles—about one person in nine—were receiving public assistance.

The camp at Tule Lake did not figure in the Supreme Court cases except as the place from which Mitsuye Endo submitted her initial petition for habeas corpus. But any account of the larger history and impact of the Japanese American incarceration must examine the brutal treatment meted out to protesters there. Originally an "ordinary" camp styled, as were the other nine, a "relocation center," Tule Lake became, on July 15, 1943, a "segregation center" into which the largely inept WRA officials intended to put all the prisoners it regarded as disloyal because of their response to its loyalty questionnaire, plus those aliens who had applied for repatriation to Japan, those citizens who had applied for denaturalization, and persons who had protested against any of its policies or had otherwise become "trouble makers." Thus perhaps 6,500 of those Tuleans whom the WRA deemed loyal, like Mitsuye Endo and her family, were moved to another of the WRA's camps. Some 6,000 Tuleans remained, but a large number of those eligible to go refused to move out, and the WRA, unwilling to use force against them, acceded to their wishes. Thus several thousand of the 18,734 of those held at the Tule Lake Segregation Center on January 1, 1945, were "loyal" in the reckoning of the WRA. It must be understood that, to a very high degree, families chose to stay together so that, in many instances, even when only one member in a family was in the disloyal category, the WRA treated the whole family as disloyal. Even babies born in a family classified as disloyal went into the WRA's records as disloyal US citizens. Release from Tule Lake, for a variety of reasons, proceeded at a much slower rate than at the other camps.

Ironically, the ultimate decision to segregate had grown out of the War Department's decision to form an all-Nisei combat unit, which became the 442nd Regimental Combat Team. During World War I the army had accepted volunteers of Japanese origin and drafted Japanese American citizens. When the draft was reintroduced in the fall of 1940, with provisions inserted by Congress forbidding racial discrimination, the army assigned volunteers and draftees of Japanese ancestry to regular army units. By November 1941, Selective Service records show 3,188 young Japanese American citizens had been drafted and others had enlisted or entered military service via National Guard units.

In the two or three weeks after Pearl Harbor, there was an uncertainty about army policies, as we have seen with Min Yasui, summoned more than halfway across the country to report for duty, but by the time of his arrival, his activation was deferred and never occurred. Most Japanese American young men who tried to enlist were rejected, but Ben Kuroki, in Nebraska, found a recruiting sergeant who signed him up for the Army Air Force. He became a tail gunner, flew fifty missions over Europe, including the almost suicidal Ploesti raid, and then volunteered for missions over Japan. By early 1942 the bulk of those Japanese Americans in the army were either transferred to the enlisted reserve—that is, released from active duty—or placed on special, often menial duties such as "kitchen police" cleaning crews, and still others were placed in labor battalions without weapons. Yet others, like Kuroki, were given advanced training and assignments.

Many draft boards ceased drafting Japanese Americans; others did not. General Lewis B. Hershey, the perennial director of Selective Service, formally protested the waste in effort and money involved in drafting and inducting Nisei only to have them routinely returned to civilian life. On March 30, 1942, a confidential telegram went to all state directors of Selective Service telling them that no more registrants of Japanese ancestry would be accepted by the army. Finally, on September 14, 1942, the confidential policy was formalized by instructions to all boards that "registrants who are Japanese or of Japanese extraction or parentage" were to be placed in category IV-C, hitherto restricted to aliens. Up to that time many boards had reclassified all Japanese registrants as IV-F, physically or mentally unqualified for service.

The effects of this rejection were devastating for many of those who experienced it. The Tule Lake project attorney later testified that some 600 Nisei men who wound up at Tule Lake had been in the army and either discharged or transferred to the reserve "at the convenience of the government" in early 1942, and that he believed this policy had had an impact not only on them but also on other men who learned about it.

The now widely understood accounts of truly heroic Japanese American military service in World War II in the Military Intelligence Service in the Pacific Theater and by the men of what became the 442nd Regimental Combat Team in the European theater are discussed later. But the disgraceful story of how the US Army dealt with the nearly 4,000 Japanese Americans who were serving in the United States has been little noted and only rarely remembered. Separate recent studies, by Shirley Castelnuovo and Linda Tamura, have lifted the veil, although further work needs to be done.

In the period between mid-December 1941, when most draft boards stopped drafting Japanese Americans, and the late-January 1943 edict by Secretary of War Stimson announcing that Japanese Americans would again be allowed to volunteer, there was no fixed policy. The two extreme cases were on the West Coast and in Hawaii. In the former, General DeWitt insisted that all Japanese American troops, like all other persons of Japanese descent, be removed from his forbidden zone. In Hawaii, under General Emmons, Japanese American soldiers continued to serve in two federalized Hawaiian National Guard regiments for the first six months of the war. Then the Nisei soldiers were organized into a segregated battalion nearly 1,500 strong; ten of twenty-four officers were Nisei. In June 1942 the battalion was shipped to the mainland for training, first to Camp McCoy, Wisconsin, and then to Camp Shelby, Mississippi. By September 1943 it was fighting in Italy, and when more Nisei troops arrived, it was incorporated into the 442nd Regimental Combat Team.

But most of the perhaps 1,500 mainland Nisei soldiers not transferred into the army reserve underwent basic training at various facilities. Some testimony suggests that they were not treated worse than other trainees. But after basic training, when most other trainees were either sent to units preparing to go overseas or sent to service schools for special training, most Nisei were assigned to permanent US military installations for duty, mostly in maintenance jobs, many of them menial. Fragmentary evidence and a good deal of individual testimony make it clear that they were not trusted by the army. Individual dossiers show that the Kibei (Nisei who has been sent or taken to Japan for schooling) among them were subject to special investigation, and that non-Kibei Nisei were interrogated to provide "evidence" of Kibei disloyalty, which some provided.

After army policy about Japanese American enlistment changed in 1943, most of the pre–Pearl Harbor draftees and volunteers still in the army were transferred to Camp Shelby and assigned to the 442nd. But others were eventually transferred to one of two "special organizations" created by the army for "subversives" who were judged "disloyal" but who had not committed any subversive action. Given innocuous designations—the 1800th Engineer General Service Detachment and the 525th Quartermaster Service Company—assignment to these organizations was a kind of punishment. Although normally soldiers were promoted to private first class on completion of basic training, soldiers assigned to either of the special organizations were demoted, permanently, to private; when discharged, they were given so-called blue discharges, which were "less than honorable" but not "dishonorable." They were not eligible for normal veteran's benefits despite years of service. The largest numbers of men assigned to these units were citizens of German birth or ethnicity. The second largest, several hundred, were citizens of Japanese ancestry; others included citizens of Italian birth or ethnicity and a variety of other presumed "subversives."

An additional variant of army attitudes toward military service for Japanese Americans—and the only one truly dictated by military necessity—resulted from the military's need for persons able to translate Japanese documents into English, transcribe radio intercepts, and interrogate Japanese prisoners. Both the army and the navy had a handful of officers who had acquired skills in Japanese or Chinese on their own. Until the army established the Japanese Language School—the direct ancestor of today's Defense Language Institute—that opened in a former airplane hangar at San Francisco's Presidio on November 1, 1941, it had done no language training at all. The school's four instructors were Japanese American; of its sixty soldier students, fifty-eight were Nisei and two Caucasian. After Roosevelt's executive order went into effect, General DeWitt insisted that the language school be moved elsewhere; the army found room for it at Camp Savage, just outside of Minneapolis.

In July 1942, when the army decided to expand the school, its commander, Danish-born Lieutenant Colonel Kai Rasmussen, fluent in Japanese, led recruiting teams to seek qualified volunteers in every WRA camp and test their proficiency. They had the authority to enlist any who qualified and escort them back to Minnesota. Many volunteered, but few qualified. Bill Hosokawa, who became an outstanding journalist after the war, and who had worked in Asia before the war, was one of the unsuccessful majority of volunteers. He wrote about flunking an exam given by Rasmussen himself, who told him, "Hosokawa, you'd make a helluva Jap." The initial groups recruited largely from the camps, 167 by the end of 1942, were not subjected to any loyalty tests. All that mattered was that they had volunteered and had done reasonably well on their language examination. Most of that first group were Kibei, a group that was regarded by most of those in charge of military and civilian security as untrustworthy. The several thousand graduates of the school played an important but secret role in the Pacific War; those who served with frontline units in the Pacific theater had to be assigned Caucasian bodyguards to prevent them from being shot by their fellow soldiers. But otherwise the army continued to bar Japanese recruits or draftees throughout 1942, although there were many, such as the army's John McCloy and the WRA's Milton Eisenhower, and Dillon Myer, who became WRA head in June, 1942, who felt strongly that military service ought to be an option for Nisei. As early as May 20, 1942, McCloy wrote that "it might be well to use our American citizen Japanese soldiers in an area where they could be employed against the Germans. I believe that we could count on these soldiers to give a good account of themselves."

By mid-July 1942 a general staff board had been organized to investigate how to utilize Nisei manpower. Its initial erroneous assumption was that there would be enough such manpower for a division, 12,000 to 15,000 troops. Within the army the chief opponents of such a change in policy were the military bureaucrats in the Provost Marshal General's Office and General DeWitt and most of his staff in San Francisco, the original military advocates of mass imprisonment.

In early 1943 war secretary Stimson, who had always had some misgivings about the incarceration policy he had approved and advocated, pursued a change in policy after gaining Roosevelt's assent. In mid-January Dillon Myer and other WRA officials were summoned to McCloy's office and informed that the army intended to recruit an all-Nisei combat team of some 5,000 men from both Hawaii and the mainland. Obviously only loyal Nisei would volunteer, but the army first wanted the loyalty of all male Nisei of military age in the camps to be determined by means of a questionnaire, although no such requirement had been called for when the volunteers for the language school had been accepted the previous summer. Those men, like other military volunteers and draftees, were required only to take a simple affirmative oath similar to the one prescribed for the president in the Constitution.

A loyalty test suited not only the WRA, whose Washington staff had been talking about segregation as early as August 1942, but also some liberals within the government. On October 6, 1942, Office of War Information head Elmer Davis and his deputy, Milton Eisenhower, had suggested in a memorandum to the president that "loyal American citizens of Japanese descent should be permitted, after individual test, to enlist in the Army and Navy." Conversely, General DeWitt and his staff in San Francisco were appalled by what the War Department proposed. They insisted that loyalty tests for Japanese Americans were useless because no white person could tell whether a Japanese was lying.

On January 28, 1943, Secretary Stimson announced the decision to form a Japanese American combat team. In an accompanying statement the War Department revealed that an all-Japanese unit of the Hawaiian National Guard, the 100th Battalion, was already undergoing training in the United States for overseas service. The announcement did not reveal that the unit, which eventually became part of the combat team, had been moved to the mainland early in June 1942 without its weapons or that the original intention had been not to train it for combat. On February 4, 1943, a letter from Roosevelt—who had been in Africa when the original announcement was made—was released by the White House. It gave his "full approval" of the proposal to form the combat team, noted that 5,000 "loyal Americans of Japanese ancestry" were currently serving in the armed forces, and added:

> This is a natural and logical step toward the reinstitution of the Selective Service procedures which were temporarily disrupted by the evacuation from the West Coast. No loyal citizen of the United States should be denied the democratic right to exercise the responsibilities of his citizenship, regardless of his ancestry. The principle on which this country was founded and by which it has always been governed is that Americanism is a matter of mind and heart: Americanism is not, and never was, a matter of race and ancestry. A good American is one who is loyal to his country and to our creed of liberty and democracy. Every loyal American citizen should be given the opportunity to serve this country wherever his skills will make the greatest contribution—whether it be in the ranks of our armed forces, war production, agriculture, government service, or other work essential to the war effort.

The president's statement was widely publicized within the camps and was hailed by JACL leaders as a vindication of the accommodationist policy that they had advocated and pursued. But many inmates surely shared the view of the young man of military age who asked why, if the president's words were true, he was in a camp. Others thought that the segregated unit was to become a "suicide group," but this was not the case. However, the fact that the vast majority of Japanese American volunteers, and later draftees, were earmarked for the combat team meant that virtually none was in the large noncombat force that supported the combat troops.

The War Department insisted that volunteers in camp fill out a questionnaire to demonstrate their loyalty. The Selective Service authorities had prepared a new form, "Statement of United States Citizen of Japanese Ancestry" (DSS Form 304A); this was but a variant of an existing form, "Alien's Personal History and Statement" (DSS Form 304). The forms included questions about family, education, religion, and foreign travel and demanded the names of non-Japanese individuals as character references. The two crucial items were questions numbered 27 and 28, which will be discussed later. What it is necessary to understand is why the WRA leaders in Washington not only agreed to issue the questionnaires to male US citizens of military age but also later decided to administer it to all camp inmates seventeen and older, citizen and alien, male and female. The reason for this was that the WRA's main concern was unclogging its all but blocked release program.

Milton Eisenhower, during his three months in charge, committed the WRA to the view that 85 percent of the Nisei were loyal—which meant that 15 percent were disloyal—and that at least half the Issei were passively loyal. He had no empirical evidence for this somewhat Nisei-friendly view. If pressed, which he was not, he probably would have said that it was his "gut feeling," or "common sense," or some such locution. His successors, sharing that belief, decided to use the questionnaire as a vehicle to get the loyal citizen majority and some of the Issei out of camp and resettled as quickly as possible. Thus they changed the title of the form to "Application for Leave Clearance" and decided to require all incarcerated persons seventeen years of age and over to complete the form. Even today, one can only ask, "What were they thinking?"

It is clear that one of the things that WRA officials were thinking about was segregation of the "loyal" from the "disloyal" regardless of citizenship. Although the WRA did not formally adopt a segregation policy, after a meeting of all camp directors on May 31, 1943, such a possibility had been considered during Eisenhower's tenure and had been given legs in the aftermath of protests in camps in the closing months of 1942. Although specific discontents arose in every camp, the authorities were particularly concerned about two events. The first was a November 1942 strike at the camp at Poston, Arizona, which was about wages and working conditions; the second was a December dispute at the Manzanar, California, camp, which began as a dispute over food between Los Angeles JACL leaders and other inmates who opposed them. The director at Poston, faced with community-wide opposition, entered into negotiations, and a peaceful settlement resulted. This did not take place at Manzanar.

There, on the evening of December 5, 1942, six masked men invaded the one-room living space occupied by Los Angeles JACL leader Fred Tayama, his wife, and their eleven-year-old daughter and began to beat him with clubs; the screams of a neighboring woman caused the six to flee. Tayama's injuries were not life-threatening but were serious enough to require hospital treatment. He told camp authorities that he recognized one of his attackers, a Nisei, Harry Ueno (1907–2004), a protester who was organizing a kitchen workers union, who denied the allegation. Despite this, the camp director ordered Ueno and two others to be taken to the county jail. Angry protest meetings demanded that the jailed men be brought back to camp, and some expressed anti-American and pro-Japan sentiments.

WRA director Dillon Myer, who was not present, later described the chief Manzanar agitator, Joseph Y. Kurihara (1895–1965), a Hawaii-born Nisei who had served in the American army in France and Germany during World War I and had been a staunch supporter of Americanization until the wartime incarceration, as one who "turned his back on America because he thought that America had turned its back on him."

The Manzanar camp director, like his colleague at Poston, was initially willing to negotiate; he agreed to have the three men brought back into camp and placed in what served as the camp jail. In the meantime, other meetings had taken place, and some groups of individuals went looking for JACL leaders and others regarded as *inu*, a Japanese word for "dog," but in this context roughly equivalent to "stool pigeon"; another group went to the hospital boasting that they would "finish off" Tayama, whom hospital workers managed to hide.

As darkness gathered, the director requested the military police, who normally manned the gates and the guard towers and remained outside of the camp, to come in and restore order. Confronting an angry, unarmed, and disorderly crowd of young men and boys, the soldiers dispersed it with the use of tear gas grenades. The crowd re-formed, even angrier about being teargassed, and a second confrontation occurred. Although no order to fire was given, shots were fired into the unarmed crowd. One seventeen-year-old boy was dead on the spot, and a twenty-one-year-old man died in the hospital. At least ten others in the crowd were wounded, as was one soldier, apparently hit by friendly fire. There was never any formal investigation of the two homicides, so no one was ever charged, no less convicted, of the killings. Nor were death benefits or other considerations given to the grieving families.

Because the killings occurred on December 6, many papers and radio stations referred to the whole dispute as a "Pearl Harbor riot," as if it had been planned in Tokyo. Throughout the incarceration, all the disputes between inmates and captors were created in America, by Americans; none was made in Japan.

The aftermath of the Manzanar tragedy shows the WRA's propensity to think of segregation as a problem solver; in actuality it was never a solution but rather a creator of new problems and further injustices. Two distinct segregation projects resulted at Manzanar. In the first, sixty-five individuals, mostly prominent JACL leaders and their families who had been threatened or felt endangered at Manzanar, were first taken into protective custody in the administration building, then sent to an abandoned Civilian Conservation Corps (CCC) camp in nearby Death Valley. A few weeks later most were processed for leave clearance and sent to Chicago. In the second, Ueno and twenty-five "trouble makers" were held, without charges, in jails in Bishop and Lone Pine, fifty and ten miles away, respectively. Ten of those individuals were eventually returned to Manzanar and not subjected to additional special confinement there. The other sixteen were shipped in mid-January 1943 via Greyhound bus and train under heavy military guard to the camp outside of Moab, Utah, which the WRA set up as its first isolation camp for dissidents. Soon the Issei among them were sent to Department of Justice internment camps, a process that continued for selected Issei from other camps throughout the WRA's existence. Eventually more than 3,100 Issei were thus transferred. In the future only Nisei dissidents would be sent to Moab or its successor, which soon had forty-nine prisoners from several WRA camps.

The Moab camp lasted only until late April, when its prisoners were transferred to a more appropriate prison camp. Most of the prisoners made the thirteen-hour journey in a Greyhound bus, but five prisoners, including Ueno, who had refused to obey the rules that the WRA invented for its segregated prisoners, were confined in what one of them told a historian many years later was "a four-by-six-foot box on a pickup truck with a hole in the back end of the box which was only about two by two feet." In his diary Ueno wrote that the "dust was so thick that I needed to press a handkerchief against my face. . . . [T]he rough movement made you feel like your insides were being forced up." The WRA officials in charge did not feel that the constitutional prohibition against "cruel and unusual punishment" applied to unruly Japanese American prisoners. Unlike their counterparts in the Justice Department camps, they were not encumbered with regulatory supervision.

The new camp, near Winslow, Arizona, had been a Bureau of Indian Affairs boarding school to "Americanize" native Indian children segregated from their parents. Named Leupp after a former government official, its accommodations were better for prisoners. The security seems excessive for a camp that received only eighty-three prisoners. It was surrounded by a "man-proof fence" with guard towers at each corner manned by soldiers with machine guns. A detachment of 150 military policemen and a few officers was stationed just outside the enclosure. The small prison camp was abandoned on December 2, 1943, when its prisoners were transferred to the renamed Tule Lake Segregation Center, for which it had been a precursor.

The WRA had announced a policy of "leave clearance" on October 1, 1942; this process enabled persons approved by the WRA to leave camp to work or attend college east of General DeWitt's forbidden zone. In theory such persons were not released, but in practice once an inmate had left camp, the WRA had no means of control. Persons released to go to Chicago, for example, could and did move to East Coast cities, especially New York. The process was very slow. In January 1943 only 3.9 persons per 1,000 left the camps, and by the end of 1943 only 17,000 had departed. At that rate it would have taken many years to empty the camps.

A substantial percentage of those camp leavers were released in special programs and circumstances. These included the Kibei who were recruited for the army language school. Even earlier, larger numbers were recruited to leave camp temporarily to help harvest crops. The first such group was released temporarily from the Portland Assembly Center by General DeWitt's Western Defense Command on May 15, 1942, to harvest crops in Malheur County in southeastern Oregon, outside of the forbidden zone; 753 "seasonal workers" so released from assembly centers simply never returned. They either remained in the area to which they were initially released or simply moved elsewhere. The same was true of an indeterminate number of those released later from WRA camps.

This was part of a nationwide response to a shortage of farm labor that eventually included tens of thousands of presumably temporary Mexican workers styled Braceros. In a press conference on October 29, 1942, largely devoted to explaining what became of that program, President Roosevelt casually remarked that "in some cases, like the Montana beet fields, they are already moving [in] some of the Japanese labor." When a reporter asked where they came from, the president's two-word answer was "concentration camps." Eventually some 10,000 Nikkei, largely male, were temporarily released from army and WRA camps during the 1942 harvest to work in western fields.

The president had also approved a more benign program that had been suggested to him by California governor Culbert L. Olson, in a plan promoted by University of California officials to allow incarcerated college students and those who wanted to become college students to attend college. The president, after consulting his Office of Education and the WRA's Milton Eisenhower, answered the governor's April 15, 1942, letter in just over a month. He assured him that "qualified American-born Japanese students will be enabled to continue their education in inland institutions." He did not promise the financial support that the California educators had envisaged, although the WRA did provide the necessary train or bus fare as it did for other camp leavers. Eisenhower persuaded Clarence E. Pickett, head of the Quaker American Friends Service Committee, to create a private organization to run the program.

In all some 4,000 Nisei went from concentration camps to college campuses during the war. Some elite institutions refused to cooperate. Princeton University, for example, assured Pickett that its refusal to admit such students even if they were "in good standing, and not under suspicion" was for some unspecified "good reasoning." Many small, obscure, private religious colleges opened their doors and found funds to support the students.

The common sense that the WRA exhibited in dealing with the students was unfortunately not applied in its execution of the army's plan for screening volunteers. Both of the issues involved with the questionnaire, volunteering for military service—with an eventual reinstitution of the draft on the horizon—and procedures for leaving camp, were controversial. Combining them was a recipe for more disorder. If the military issue, which the War Department insisted upon, had been treated separately and restricted to young male citizens of military age, a less disruptive result might have ensued. At the root of the WRA's insistence on having everyone over seventeen years of age fill out its form was its desire to identify who was disloyal. Then, its leaders foresaw, it could segregate the disloyal minority in a separate camp, along with troublemakers of any kind, and proceed with its all but stalled program of release and relocation.

The registration process began on February 8, 1943. It had gone forward with haste and secrecy: few, if any, beyond top WRA executives in Washington knew what was coming. Apart from changing its title, the WRA accepted the questionnaire as it came from the military. While the entire questionnaire was an affront to many in the camps, the focus of complaint and eventual resistance was on two questions:

27. Are you willing to serve in the armed forces of the United States on combat duty, wherever ordered?
28. Will you swear unqualified allegiance to the United States and faithfully defend the United States from any or all attack by foreign or domestic forces, and foreswear any form of allegiance to the Japanese emperor, to any other foreign government, power or organization?

Within four days the WRA realized what should have been self-evident: however appropriate the questions may have been for its initially intended recipients, male US citizens of military age, it was utterly inappropriate for the camps' aliens and women. More suitable language for aliens was soon provided; they were asked, "Will you swear to abide by the laws of the United States and take no action which would in any way interfere with the war effort of the United States?" It was possible, in some cases, to submit amended or initial questionnaires as late as September 1943.

The WRA's tabulation of the final answers to the revised question 28 on the loyalty questionnaire, in which there are minor inconsistencies, was as follows. A total of 77,957 persons were told to complete the questionnaire: 40,311 citizens (21,061 males, 19,250 females) and 37,646 aliens (22,281 males and 15,365 females). Three thousand two hundred fifty-four persons, some 4 percent of the total, refused to fill out their questionnaires; 1,386 citizens (654 males, 732 females) and 1,868 aliens (1,280 males and 588 females). They were treated as if they had said no.

Of the 74,703 persons who filled out questionnaires, 68,018, or 91 percent of the total, said yes. The 5,376 who answered no, plus the 1,041 who qualified their answers and the 234 who left that answer blank, were treated as if they had said no. Of the 7,181 citizens regarded as saying no, 4,612 were male and 2,569 were female. This was just below 18 percent of the citizens in the camps. But looking at the results for each of the ten camps reveals a wide divergence in the percentage of "no" responses from citizens. Those from two camps, Central Utah and Gila River (AZ), closely bracket the 18 percent mean. At five camps the figures were sharply below the mean: just over 10 percent said no at Colorado Rivers (AZ), as did fewer than 9 percent at Rohwer (AR), fewer than 5 percent at Heart Mountain (WY), and fewer than 3 percent at Minidoka (ID). At Granada (CO), the figure was so low—0.4 percent—that one suspects that the camp's administrators, like some contemporary school principals faced with No Child Left Behind mandates, had cooked the results. At the other end of the spectrum of results, at three camps—Manzanar and Tule Lake (CA) and Jerome (AR)—around a quarter said no. Scholars have attributed the high numbers at Manzanar to the disputes there culminating in the riot, while the high degree at Jerome is often charged to the presence of a goodly number of Hawaiians, largely family members of persons in DoJ camps, and the presence of a highly authoritarian camp director who tried to stifle all dissent. No reasons have been given to explain Tule Lake's place in the high category. It should be noted that while a relatively average number of Tulean citizens, 1,114, actually said no, an even larger number of its citizens, 1,360, chose not to fill out their questionnaires. Counting both Issei and Nisei responses, 3,218 Tuleans simply refused to participate, an option recorded for only a total of 36 inmates in the other nine camps. In 1980 a Tule Lake survivor remembered that during the registration process we "had voted as a block, not to sign the loyalty oath."

Whatever the reasons, it is clear that a propensity for collective action had developed at Tule Lake. Upon reflection, it seems that rather than an indication of the incidence of disloyalty in a given camp, the results of the infamous loyalty questionnaire should be regarded—if they are regarded as anything—as a measure of the relative comfort/discomfort levels among the imprisoned people.

The War Department had expected to get 3,000 volunteers from the mainland, mostly from the camps, and anticipated only 1,500 from Hawaii. Its supposed experts were obviously clueless. Recruiting in the camps produced only 805 volunteers, while in Hawaii recruiters were overwhelmed by some 10,000 applicants, of whom 2,600 were immediately accepted. That many military leaders could not anticipate that free men would behave more positively than those unjustly imprisoned is perhaps indicative of how little they understood democracy.

While the War Department continued to modify its policies toward Japanese Americans based on its experience, the WRA continued to develop its plans for total segregation despite the increasing difficulties its policies were creating. Myer's memoir explains that he had handpicked almost the entire top WRA staff from among those he had learned to trust at the Agriculture Department. Apparently, few alternative views were put forward at staff meetings. Myer did admit that some of the wording in the questionnaire had been a "bad mistake," an "egregious oversight," but never once acknowledged that he and his colleagues had erred in transforming an agency created to house, feed, succor, and resettle a guiltless people in such a way that one part of its system of generally benign custodial confinement was turned into a prison, and inside that prison a stockade was constructed within which brutality and torture became routine.

The segregation policy had a long history. In late 1942 both the WDC and John McCloy had suggested some kind of segregation policy to the WRA, but their proposals focused on segregating entire categories of persons, Kibei and Issei, and were rejected by the WRA. After the data from the questionnaires had been sorted and evaluated, the WRA, bent on segregation, had to decide where to put the persons to be segregated and those family members—most of whom would be children who were US citizens—who would accompany them. Because most of the inmates of the segregation center would not be eligible for resettlement, the site chosen needed to be a large one with a surrounding agricultural environment able to provide significant employment. Three of the camps, the two on

Arizona Indian reservations and Tule Lake, met those requirements. The fact that Tule Lake had a significantly higher number of persons to be segregated was a major factor in its selection because it meant fewer persons to be transported.

Raymond Best, who had made his reputation as a hard-nosed disciplinarian at the Leupp prison camp, became director of the Tule Lake Segregation Center on July 1, 1943. This was a clear indication of the kind of regime the WRA expected to be instituted there. Evaluating Best's Tule Lake performance in 1971, Myer said of him that "Ray . . . carried on with honor."

It took most of the spring and summer of 1943 for the WRA to prepare for the series of exchanges between Tule Lake and the nine other camps. On July 15 Myer announced the segregation program on a national radio network. He told his audience that "some people" in his camps had indicated a preference to be Japanese rather than American, and therefore the WRA was going to segregate such persons "as soon as transportation can be obtained to move them." He insisted that his organization's camps were not desirable institutions. "It is not the American way to have children grow up behind barbed wire. It is difficult to reconcile democracy with barbed wire." Yet, when the transferees to Tule Lake began to arrive, bringing many children with them, they found, in preparation for their coming, a camp in which security measures had been heightened. An "eight-foot-high double 'man proof' fence" replaced the several strands of barbed wire surrounding the facility, the platoon-size MP detachment had been increased to a battalion of a thousand men, and a few tanks had been added to cow any demonstrators.

Two days after Myer's public relations effort, war mobilization director James F. Byrnes made a blunt and comprehensive statement aimed at reassuring Congress and others that most curbs on releasing Japanese Americans would stay in place: "The present restrictions against persons of Japanese ancestry will remain in force as long as the military situation so requires." The former Supreme Court justice then revealed that the normal presumption of innocence would be reversed when allowing Japanese Americans to leave the camps: "If there is evidence from any source the evacuee might endanger the war effort permission for leave is denied." He made a strong positive statement about the performance of Japanese American troops and revealed for the first time that some American solders of Japanese descent had performed "useful and hazardous service" in the Pacific theater, and "a number have already been decorated for meritorious services." The policy was hailed by many in Congress and most newspapers that bothered to discuss it, and was approved by the Japanese American Citizens League.

The army, which controlled the railroads, provided thirty trains with guards to transport the "loyal" Tuleans out and bring in the "disloyal" from the other nine camps. At Tule Lake, however, a substantial number of those slated to move out protested that they did not want to go. Like almost all of the inmates, they had been moved at least twice and did not want to move again. The WRA, perhaps unwisely, acceded to their request. This meant that there were some 6,000 so-called Old Tuleans staying on, almost evenly divided between "loyal" and "disloyal."

Two congressional bodies, a subcommittee of the Senate's Committee on Military Affairs, and the infamous House Committee on Un-American Activities, then known as the Dies Committee, had been conducting hostile and irresponsible investigations of the camps, the former charging that the WRA was "pampering" its Japanese American prisoners, the latter that the camps were filled with dangerous subversives who were a threat and should not be released. Just before beginning a long recess in early July 1943, the Senate had sent a resolution to the White House asking the president to issue an executive order directing the WRA to segregate the loyal and the disloyal in the camps and to have a comprehensive statement issued on conditions in the camps and describing plans for future operations.

In a letter released on September 14, 1943, and timed to coincide with the beginning of the segregation program, Roosevelt informed the Senate and the nation that such a program "is now underway." He said that he had asked Byrnes to issue the July 17 statement noted earlier, and that a fuller version "is being made today" and "a further Executive Order is not necessary." The president went on to explain the planned program of segregation:

> The segregation program . . . provides for transferring to . . . the Tule Lake Center . . . those persons . . . who have indicated that their loyalties lie with Japan. . . . They will be adequately fed and

housed and their treatment will in all respects be fair and humane; they will not, however, be eligible to leave the Tule Lake Center while the war with Japan continues or so long as the military situation requires their residence there.

The president went on to promise that once segregation was complete, the WRA would "redouble its efforts" to resettle loyal "Americans of Japanese ancestry" in communities away from the West Coast. And for the first time the president promised, "We shall restore to the loyal evacuees" the right to return to the West Coast as soon as the military situation permitted. As he liked to do, he closed his message with a broad positive statement:

Americans of Japanese ancestry, like those of many other ancestries, have shown that they can, and want to, accept our institutions and work loyally with the rest of us, making their own valuable contributions to the national wealth and well-being. In vindication of the very ideals for which we are fighting this war it is important to us to maintain a high standard of fair, considerate, and equal treatment for the people of this minority as of all other minorities.

The phrase "with the rest of us" was a retreat, perhaps unconscious, that deviates from the typical universality of Roosevelt's rhetorical democracy. Even more striking, in view of what actually took place, is the pledge that the segregated "disloyals" would get fair and humane treatment.

In mid-September the first trains transporting inmates in and out of Tule Lake began, a process that took about four weeks. Some 8,500 persons were brought in while some 6,500 were shipped out. Because of the larger number of Old Tuleans staying on, some 1,900 persons designated as segregants could not be accommodated until more barracks were built, and were being held at Manzanar. Thus conditions remained in flux well into 1944.

The majority of the new arrivals seem to have chosen to come seeking what one scholar described as "a haven from the fears, worries, and frustrations which they had experienced in the relocation centers." If that had been the case, most were quickly disabused. They entered the camp through the newly installed heavy duty man-proof fence, similar to but much larger than the one Director Best had installed at the prison camp at Leupp, and they saw newly erected additional guard towers and blockhouses. Looking out through the fence that confined them, they could see elements of the 752nd Military Police Battalion commanded by a lieutenant colonel, with armored cars and tanks, not normal equipment for military police, parked in full view. Although the WRA insisted that segregation was not punishment, the authorities obviously expected trouble.

The newcomers, who had been able to leave their camps for shopping and other reasons, quickly discovered that they could not leave their new camp except on work details, and that although leave clearance was still possible according to WRA regulations for those who had come as family members, and for the loyal Old Tuleans, director Best had dissolved the existing leave clearance apparatus, and the officials in charge of it had been assigned to other duties. In addition, community government had been abolished. As had been the case in other camps, only citizens could vote and hold office. At Tule Lake, Issei were given a voice by the creation of a planning commission of Issei residents as an advisory body. Best, as he had done at Leupp, was prepared to listen to complaints but not to negotiate about them. He later created a group of representatives, one citizen in each block, appointed by him.

Information about inmates wishing to go to Japan began to be collected by General DeWitt's Wartime Civil Control Administration in early 1942. The WCCA created two different lists. One was a list of names sent by Tokyo via the protecting power, Spain, to the State Department of persons Japan would be willing to accept in the forthcoming prisoner exchange. When contacted, most of those named by Japan "declined interest in exchange." Similarly, the "bulk" of all persons on the early lists of those who told either the WCCA or the WRA that they wished to go to Japan had not been on the list sent from Tokyo. On November 15, 1942, the WCCA transferred the files on what both agencies described as "expatriation" and "repatriation" to the WRA. By the end of 1942, the WRA had a list of some 2,200 persons who had applied to go to Japan. That represented one person in fifty of those held by the WRA. Two years later, as the WRA stopped accepting such documents, the total had reached 20,000, one person in six. But the only WRA prisoners able to go to Japan prior to November 1945 were the 318 passengers on the second voyage of the Swedish exchange ship *Gripsholm* described in the next chapter.

It is apparent that the primary factor in the steadily increasing growth in applications was the growing dismay by more and more of the WRA's captives at their continuing confinement and a sense that there was no place for them in America. But WRA spokesmen, most congressmen, and the press equated it to a fanatical loyalty to Japan. It is certainly the case that many Issei and more than a few Nisei were rooting for Japan "to win the war." Few if any expected Japan to conquer the United States. Those in Tule Lake and elsewhere who listened to Radio Tokyo on crude, improvised radio sets heard nothing about pending invasions of the United States, but they were heartened by claims about the impregnable defenses of the homeland and the indomitable spirit of its defenders. At the same time American prisoners of war in German stalags were similarly heartened by hearing BBC reports on their illicit sets about Allied military progress on the road to Berlin.

The American citizens who came to Tule Lake, very few of whom could understand the Radio Tokyo broadcasts, had a range of immediate ambitions. Most of the adults probably felt that Tule Lake was a good place to sit out the war, and hoped to do so and try to resume their interrupted lives when peace finally came. Very large numbers were children who had little or no choice in the matter. Most families adhered to one choice or the other, although a few children and even fewer wives of male segregants chose to remain in one of the relocation centers.

A minority of the young male segregants had become radicalized and formed or joined explicitly pro-Japan organizations. These were overt rather than covert groups. They held pep rallies and marched up and down in a threatening manner blowing bugles and shouting pro-Japan slogans, which made them feel good and enabled them to let off steam. Inside the barracks many cajoled or threatened others to join them.

All this scandalized officials, provided good copy for hostile West Coast newspapers, and delighted West Coast politicians by giving them more talking points to make in their crusade to keep Japanese Americans from returning to their former homes. But despite growing disillusionment about life at Tule Lake, the events that triggered the first serious violence there had nothing to do with patriotism or politics: they grew out of garden-variety labor disputes about working conditions and wages.

On October 7, 1943, a group of forty-seven workers on the coal crew that distributed fuel for the potbellied stoves that heated the individual "apartments" had been fired for protesting the prior dismissal of three workers for insubordination. These men were Old Tuleans, who had most of the good jobs in the camp, and some of their number went to two of the known leaders of the segregant newcomers, who succeeded in getting the fired men reinstated. One of the granted demands was for a second breakfast at 10:00 a.m. for the coal crews, as it was agreed that the normal breakfast did not provide enough calories for men doing heavy labor.

On October 15 a truck carrying farmworkers overturned, injuring twenty-seven workers, five seriously, one of whom died shortly after being taken to the camp hospital. News of this caused hundreds of farmworkers to leave the fields, vowing not to return until better safety arrangements were made and compensation provided for the injured workers. The cause of the fatal one-vehicle crash was attributed to a sixteen-year-old driver who was speeding and tried to pass a slower truck. It was harvest time, and the 800 acres of crops grown on the fertile, dry lake bed that gave the camp its name were a major source of food for Tule Lake and other WRA centers. Not surprisingly, some of the leaders among the striking farmworkers asked the men who had successfully negotiated the reinstatement of the fired coal crew members to take up their cause, and they agreed.

At the same time, some saw an opportunity to use the feelings of solidarity for the farmworkers as a way to recreate a kind of community government. On the evening of October 16, meetings in every one of the sixty-four large blocks of barracks elected one person as a representative to an all-camp council. Unlike WRA-sanctioned elections, all adults, including aliens, could vote and be elected. The resulting body was given a Japanese name, Daihyo Sha Kai (DSK), which means "representative body." It began discussions about what its goals ought to be in addition to the farmworkers' demands and asked permission to hold a large public funeral for Mr. Tatsuto Kashima, the farmworker who had been killed. The degree to which the camp authorities were aware of the organizational efforts other than the funeral request is not clear.

On October 20 the administration issued an ultimatum to the strikers to send an official representative to discuss terms for completing the harvest the following morning or the army would be called upon to do it. The workers responded that they had delegated responsibility to a DSK committee; director Best said that he would meet with "any representative committee to discuss any problem." The committee asked permission to hold the funeral, which Best denied. The DSK held the mass funeral on October 23 anyway, and it was neither facilitated nor obstructed by the administration.

On October 26 the DSK negotiators were finally ready to meet with Best. He listened to their requests, the most important of which was a request for "resegregation," that is, removal of all "loyals," which was what the WRA had originally planned. Best was courteous and even affable. He gave the negotiators no encouragement about the farmworkers' issues and other matters but seemed amenable to recognizing the DSK as a legitimate governing body. Two days later their optimism was shattered when Best announced that the entire 800-man farm crew had been fired; the next day they learned from the press that Best was bringing in 232 strikebreakers recruited from the "loyal" inmates at Topaz and Poston, with more to come from other camps. Best had begun his secret arrangements with other camp directors immediately after the mass funeral. The strikebreakers were housed outside the camp limits. The Tuleans, old and new, were outraged at their "double crossing" compatriots and were further angered when they discovered that the strikebreakers were being paid a dollar an hour for work that the Tuleans had been doing for sixteen dollars a month. Best mandated an eight-hour day, seven days a week, but refused to pay time and a half for overtime.

On November 1, 1943, WRA director Dillon Myer arrived for his first visit to Tule Lake as part of an inspection of a number of camps. As he tells it, while he was having lunch in the mess hall for administrators, Best came to tell him that "unauthorized announcements" had been distributed urging everyone to come to the administration building to confront Myer. Several thousand came, with women and children leading to show peaceful intent. Most of the same committee that had met with Best asked to meet inside with Myer, which was agreed to. They repeated similar requests, adding that, because he had brought in strikebreakers, Best and some of his aides should be fired. Myer responded that he "would not negotiate on the basis of demands," but that Best would "entertain recommendations or requests" from "a properly constituted group" and told those he faced that he doubted their legitimacy.

Myer then went outside with the committee and faced the crowd. Two members of the committee described the results to the crowd in Japanese, and Myer followed in English. There was no crowd reaction to either, but most bowed to the speakers before leaving quietly.

There was a brief violent episode in the hospital while the meeting was going on in which, as Myer described it in 1971, "some toughs" beat the hospital's chief physician, a Caucasian, "rather badly." A later detailed FBI report said that the doctor gave as well as received blows, and may have struck the first one. It detailed his injuries as "a blackened right eye, a laceration on the right cheek, severe contusions on his right forearm, and numerous lacerations on his left shin. None of them were of a serious nature." The doctor finished his shift and drove himself home. All accounts agree that there was no further violence, although there was minor vandalism of cars in the administration parking lot. According to Myer, "hysterical employees" told wild stories about violence and threatening behavior to journalists and others, although there had only been the one violent episode. Within the camp many employees said they feared for their personal safety, and on November 2 and 3 WRA staff members held at least two meetings convoked by middle-level supervisors to discuss their concerns. Myer, before leaving for the Pacific Northwest, spoke to staff members to say that they were safe and would be protected. After Myer left, another meeting of staff appointed a committee to ask the Military Police commander, Lieutenant Colonel Verne Austin, for protection. He told them that a request from the camp director was required for him to intervene inside the camp. On November 3 Best gave employees assurances similar to those given by Myer but, like him, provided no specifics. However, on the afternoon of November 4, perhaps as a consequence of those concerns, construction began on an internal high-security fence. It would separate the area where the employees worked and some lived from the part of the camp where the inmates lived, often referred to as the "Japanese colony." Inmates could come to the administration building and the hospital only through a gate manned by armed soldiers; none of the WRA security personnel was armed.

That evening—November 4, 1943—what the WRA called the "Tule Lake incident" occurred. It was a minor clash between Japanese American workers and three security guards, one of whom tripped, hit his head on a rock, and then was kicked and hit with clubs, followed by an alleged threat against the camp director, which caused him to phone the MP commander to come in and take charge. It is difficult not to conclude that Best had been waiting for an excuse to do so.

The Military Police remained in full charge until January 15 and instituted a two-month reign of terror during which suspects were beaten by officers, enlisted men, and civilian personnel during interrogations. The army caused a stockade to be built—a prison within a prison camp—in which large numbers of men were held under conditions forbidden by both civil and military law. A detailed investigation by FBI agents, whose unredacted report is now available, exposed both civilian and military violations of basic human rights. The report was, or should have been, available to the War Department and the attorney general, but neither took any action against the alleged federal perpetrators.

Press accounts of events at Tule Lake, which magnified and sometimes invented violence by inmates and largely ignored that by the army and the WRA, came to the attention of Tokyo, which broke off previously successful mutual exchanges of nationals interned in each country. Secretary of State Hull, concerned about the status of the prisoner exchange, insisted that the "martial law" at Tule Lake be ended, while the War Department was properly concerned about possible effects on American prisoners of war in Japanese hands.

Accordingly, an official announcement was made on January 14, 1944, that the Tule Lake Center had been "transferred back" to WRA control, but the army continued to control internal security and operate the stockade until May 23, 1944, when Best insisted that the troops be removed after continued disagreements with Lieutenant Colonel Austin about policy. For a time the MP force remained at about a thousand, but soon it was reduced to 650.

Continuing mistreatment of prisoners at Tule Lake by the WRA officials should have alerted the national ACLU, but it took no action, as Baldwin was assured by Dillon Myer, who had become his friend, that all was well. Against Baldwin's wishes, Ernest Besig made the 400-mile drive from San Francisco to Tule Lake—ten hours plus at wartime speed limits—and began to interview prisoners in the stockade that the WRA had taken over from the army, with, as Besig put it, WRA monitors "in my lap." Besig arrived with a stenographer on July 12, 1944. On July 14, Best, exasperated by Besig's continuing investigations and hostile attitude, telephoned Roger Baldwin in New York to complain; Baldwin suggested that he invite Besig to leave. At Best's orders, security officers escorted Besig to the guarded parking lot for employees and visitors, where he discovered that his car's gas tank had been filled with salt.

The events at Tule Lake gave added ammunition to those in Congress and the government who wanted to strip dissident Nisei of their American citizenship. The Department of Justice, as Edward Ennis, who drafted what became the law, explained, had two fears and a hope. It feared that the court might eventually declare continued detention of citizens illegal, and order that both "loyals" and "disloyals" be freed, and that militant disloyals, released, might be dangerous; and hoped that militant disloyals would renounce their citizenship, making it easier to hold them. A bill legalizing renunciation of citizenship in wartime based on Ennis's draft was introduced in Congress in February 1944 and signed into law by President Roosevelt on July 1, 1944. The Justice Department had advised Congress that it expected from 300 to 1,000 Japanese American citizens to avail themselves of the new law by applying for denaturalization in writing. In the eighteen months after the law went into effect, some 5,500 American citizens imprisoned at Tule Lake formally applied for and were granted denaturalization under the act, which created a new legal category—native-born American aliens—and a new set of Japanese American cases, which will be discussed in the next chapter. Besig, aware of the dangers created by the new law, had advised the prisoners he talked to at Tule Lake not to apply for it and, if they had already done so, not to sign any papers about it.

On January 20, 1944, as President Roosevelt had said would be the case, Secretary Stimson had announced that Selective Service procedures were again to be applied to Japanese Americans both in and out of camps, and draft boards were told to remove them from the IV-C category; the draft was not applied to "disloyals" at Tule Lake. The reinstatement of the draft was hailed by national JACL leaders as a further vindication of the policies they had followed. But much of the response in camps was negative and greatly increased the numbers of a new group of resisters in many camps: draft-age men who had said yes to question 28 and thus were "loyal" but argued that men in a concentration camp should not be subject to the draft even before the draft had been instituted. The earliest leaders of the antidraft resistance movement at the Heart Mountain, Wyoming, camp, the Fair Play Committee, were eventually sent to Tule Lake as troublemakers, marking them in the WRA's records as "disloyal" even though they had answered yes.

One of their leaders had written to Roger Baldwin in April 1944, asking for ACLU support. Baldwin responded, in a letter he made public before it reached its recipient, that although the men had a "strong moral case," they had "no legal case at all." He went on to say that "men who counsel others to resist military service are not within their rights and must expect severe treatment."

When draft call-ups began, based on the actions instituted by various local draft boards, the Selective Service System ruled that, unlike the physical examinations for volunteers, which had taken place in camps under army auspices, the physicals for draftees would not take place in camps. The army and the WRA then agreed that there would be no preinduction physicals for men in camp and that the men to be drafted would be inducted into the army in camp without physicals. Thus men in camp who wanted to resist induction had to do so without a preinduction physical, which many of them would surely have failed.

Most Nisei who received draft calls in camp obeyed and were sworn in during a camp ceremony. They then boarded a bus to an army facility for physical examinations and processing for those who passed; those who did not pass were returned to camp. The ploy of taking the oath in the hope of failing the physical and, if one did not fail, intending to balk at serving, was not viable. In the latter instance any Nisei would have already been soldiers and subject to courts-martial, and could be tried for mutiny, which, in wartime, could result in a death sentence.

During the period, nearly a year, when Nisei could enlist but not be drafted, 1,943 had successfully volunteered for military service from the ten WRA camps. Between January 20, 1945, and the closure of the camps in the fall of 1945, a total of 2,275 Nisei were drafted from the camps and actually entered the army, and 315 refused and were indicted, almost 14 percent of those called. Unlike the situation during World War I, when draft resistance was not unusual, there was relatively little open resistance to the draft during World War II, so these cases were exceptional. But they were little remarked by the contemporary press and ignored by the early decades of scholarship about the Japanese American wartime experience. The incidence of draft resistance varied greatly from camp to camp. Of 290 men brought to trial, almost 60 percent were from just two camps (104 from Colorado River and 63 from Heart Mountain), while two other camps, Poston and Gila River, had none, and the two Arkansas camps had 4 between them.

The first of these trials and the largest trial for draft resistance in American history, took place in Cheyenne, Wyoming, where sixty-three draft resisters from Heart Mountain were tried in federal district court. The JACL, with the support of the government, intervened in an effort to get the defendants, or some of them, to recant and agree to induction, in which case, its leaders had been assured, the government would drop charges for any who did so. The 1942 protester Min Yasui, who had done his time and relocated to Denver, joined the JACL effort and visited the men in jail urging submission, but all remained steadfast.

At the trial, Samuel D. Menin, an experienced Denver attorney, argued, in mitigation, that his clients had been seeking a test case to clarify their status, and that no felonious intent was involved. Like several of the attorneys in the cases contesting DeWitt's orders, Menin waived trial by jury. It seems to me that this, regardless of result, was a lawyerly error. Had the Heart Mountain defendants, or some of them, taken the stand and made their case in open court, some journalists, especially those who were stringers for the wire services or metropolitan newspapers, could have written stories that told what the cases were about in human terms. The tactic chosen contributed to the all but universal ignorance of these cases that came to prevail.

Later generations of civil rights attorneys would learn that, in the final analysis, the court of public opinion was a venue they could not ignore. The judge would have none of Menin's argument, found the men guilty, and on July 19, 1944, sentenced all to three-year terms in federal prison. An appeal to the Tenth Circuit in Denver was rejected, and the Supreme Court refused to review the case.

The same federal grand jury that had indicted the Heart Mountain sixty-three in May 1944, had also indicted seven members of the Fair Play Committee and James Omura (1912–1994), a Nisei journalist living in Denver, for conspiracy to counsel, aid, and abet, violations of the Selective Service Act. Omura, who had resettled in Denver before General DeWitt had forbidden egress from the prohibited zone, had taken over an ethnic newspaper there. He had corresponded with some members of the Fair Play Committee and written about their struggle but had never met or even spoken to any of them. The committee members were defended by A. L. Wirin, and Omura by a Denver attorney, Sidney Jacobs, who tried unsuccessfully to get a separate trial for him. In early November 1944 the jury convicted the Heart Mountaineers but acquitted Omura. When the federal attorney, who had been cocksure of convicting all eight, asked jurors why they had acquitted Omura, he was told that none of the evidence showed him to be a conspirator as opposed to counselor. The judge differentiated between the defendants, sentencing those he believed more influential to four years, the others to two. For the two defendants who had been part of the sixty-three, he ruled that their sentences should run concurrently. Wirin's appeal was successful as the Tenth Circuit ruled on December 26, 1945, that the judge's failure to instruct the jury of the possible relevance of Wirin's insistence that it was a test case was reversible judicial error. The federal prosecutor wanted the reversal appealed to the Supreme Court, but the Justice Department refused to allow it. After all, the war was over, and all the camps but Tule Lake had been closed down.

As Eric Muller has shown in his splendid study *Free to Die for Their Country*, a number of other trials followed a course similar to the one in Wyoming, but without an ensuing trial for conspiracy. In all the trials save one, the defendants lost. That trial was another matter altogether.

In July 1944 federal judge Louis E. Goodman of the Northern District of California traveled with his law clerk from his base in San Francisco on an annual trip to hold court for a week in Eureka, population 28,000, near the Oregon border. He found waiting for him a case involving twenty-seven draft resisters from Tule Lake, which became *US v. Kawabara*. Trials for draft resistance by WRA prisoners seemed so cut-and-dried that no attorneys from the Justice Department bothered to show up at the out-of-the-way venue. A federal prosecutor, Emmet Seawell, up from Sacramento for the week, would show no awareness of the issues and assumed that the matter would be pro forma, as the Heart Mountain case had set a precedent. Goodman, appointed to the federal bench by President Roosevelt in November 1942, had no prior judicial contact with Japanese American cases, but as a San Franciscan he was aware of the issues and had some knowledge of the draft situation as a member of a local draft board between the passage of the 1940 Selective Service Act and his appointment to the bench. When court opened on Monday, the defendants were marched from the jail to the courthouse for arraignment. Because they had no counsel, Goodman appointed two local lawyers and told them to enter motions the next day. The local attorneys came back and filed guilty pleas for the first group of defendants. It is not known precisely how and when Judge Goodman decided to prevent what seemed the certain conviction of the Tule Lake twenty-seven—he died suddenly at age sixty-nine and left no memoir—but it had clearly become a matter of conscience. Either Tuesday evening or Wednesday morning he called Blaine McGowan, a friend from law school and a local lawyer, asking him to take over the defense. On Wednesday, after meeting with the prisoners and assuring them that he would win their case, McGowan appeared in court and moved to withdraw the guilty plea. Goodman approved and told him to file appropriate motions the next day.

On Thursday McGowan moved to quash the indictment and terminate proceedings, justifying his action on both constitutional and statutory grounds. He argued that, since the defendants "were at all times during all proceedings . . . under duress, personal restraint, confinement and fear" because of their "confinement in a Concentration Center, without due process of law, and contrary to the provisions of Amendment 5 of the Constitution of the United States of America," their prosecution was unjustified. He also claimed that the men were unacceptable for military service under the Selective Service Act, and finally, that since the men had applied for expatriation to Japan, they were not acceptable to the army.

During oral argument Judge Goodman asked Seawell how, in view of McGowan's argument, he would show that the prisoners were, in fact, free agents, capable of legally binding decisions. The government attorney, obviously unprepared, answered that he had asked the Justice Department for instructions and expected an answer by Saturday morning. The answer, from Assistant Attorney General Tom Clark, did not seem to recognize the nature of the constitutional claim and noted that the judge in the Heart Mountain case had raised no such questions.

It seems clear that Goodman, having decided to dismiss the cases, had two options. As McGowan had waived the defendants right to trial by jury, he could have staged a brief trial and found the defendants not guilty. Such a verdict, like an acquittal in a jury trial, is not appealable. He chose not to do that and instead dismissed the charges with an opinion, which could have been overruled by a higher court, in this instance, the Ninth Circuit.

But the Justice Department chose not to appeal, for reasons that are not clear; the government alleges that the department's files on *Kawabara* no longer exist. Assistant Attorney General Herbert Wechsler wrote to Attorney General Biddle explaining that the solicitor general chose not to appeal because the defendants were not acceptable by the army.

The facts of that matter are quite clear: not one single individual from Tule Lake was ever drafted. Whose excess of zeal was involved cannot now be stated. Judge Goodman's bold act of conscience spared twenty-seven men from having to spend time in prison, but it changed very little beyond that. His next intervention in Japanese American cases was of much more moment.

Legal scholars have pointed out that Goodman's hurried opinion is not well crafted, and it is possible to argue that his stage managing of the defense from the bench violated judicial ethics. But among the other final decisions on the wartime Japanese American cases, his words "It is shocking to the conscience that an American citizen who had been confined on the ground of disloyalty, and then, while so under duress and restraint, be compelled to serve in the Armed Forces, or be prosecuted for not yielding to such compulsion" are in stark contrast to the callous opinions of other American judges and judicial officials besotted with the notion that the urgencies of wartime simply nullified constitutional restraints. To be sure, they never went as far as their French and German wartime counterparts, but, after all, no one asked them to.

CHAPTER FIVE

Postwar Changes

As the war came to an end, Japanese Americans continued to be a people in motion. Since the spring of 1942 almost all of the 120,000 who became WRA prisoners had moved at least three times, and many moved a good deal more than that. The same was true for the thousands interned in Department of Justice camps. The extreme dispersion to a handful of families in each of America's 3,000 counties, a pipe dream that Franklin Roosevelt mused about but probably did not really believe in, was always a nonstarter. Nikkei internal migration, like almost all such in the twentieth-century United States, was primarily rural to urban or urban to urban, with an increasing concentration in large cities and metropolitan areas.

There was a shift in the regional distribution of Japanese Americans, with most of those who had resettled elsewhere later returned to the three Pacific states: they held 89 percent of mainland Nikkei in 1940 and just 69 percent in 1950. The nearly 15,000 living in other states in 1940 had almost tripled by 1950.

The case of Chicago illustrates the transitory nature of much wartime resettlement. The Windy City contained 390 persons recorded as of Japanese ethnicity in 1940, and 11,051 in 1950. There had been an intercensal peak of perhaps 23,000. While some of these temporary Chicagoans moved to other locations in the area of resettlement, most returned to the West Coast, but not necessarily to their original location. Despite WRA efforts to place Nikkei on farms, few resettlers went to rural areas. In Illinois, which in 1950 was second only to California in Nikkei population, just 595 of them were beyond the city limits of Chicago, and most of those were in other urban settings. Except in the intermountain West, not one in twenty postwar Nikkei living away from the Pacific states were in agricultural pursuits.

For the two-thirds of the Nikkei who returned to the West Coast, it was not a particularly happy homecoming. In 1942 various federal officials had given vague assurances that were not quite promises about taking care of Nikkei property during the absence of its owners, but these came to nothing. Many returners had lost their homes and their farms. Some farmers were forced to become sharecroppers on land they once leased as proprietors; farm owners often found that tenants had not maintained farms and equipment properly; and many former farmers could not find any foothold in the rapidly expanding economy.

Urban returners discovered that possessions thought safely stored had been discarded, stolen, or exposed to decay. In San Francisco motor vehicles owned by Nikkei were stored in a fenced but unguarded lot near what is now Candlestick Park. What looters and vandals did not destroy, the elements did. Some possessions safely stored were simply never reclaimed; one such trove was rediscovered in a Seattle workingman's hotel in the twenty-first century.

In the postwar West Coast states Japanese Americans of both generations remained more heavily engaged in agriculture than the general population, but the incidence of their production was greatly reduced. The 1940 census showed that two of five Japanese Americans employed in the three West Coast states, 41.4 percent, were in agriculture; the 1950 census showed that almost one in three Nikkei, 32.4 percent, were so employed. In California by 1960, just over a fifth of working Nikkei were in agriculture; the parallel datum for "whites" was less than a fiftieth, 1.7 percent.

The capital available to the postwar West Coast Japanese Americans was greatly reduced. In addition to the loss of many income-producing assets, businesses, farms, and leaseholds on agricultural property, much of the prewar community's savings had been in American branches of major Japanese banks. Although the American clients had put in dollars, one set of the branches' books showed them in yen. The Treasury Department seized and shut down those branches in the days after Pearl Harbor, which denied the depositors the use of their savings in a time of great need. After the war, when the assets were freed and made available to depositors, the Treasury Department used the postwar yen rate of 360 yen to a dollar, established by the American occupation authorities, as opposed to the prewar rate of 4 yen to the dollar. Thus a person or heir who had had $1,000 in the bank, recorded as 4,000 yen, would receive, after the war, about $11.

The state of California did worse than that. Someone in Sacramento kept an eye on the casualty lists and had the local real estate records searched for names of Japanese American military dead. If the dead soldier was on the real estate rolls as an owner of agricultural land and had left his estate to his Issei parents, the California attorney general's office instituted escheat proceedings and in eighty instances seized the land for the state. Queried about those actions in 1967, Robert W. Kenny, the liberal Democrat who was California attorney general during Earl Warren's first term as governor, admitted, "We really shouldn't have done that." On the other hand, it must be noted that in the November 1946 general election California's voters soundly rejected a ballot proposition to incorporate the existing Alien Land Law into the state's constitution by almost three-fifths of the nearly 2 million votes cast. All previous anti-Asian measures put on the state ballot had succeeded.

Although in early 1942 the congressional Tolan Committee had strongly recommended that either the Alien Property Custodian or the Federal Reserve Bank in San Francisco be made responsible for the protection of the property of "evacuated persons," neither organization lifted a finger to do so. The WRA produced a small postwar volume titled *The Wartime Handling of Evacuee Property*, which largely documents its failure to do so effectively. Its two-paragraph conclusion, after a hundred-plus pages of specific examples, cites the estimate of an agency official that the "evacuated people" left behind more than $200 million worth of real, personal, and commercial property and reported losses of "many millions." A more precise estimate of the most significant category of loss by two experts in the Department of Agriculture's Bureau of Agricultural Economics calculated that in the three West Coast states, "ownership transfers to non-evacuees . . . reduced [Nikkei] farm ownership interests to less than a fourth of the total of prewar Japanese land holdings, including leaseholds." The report also noted: "Many lost their chance of income and security in their old age through inability to keep up payments on their insurance policies. Others have lost property through inability to pay taxes. Individual losses vary in amount from a few hundred to many thousands of dollars."

Added to these detailed accounts of loss must be the observation that, apart from those actually involved in combat, the American people, in the vernacular of the time, "never had it so good." Unemployment disappeared, and national income rose significantly, as did personal savings. Farm income rose to its highest levels, while most Nikkei farmers were reduced to doing agricultural labor at nineteen dollars a month on WRA holdings or as wage workers on farms in the intermountain West at the lowest legal rates for hard, dirty work at harvest time.

There was almost no talk about any kind of redress during the war. The only example I have discovered in wartime by a ranking official was a suggestion to President Roosevelt by Milton Eisenhower prior to his resignation from the WRA that, after the war was over, there should be some kind of redress for what the WRA captives had suffered. By the end of the war Roosevelt was dead, and Milton Eisenhower, who had left government service in 1943 to become president of his alma mater, Kansas State College, seems to have made no effort to influence postwar policy toward the Nisei. The WRA itself, as part of its final accounting in 1946, would recommend only a very limited form of redress in what it called "Unfinished Business": the creation of an evacuee claims commission to consider property losses attributable to their exile.

In November 1945, as the last of the relocation centers were pushing out their remaining inmates, the first of the postwar shipments of WRA inmates to Japan began from San Francisco and Seattle. The only wartime shipments to Japan were under the auspices of the State Department, which had chartered the Swedish liner *Gripsholm* to effect exchanges of civilian prisoners between the United States and Japan. Although the conflict between the United States and Japan was what John Dower has correctly called a "war without mercy," the two little-noted civilian prisoner exchanges in 1942 and 1943 were carried out punctiliously by both sides. The exchanges had been conducted through the Spanish government, which was the "protecting power" of Japanese interests in the United States, and the actual exchanges took place in Lourenço Marques, Mozambique, in East Africa.

Altogether, 3,003 Nikkei were sent east from New York. Some 90 percent of them were either Japan's diplomatic personnel from the United States and other New World nations, plus Japanese nationals interned by the Justice Department, including some who had been rendered from Latin America. The remainder were 318 persons drawn from all ten WRA camps: 138 were aliens, 180 US citizens. Of the Nisei 113 (63 percent) were under eighteen; most of the 38 adult Nisei women were married to alien males. All of the adults went willingly, and many other incarcerated adults who had expressed a desire to go could not be accommodated.

The postwar shipments were a different matter. They were enabled by President Truman's proclamation of July 14, 1945, that "alien enemies now or hereafter interned . . . shall be subject upon the order of the Attorney General to removal from the United States and may be required to depart therefrom in accordance with such regulations as he may prescribe." The Justice Department used that authority not only to deport interned alien enemies but also to deport renunciants who had neither been interned nor declared enemy aliens. All that their official notice of change of status had said, in a form letter, was that "you are no longer a citizen of the United States . . . nor are you entitled to any of the rights and privileges of such citizenship."

As opposed to the wartime shipments which had to be agreed to in advance through intermediaries by both warring parties, the postwar shipments cannot be precisely accounted for. The WRA provided good data, but the reports made by the Department of Justice were deliberately vague and misleading and are best described as dodgy. The WRA reports about the three postwar shipments of its captives involving several sailings between November 25, 1945, and February 23, 1946, enumerated 4,406 persons, all from Tule Lake; 1,767 were US citizens, 1,116 were renunciants, and 1,513 alien Issei. Of the citizens all but 49 were under twenty years of age, and 1,418 were under fifteen. Most were accompanying repatriating or expatriating parents. None of the US citizens forfeited their citizenship, but existing citizenship law provided—as had been the case for the citizen children on the *Gripsholm*—that minor citizens residing abroad who reached their twenty-first birthday had to affirm their citizenship formally or lose it. It is not known how many of the expelled citizen children did that, or returned to the United States. The WRA had, over the years, shipped 3,121 persons to Department of Justice internment camps, some of whom were surely included among those sent to Japan by the Justice Department.

Some future "archive rat," a term of art that no longer describes me, may well be able to piece together the details of the Department of Justice's share of the postwar deportations of persons to Japan who were, or had been, US citizens. One thing that seems clear is that the department's original intention had been to deport, in addition to most enemy aliens in its custody, all 5,133 Japanese American citizens whose applications for denaturalization had been approved by Attorney General Francis Biddle. All but 89 of them were approved between March 22 and May 5, 1945; none were approved after the latter date. That the department did not succeed in doing this is due to the attorneys of the NCACLU, particularly Wayne Collins, whose bleak struggle of Dickensian proportions began in August 1945 and ended only on March 6, 1968.

Tom Clark, who replaced Biddle in June 1945, signed annual reports that are curiously reticent about the numbers of deportations to Japan as opposed to those to Europe and Latin America. In his 1945 annual report Clark is forthcoming about deportations to Europe: "1,379 alien enemies were repatriated to Europe." Nothing was said about those shipped to Japan. The report did say: "Because of pro-Japanese demonstrations and disturbances at the Tule Lake Segregation Center, 1,516 Japanese natives and persons of Japanese ancestry were transferred to internment camps operated by the Immigration and Naturalization Service, after evidence of their participation in such disturbances had been revealed in hearings held by Departmental representatives." As will be discussed later, those hearings were not an investigation into the 1944 violence at Tule Lake but hearings about the renunciation of citizenship. The word "renunciation" first appears in the annual report for 1947.

The 1946 annual report provides two sets of numbers for overlapping time periods in separate adjoining sentences about deportation. In the first, covering January 1 to December 31, 1946, "10,764 persons departed from [all detention] facilities . . . the majority of which were Japanese repatriated to Japan." In the second, covering May 7, 1945, to June 30, 1946, "9,331 alien enemies had been repatriated to Germany, Italy, and Japan and 569 such nationals had been returned to Latin American countries from which they had been brought by the State Department." If these numbers are accurate, we can only say that at least 5,383 persons of Japanese ancestry were sent to Japan by the government.

Clark's 1947 annual report says no more about deportation of war-related prisoners but does, for the first time, refer to renunciation. In an inaccurate passage the report speaks of "the so-called 'Tule Lake' cases in which restoration to citizenship was requested by 1,400 citizens of Japanese ancestry while in detention at the Tule Lake, California, segregation camp."

We know very little about the lives of these and other Americans exiled to devastated postwar Japan. The entire Japanese people who had survived the horrors of aerial bombardment—accounts of Tokyo during attacks of explosive and incendiary bombs speak of the water boiling in its canals—had to cope with food shortages, a damaged, disrupted infrastructure, and a disintegration of social services. A pioneering 1955 study of renunciants in one Japanese prefecture by Gladys Ishida (Stone) found that while Kibei had been able to adjust to the cultural differences, the other Nisei were not equipped with the proper cultural tools to live in Japan. "After nearly a decade of postwar residence . . . these Nisei renunciants still continue to look forward to the day they can return to America; they consider their stay in Japan as temporary. How many did return after 1959 when American law permitted it, is not known."

Eileen Tamura's recent biography of the most prominent of the renunciants, the Manzanar agitator Joseph Y. Kurihara, who left on one of the first two vessels carrying postwar exiles to Japan, shows that his life in Japan was consistent with some of Ishida's generalizations, although Kurihara always assumed that Japan would remain his home. He never came close to mastering Japanese, and, like many renunciants and other Nisei who had been trapped in Japan, his initial economic survival was assured by his employment by the military occupation authorities. While army intelligence officers looked askance at the employment of such persons, their objections were overridden. The employment of renunciants was a matter of authentic military necessity.

The only renunciant I have ever knowingly spoken to was an infant who remained unaware of her American birth until she was an adult. A professor at a Japanese university when I spoke to her in 2004, she had been trying, without much success, to gather reliable information about the Japanese experience of her father and other American renunciants. That chapter of trans-Pacific history remains largely unwritten.

That the Department of Justice did not ship more renunciants to Japan was due to the efforts of West Coast civil rights attorneys. Ernest Besig's aborted July 1944 visit to the Tule Lake camp, which alerted NCACLU attorneys to the scandalous conditions there, was followed up on by Wayne Collins, who was initially also denied access. In August 1944, after he had threatened to file habeas corpus suits, director Raymond Best, under instructions from Washington, yielded and even sent the project attorney up to Klamath Falls to meet him and drive him back. Collins's main complaint was that citizens had been incarcerated in the stockade for long periods without charges being leveled against them. Collins met with the prisoners. After a conference with Best and the project attorney, the camp officials agreed to release the prisoners, and Collins was able to meet with them.

According to a 1958 account in his files, Collins, preparing to go back to San Francisco, learned that some other inmates wanted to meet with him, and a room was provided. In this meeting, Collins learned from parents of younger renunciants of the renunciations and the threatened deportations, apparently for the first time. His immediate reaction was that renunciations of citizenship while incarcerated were invalid. He wrote out on the spot copies of a sample letter to the attorney general for renunciants and the parents of minor renunciants to submit, arguing that the renunciations they had submitted were "void for being the proximate result of both government duress" and threats of violence and other retaliation from camp militants.

Some WRA captives had submitted requests to be allowed to go to Japan as soon as mass incarceration began. In 1942 the government received 2,225 such requests, almost three-fifths of them from aliens; more than half the rest came from persons younger than eighteen; the Justice Department used eighteen rather than twenty-one as a dividing line because draft eligibility began at that age. By the end of 1943, 6,673 additional requests to go to Japan had been received; none of them or others received in the first half of 1944 could be acted upon, but their existence was an important argument for the renunciation law, which Roosevelt approved on July 1, 1944. Many of them were driven by the loyalty questionnaire; more than two-fifths of the 1943 requests were received during the ten-week period of the "registration." Other triggers were the reinstitution of the draft for Japanese Americans in January 1944 and Dillon Myer's announcement in the wake of the *Endo* decision on December 18, 1944, that all WRA camps would be closed within a year. By the day after Christmas in 1944, 2,000 additional applications for renunciation were received, and army officers conducting interviews of applicants were asking citizens, "Do you want to go out"—that is, leave Tule Lake and go somewhere in the United States—"or do you want to renounce your citizenship?"

As the applications for renunciation continued to pour in during the new year, Ennis and his deputy Burling, seeing that they had created a situation far more serious than they had expected, went to Attorney General Biddle and asked him to stop the renunciation program. Biddle refused, according to Ennis, insisting that he could not shelve a program that he had begun. Burling and a team of four other Justice Department lawyers were sent to Tule Lake to administer hearings. Burling testified that he had explained to his team that "the entire evacuation has been a tragic mistake" and urged them to impress on the applicants the negative possibilities inherent in renunciation.

Actually, by the time the attorney general got around to approving large numbers of the requests, many renunciants had begun to rethink their position. A major factor was worsening war news for Japan, one Issei poet noting:

> The colors of the war maps
> Having lately changed,
> No longer can we smile.

The hearings conducted by Burling's team ended on March 17, 1945. By that date only 84 individual requests for denaturalization had been approved under the terms of the 1944 law. Between March 22 and May 5, 1945, the attorney general approved 5,049 more. By the time he finished his approvals, written requests for withdrawal of approved or pending applications were piling up, but Attorney General Biddle insisted that it was impossible to revoke an application for renunciation once granted, a policy continued by his successors, Tom C. Clark, whom Truman appointed to replace Biddle in late June 1945, and J. Howard McGrath, who succeeded him in July 1949 after Truman named Clark to the Supreme Court. In 1981 Ennis testified to the federal Commission on Wartime Relocation and Internment of Civilians (CWRIC) that the renunciation program had "failed" without making clear that he was an author of the program and had drafted the law that made it possible, and that after he realized it was a failure, he continued to defend it.

Of slightly more than 6,000 requests under the new law, 5,589 were approved. Apparently the few hundred persons who were not approved were never informed of the status of their applications, nor do we know why they were not approved. Of those in its custody who successfully denaturalized, the WRA provided a brief account, with statistics, in 1946.

The Justice Department had informed the WRA that it was to keep the new noncitizens in an interned status and not to release them until told to do so by the attorney general, and eventually the Justice Department took legal custody of the renunciants held at Tule Lake. Thus, although the law said nothing about detention or status, the Justice Department treated them as enemy aliens. The WRA reported that about half of the renunciants, 2,785, had been released and relocated. Thirty percent (1,657) were sent to Justice Department camps, and some of them were subsequently sent to Japan. Four died at Tule Lake, 6 were allowed to leave before approval had been received, and 4 were sent to mental institutions. The WRA accounting leaves the fate of 1,133 renunciants unaccounted for and unexplained.

The Justice Department had expected the shipments to Japan to continue, but Wayne Collins, with the support of Besig and over the continuing objections of the national ACLU, filed a number of lawsuits that not only blocked further deportations but also encouraged release, as Myer resisted keeping Tule Lake open, and the capacity of the Justice Department camps was limited. Although Collins failed to prevent the early group of postwar deportations, his lawsuits threw a monkey wrench into the Justice Department's plans for continuing deportations.

Collins's first two renunciant cases, class action suits, *Abo v. Clark*, a suit in equity, and *Abo v. Williams*, a habeas corpus petition, were originally filed in the San Francisco Federal District Court of Judge St. Sure on November 13, 1945. (Clark was attorney general; Ivan Williams was his regional director of the Immigration and Naturalization Service and legal custodian for the Tule Lake prisoners in consequence of the *Endo* decision, although the WRA continued to run Tule Lake until its closure on March 28, 1946.) A few days later, as Collins told the story, he boarded one of the first army transports due to take renunciants to Japan and brought off an unspecified number of his clients whose names were on his petition. At that time Collins had the signatures of "only" 987 of the renunciants; he continued to collect signatures and eventually secured a total of 4,754, which made 85 percent of all renunciants his clients. His contentions throughout were that all his clients had suffered from coercion and duress not only from pro-Japanese individuals and organized groups within the imprisoned population but also in some instances from their own family members. He also charged duress by government officials plus the fact that the government failed to protect his clients from inmate coercion.

Within a month of Collins's successful filings, the Justice Department reversed itself and announced on December 10, 1945, that it would hold "hearings in mitigation" for renunciants attempting to revoke their renunciations. These, managed by Burling and other Justice Department lawyers, were properly conducted. Early in the new year Judge St. Sure put the cases on hold pending the outcomes of the hearings. As a result of 3,186 individual mitigation hearings lasting into the spring of 1946, 2,280 persons were granted stays of deportation orders. On September 23, 1946, some ten months after the institution of the suits, the Justice Department responded. Although admitting much of the coercion charged by Collins, it nevertheless insisted that all the defendants had been dual nationals so that their loss of American citizenship made them citizens of Japan, and thus alien enemies subject to deportation. It ignored the facts that it had little or no evidence of dual citizenship, even for Kibei, and that the United States did not recognize dual citizenship. It did admit that some of those denaturalized had been minors, but still argued that they too had become citizens of Japan, and that none of the renunciants had been "coerced or led by any form of duress to renounce" and "were voluntary and active participants . . . with full knowledge and consequence of their act."

On October 14, 1946, Collins moved that the requested writs of habeas corpus be granted while the government asked that they be denied. Judge St. Sure agreed to rule on the basis of the arguments and affidavits already filed. Before he could issue a ruling, however, he became seriously ill, and on February 20, 1947, the cases and the large and growing collection of documents associated with them were transferred to the court of the other San Francisco–based federal judge, Louis Goodman. After a little more than four months, Judge Goodman handed down his decision on June 30, 1947. Borrowing some of the language he had used in the 1944 case of the Tule Lake draft resisters, *US v. Kawabara*, Goodman challenged the whole process of renunciation, writing that it was "shocking to the conscience that an American citizen be confined without authority and then, while still under duress and constraint, for his government to accept from him a surrender of his constitutional heritage."

Goodman went on to accept Collins's central argument that all the renunciations were tainted by endemic coercion and duress from government, ethnic militants, and even parents and other family members, finding that the prisoners had acted in "fear, anxiety, hopelessness, and despair." The effect of his order was to suspend the deportations and restore the citizenship of thousands of Nisei. Since Tule Lake had closed on March 26, expelling its final residents into a world they feared would inflict more pain upon them, the 4,500 released renunciants were indistinguishable from the rest of the mainland Nikkei and could, if they wished, exercise all of their rights of citizenship with impunity. The renunciants released from confinement had been paroled to their attorney and allowed to re-settle pending the outcome of the government's appeal. At this stage the intelligent move would have been for the government simply not to appeal. With the presumption now in favor of the litigants, and with no evidence against the mass of the defendants except their own words now disavowed, there was little if any real hope of victory. But a succession of less than outstanding attorneys general allowed the cases to drag on; some lasted for an additional twenty-one years.

After Collins's initial success the able and aggressive A. L. Wirin was able to get a very tiny piece of the Tule Lake action, signing up four renunciant clients, Miye Murakami, Yuichi Inouye, Tustako Sumi, and Mutsu Shimizu, for a very different approach. After winning an initial case in a Los Angeles federal district court and having it dismissed on a technicality, he had the same clients apply for passports and, when the State Department refused to issue them, sued the secretary of state to restore their citizenship and issue the passports. On August 27, 1948, Los Angeles federal district judge William C. Mathes, a 1945 appointee of President Truman, ruled in favor of the plaintiffs in *Murakami v. Acheson*. The government appealed to the Ninth District, where Judge William Denman, now chief judge, sustained the verdict of the district court on August 26, 1949. The State Department did not appeal and issued the passports, having recognized their citizenship. In his opinion Denman made a scathing attack on the government's "unnecessarily cruel and inhuman treatment" of Japanese Americans at Tule Lake and took judicial notice of "some four thousand similar cases who are seeking similar relief." Misinformed public speculation suggested that a sweeping victory for all of Collins's clients would follow. When this did not occur, Collins and Besig, who resented what they regarded as Wirin's poaching on their territory, and had other long-standing issues with him as well, put it out that it was his case that caused Denman to insist on having coercion established in each individual case. Even more important for the record, Collins and Besig, in separate 1972 interviews with the first professional historian to write about the renunciation cases, were highly critical of Wirin, who brushed off the historian's request for an interview. It came to be an article of faith with latter-day Tule Lake activists that Wirin was responsible for the long delays.

In Collins's cases the government contended in what had become *McGrath v. Abo* (J. Howard McGrath was Truman's second attorney general) that coercion had to be established in each individual case. It appealed to the Ninth Circuit, where, on January 17, 1951, Judge Denman, in an opinion joined by two other judges, accepted some parts of Goodman's ruling but overruled others. All those who were under twenty-one years of age at the time they renounced were reaffirmed as American citizens. This voided perhaps 2,000 of a putative 4,315 renunciations under consideration. Citizenship was also restored in eight instances in which the renunciants were legally incompetent, and in fifty-eight other cases in which the evidence was inconclusive.

Denman continued to condemn the government's administration of Tule Lake. The evidence shows, he ruled, that prevailing "oppressive conditions" caused or made possible by the WRA created a "rebuttable contention" that the "acts of renunciation were involuntary." Denman thus rejected Collins's and Goodman's contention that government misconduct voided all renunciations, but he placed the burden of proving the legitimacy of individual renunciations on the government, and not, as the Justice Department had contended, on the individual renunciant.

It is not at all clear that even one individual effectively lost his or her citizenship in all this lawyerly filing and argumentation. Neither the government nor Collins knew where all the scattered defendants were, although Collins surely had a better grasp than federal officials. The leading Japanese American editor of the time, Yasuo Abiko, told the *New York Times* that the defendants were scattered widely and that about 200 were in the US Army, and he assumed that some were fighting in Korea. Collins's herculean task, with few helpers and minimal assets, was to somehow cobble together an effective set of documents to fit each case once he had located the defendant. His primary weapon was the individual affidavit he filed for each defendant or family of defendants. It was the government's burden to rebut each defendant's claim, and in all but a handful of cases it had no evidence beyond the now compromised and repudiated words of the defendants themselves. Rather than separate trials, Judge Goodman now had to rule on individual cases in camera as affidavits and other documents were presented to him, primarily by Collins as the government usually had few documents to present. A good example is the affidavit for his lead defendant.

Tadayasu Abo (1911–1989), who became the lead client in Collins's two main suits by virtue of alphabetical precedence, turned out to be not unrepresentative of the renunciants. Tada, as he was called, and his wife, Yukiko (1919–2011), were both Kibei born in rural Washington and had limited facility in English. He had spent the decade after his sixth birthday in Japan and returned there for a visit during 1935–1936 in which he entered into an arranged marriage with Yukiko. She had been taken to Hiroshima shortly after her birth and been educated in schools there until their marriage in 1936. The new couple soon returned to the United States and settled into the small Japanese communities of oyster workers in sheltered bays at the southern tip of Puget Sound near Olympia. Other family members worked there and in other Japanese enclaves in southwestern Washington. They were employed, at low wages for long hours of labor: Tada tending and harvesting the seed oysters imported from Japan, Yuki culling and shucking them in the packing shed. They lived in a company float house without electricity or plumbing. After war came, they and their two-year-old son, Joe, were seized and shipped directly to Tule Lake in mid-1942 along with other Nikkei in that part of Washington. While they were in camp a daughter, Nancy, was born in October 1943. Yukiko told twenty-first-century interviewers that at Tule Lake while Tada worked in a mess hall, she had the first vacation of her life, with time to take care of her children and learn to sew.

When the 1943 loyalty questions had to be answered, both Ados either said no or, like so many of their neighbors at Tule Lake, refused to answer. As Yukiko later put it, "We not obeying Japan, we not obeying America." Tada, in his eventually successful affidavit submitted by Collins in 1956—we do not know why it was so long delayed—expressed his many fears in explaining his reasons for renouncing his citizenship in November 1943, which are similar to those expressed by Yukiko more than half a century later. Among the several iterations of Tada's reasons for renouncing are the following:

My wife and I, both natural born citizens, were evacuated and confined like aliens, and we resented and felt bad about such unfair treatment to us. . . . I was afraid that we would be forced to relocate with small children where people would be unfriendly toward us. . . . Personal safety for my family was a constant worry and we believed from everything that was done to us that the U.S. government had given up on us as citizens and the only thing left was to find the best way for family to live. . . .

From the time I was evacuated into a camp until the time I renounced my citizenship there were many violent incidents in the camp that kept us in fear. These reasons influenced me to renounce in order to be left unmolested in the camp.

Tada testified that he thought he had applied for renunciation in November 1943 and that he did not learn that it had been accepted until he was so notified on August 24 or 25, 1945. He subsequently learned that it was possible to withdraw his renunciation, and in October 1945 he joined the mass suit and sent a letter, provided by Collins, to the attorney general requesting that his renunciation be canceled. Yukiko's actions probably mirrored his. They were released on parole in the closing weeks of 1945, with Collins as their custodian. They lived for a short time in Red Bluff, California, where Tada worked for the Union Pacific Railroad. When they learned from friends and relatives that the local oyster company was hiring back all its prewar Nikkei employees, they returned home to the same jobs and moved back into the same float house. Only on August 9, 1956, did Tada complete a satisfactory affidavit, which was received by the Justice Department on August 20; it did not challenge Tada's various claims, so Judge Goodman issued a final order on February 7, 1957. Collins wrote Tada in the letter he sent along with Goodman's order: "You need not be ashamed of the fact that you once renounced your citizenship. . . . You did so because the government took advantage of you while it held you in duress and deprived you of practically all the rights of citizenship."

Both Abos continued to work in the oyster industry until 1965, including a period when they attempted, without success, to establish an oyster operation of their own. By 1972, with the help of their children—two more had been born after their return—they were able to build a house overlooking the bay where they had worked for so many years. Yukiko, who survived her husband by almost a quarter of a century, became part of a community circle of senryu poets. Senryu poems, similar in form to the more familiar haiku, focus on ordinary events of everyday life. One of Yukiko Abo's poems depicts

> Sliding from their box,
> Seed oysters gleam in the sun
> Of a foreign land.

Judge Goodman continued to deal with decreasing numbers of cases, restoring citizenship based largely on renunciants affidavits until his death from a heart attack on September 15, 1961. His *New York Times* obituary credited him with restoring citizenship to 2,700 Japanese Americans who had been confined at Tule Lake. The last seven years of Collins's remaining cases were settled in the court of

Judge Alphonso J. Zirpoli, who, as an assistant US attorney in San Francisco during most of the war, had a minor role in some of the wartime Japanese American cases. He had been appointed to a newly created judgeship by President Kennedy on the day before Goodman died. On March 6, 1965, Judge Zirpoli ordered the withdrawal and dismissal of charges against Collins's final plaintiff. Collins's remark that closing the case "brings to a conclusion . . . equity proceedings instituted on November 13, 1945. . . . an infamous chapter in our history has come to an end," is accurate from the attorney's point of view, but the episode was far from ended.

The years of disgraceful behavior by American officials responsible for the administration of justice, including eight attorneys general running from Tom Clark in 1945 through his son Ramsey in 1965, are only rarely remembered; early in the postwar period both the Interior Department and the State Department withdrew from the suits, but the Justice Department, in the name of a foolish consistency, insisted on dragging the process out to what was, for the department, its bitter and fruitless end.

The burden of Tule Lake still lies heavily on the only people who continue to care deeply about it, many members of the mainland Japanese American community. For many of the majority of Japanese American families whose incarceration experience and traditions were associated with one of the other main WRA camps, Tuleans were those who had soiled their collective reputation. For the minority who had actually been at Tule Lake, it was a shame, even for those who met the capricious standards of wartime loyalty. Such former Tuleans often did not volunteer the name of their camp and sometimes even concealed it from postwar children or those too young to remember where they had been. Tuleans in general and renunciants in particular are the only groups of wartime Nisei who have never been celebrated, never been forgiven.

Clearly the Tule Lake cases are not well understood even by many contemporary community activists. The one thing generally agreed upon is that Wayne Collins is a very special hero. Even though many legal scholars are critical of Collins's legal knowledge and methods, it is difficult not to agree with Michi Weglyn's dedicatory comment that the San Francisco attorney "did more to correct a democracy's mistake than any other person."

Apart from signing the proclamation enabling the Justice Department to proceed with the deportation of renunciants, Truman spent eight months as president without taking official notice of Japanese Americans. When Eleanor Roosevelt wrote him in mid-December 1945 about allegations that had been sent to her about vigilante attacks against Japanese Americans returning to their homes in California's Central Valley, he ordered Attorney General Tom Clark to investigate. When that investigation, and one instituted by California governor Earl Warren, confirmed such attacks, it apparently focused the president's attention on the marginal position of Japanese Americans in American life, although Truman has left us no clear paper trail demonstrating this.

In April 1946 the White House sent a proposal to Congress calling for the creation of a commission to adjudicate claims against the government for property losses sustained by Japanese Americans because of "evacuation," which may have originated in the WRA, but no such legislation was enacted. On July 15, 1946, Truman, who as senator had silently voted for or not objected to all the major legislative acts enabling wartime incarceration, firmly and publicly announced himself as a supporter of the not yet popular Japanese Americans.

In a ceremony that he ordered and his staff stage managed, a late-returning element of the already storied 442nd Regimental Combat Team was marched onto the Ellipse behind the White House for a ceremonial presentation of its seventh Presidential Distinguished Unit Citation on July 15, 1946. Before personally affixing the ribbons to the unit's banner, the president briefly addressed the troops:

> You fought for the free nations of the world along with the rest of us. . . . You are now on your way home. You fought not only the enemy, but you fought prejudice—and you have won. Keep up that fight, and we will continue to win—to make this great Republic stand for just what the Constitution says it stands for: the welfare of all the people all the time.

Truman's cautious approach to a civil rights program began with his December 1946 creation of the President's Commission on Civil Rights, which he ordered to investigate the status of civil rights in the nation and recommend "more adequate and effective means and procedures for the protection of the civil rights of the people of the United States."

The report—*To Secure These Rights* (1947), a small book of 176 pages—is rightly regarded as an important step in the evolution of federal civil rights programs. But it was also in many respects a timid report, which pulled its punches. A section on what it styled the "wartime evacuation of Japanese Americans" began by calling it, correctly, the "most striking mass interference since slavery with the right to physical freedom" and pointing out that the "evacuation of 110,000 men, women and children, two-thirds of whom were United States citizens, was made without a trial or any sort of hearing, at a time when the courts were functioning." Yet the commissioners could not bring themselves to condemn it and used a feckless medical analogy likening the wartime incarceration to "a sort of mass quarantine measure." The committee did call for "further study" and called attention to the unresolved matter of property loss.

On December 27, 1947, President Truman announced the traditional annual list of pardons, which was limited to violators of the Selective Service Act. In prior clemency actions Truman had pardoned some 1,400 violators who had subsequently served in the armed forces. The president followed the recommendations of an amnesty board headed by retired justice Owen J. Roberts, which he had created to advise him about which of the remaining draft violators to pardon. Truman's subsequent clemency cleared the records of 1,523 of 15,805 violators. The fortunate, all of them conscientious objectors as opposed to what the board styled "10,000 willful violators," included the Nisei convicted of draft violations. A. L. Wirin had filed a petition for the Nisei and supported it with testimony.

The pardon for the Nisei drew little attention in the nation's press. Most of the criticism reported focused on the two categories of conscientious objectors the board refused to pardon. One was the relatively small group of nonreligious pacifists, the other was the 4,300 Jehovah's Witnesses who claimed a clerical exemption for each of its members. Critics such as the American Friends Service Committee's Clarence Pickett condemned the failure to pardon all who claimed conscientious objector status. The ethnic press did take notice of the pardoned Nisei, and not all its comments were favorable: the JACL's

Pacific Citizen, as Eric Muller points out, argued that the resisters' attitudes had been "inexpedient," and "threatened to disrupt" the return of the Nikkei to their prewar homes. Some Nisei veterans' groups have continued their public resentment of the resisters into the twenty-first century. An even larger group of Nikkei, as well as other Americans, have never forgiven the renunciants. Many public figures have pretended that they did not exist.

On February 2, 1948, Truman sent his landmark civil rights message to Congress, laying out a ten-point program. Not surprisingly, the points dealt chiefly with the concerns of African Americans; the last three items—Hawaiian statehood, the prospect of color-blind naturalization, and some reparation for property losses resulting from the forced exile from the Pacific states—were of concern to Japanese Americans.

The results were mixed. Hawaiian statehood came only in 1959. Color-blind naturalization was achieved in the 1952 McCarran-Walter Act, which became law despite Truman's veto. Only the third item, the call for some recompense, was achieved in a form acceptable to President Truman.

Congress responded by passing the 1948 Japanese-American Claims Act. The Senate report on the bill insisted that "the question of whether the evacuation of the Japanese people from the West Coast was justified is now moot. . . . responsible government requires that there should be compensation for such losses." The House report described the property loss as one "inflicted by a voluntary act of the Government without precedent in the history of the nation."

During the congressional hearings, former government leaders Francis Biddle, John McCloy, and Dillon Myer all supported the pending legislation, which became law in July 1948. This act, later modified and extended, covered only "damage to or loss of real or personal property" and made no provision for goodwill, anticipated profit, earnings, or interest. Under those restrictions some 23,000 claims were filed, aggregating stipulated losses of $121 million, but Congress appropriated $38 million to settle all claims. The Justice Department contested claims vigorously, and the settlement of the pared-down claims stretched out over seventeen years. What is striking in reading the record of what the 1948 House report called "redress" is the complete lack of discussion of incarceration, or even the slightest inclination to consider such standard legal damage claims as pain and suffering.

In an era when the nation began what historians have termed the Second Reconstruction, whose first major achievement was the stunning reversal of the "separate but equal" doctrine in *Brown v. Board of Education* in 1954, it was not surprising that discriminatory statutes of all kinds were negated in various ways. The hated alien land laws had become meaningless when the McCarran-Walter Act abolished the category "aliens ineligible to citizenship" at whom the laws had been aimed.

Discrimination in employment and housing was made more difficult but not eliminated by the adoption of fair employment statutes in Oregon and Washington in 1949, and in California ten years later. A variety of federal and state actions gave Social Security credit for time spent in WRA camps, while those who had been federal and state civil servants received retirement credit for their time in camp.

One little-remembered act of Congress referenced the wartime incarceration in a very different way. In the summer of 1950, during the early months of the first modern American undeclared war, a Congress already in the grip of Cold War hysteria massed bipartisan support for a comprehensive group of extreme internal security measures known collectively as the Internal Security Act of 1950. Most of its distinct and uncoordinated parts were authored by conservative senators in both parties, with Nevada Democrat Patrick A. McCarran and South Dakota Republican Karl E. Mundt most prominent. The measure passed in both houses overwhelmingly, and President Truman's prompt veto was easily overridden; only ten senators voted to sustain the president's veto.

In the debates on the bill and the subsequent veto, it was argued that many parts of the act were unconstitutional, and eventually a number of sections were so declared by the Supreme Court. But one major component of the bill, its Title II, the Emergency Detention Act of 1950, was heralded as "acceptable to the Supreme Court" because it was modeled explicitly on some elements of FDR's 1942 executive orders, although the court had avoided endorsing those documents even while accepting much of their consequences. It was sponsored by six liberal Democratic senators—including Minnesota's

Hubert Humphrey, New York's Hebert Lehman, and Tennessee's Estes Kefauver—who were eager to show that their party was attuned to the national anticommunist obsession. After a baker's dozen paragraphs of turgid rhetoric about how and why "the world communist movement" was "a clear and present danger to the security of the United States," the law authorized: "The detention of persons who there is reasonable grounds to believe probably will commit or conspire with others to commit espionage or sabotage is, in a time of internal security emergency, essential to the common defense and to the safety and security of the territory, the people and the Constitution of the United States."

The bill then created the necessary mechanism. In the case of any one of three kinds of events—invasion of the nation or its territories, a congressional declaration of war, or an internal insurrection within the United States in aid of a foreign enemy—the president was authorized to proclaim an internal security emergency. In such an instance the law provided: "The president, acting through the Attorney General, is hereby authorized to apprehend and by order detain, pursuant to the provisions of this title, each person as to whom there is reasonable ground to believe that such person will probably engage in or probably will conspire with others to engage in acts of espionage or sabotage."

The parallels with the Japanese American incarceration are unmistakable. The president issues an order and authorizes a cabinet officer to lock up persons who have been neither charged nor indicted. As was the case under Executive Order 9066, no overt act was necessary, merely the judgment of an unelected official. Unlike the 1942 instance, provision was made for individual hearings, but these were to take place *after* incarceration, not before. Realizing that in 1942 there had been a delay of several months before the camps were ready, the law ordered the Justice Department to keep some such places in readiness. As if to underline the continuity, Tule Lake was chosen for one of the standby camps.

CHAPTER SIX

The Struggle for Redress

The struggle for what Japanese Americans learned to call redress became the dominant issue in community life between the early 1970s and on into the 1990s, and arguments about the meanings of redress remain important issues in the ethnic community. But that struggle cannot be understood without an awareness of the transforming events in the 1960s that now seem to separate quite different eras in American life. The misbegotten war in Vietnam; the changing nature of attitudes toward race, ethnicity, and eventually gender; and the cascading series of technological changes, including television, increasing automation, and eventually the computer, transformed the nature of both work and leisure. Well into the 1960s a kind of postwar American triumphalism—which Henry Luce and his magazines had styled the "American Century"—seemed to prevail. Before the sixties ended, the nation seemed increasingly polarized in both culture and politics. These changes in ideology and lifestyle clearly impacted the Japanese American community and the attitudes about it held by the larger community.

By 1960 most Americans old enough to remember the war had forgotten most of what little they had known about Japanese Americans. That was certainly true of Senator John F. Kennedy, the young Democratic nominee for president, who had been twenty-seven in 1942. Campaigning in Los Angeles as the Democratic nominee, he spoke briefly to a Japanese American audience and realized, without knowing why, that he had laid an egg. When his younger brother and campaign manager, who had not been present, sought to discover what had gone wrong, he learned that his brother, using a Democratic ploy that worked well with most ethnic audiences still connected to immigration, had trashed the McCarran-Walter Act. That, of course, was the law that had enabled the remaining Issei to become citizens and reestablished immigration from Japan after a twenty-eight-year ban. Most mainland Nikkei who voted in that presidential election probably voted for Richard Nixon.

It was a different matter in newly admitted Hawaii, whose residents, able to take part in a national election for the first time, voted narrowly for Kennedy. More striking, two members of the new state's three-person congressional delegation were the first two of the continuing line of Asian Americans sent to Congress from the Aloha State. (The first Asian American sent to Congress was India-born Dalip S. Saund, a three-term representative from California first elected to the House in 1956.) Daniel K. Inouye, the first Nisei in Congress in 1959, stayed there fifty-three years. He and others, as their number increased and they gained seniority, would play an increasingly important role in shaping the Japanese American and Asian American futures.

Those too young to remember anything about the wartime fate of the Japanese Americans were not likely to have learned much, if anything, about it in school. Of college history texts available in the early sixties, only one even mentioned it. That 1957 text, whose lead author was the iconic Columbia University historian Richard Hofstadter, could give it only one long sentence, under the heading "Civilian Mobilization": "Since almost no one doubted the necessity for the war, there was much less intolerance than there had been in World War I, although large numbers of Japanese-Americans were put into internment camps under circumstances that many Americans were later to judge unfair or worse."

And there was no mention at all of *Korematsu* or any of the other Japanese American cases, which, I have been assured, were not much discussed even in the nation's law schools. While the college texts did somewhat better later in the 1960s, no high school text before 1967 even mentioned the wartime incarceration; that year's *Land of the Free*, written by UCLA's John W. Caughey, John Hope Franklin, and Ernest R. May, gave it a thorough treatment, better than that in most existing college texts.

The 1960 census described a greatly changed Japanese American population. The incorporation of Hawaii, admitted to the Union in 1959, caused the number of Nikkei included in the national count to soar; it approached half a million in a nation of 179 million. Hawaii and the four West Coast states each had about 200,000 Nikkei, and between them accounted for 86 percent of the national total, with 14 percent living east of California. The general life experiences of Japanese Americans were quite different in each of those regions.

Hawaii's Nikkei, few of whom had been incarcerated during the war and now enjoying access to political power, soon dominated not just the federal elective offices but the state legislature, the governor's chair, the state's courts, and such prestigious positions as the presidency of the state university. But economic power remained largely in the hands of *haoles*, a Hawaiian word originally meaning any foreigner but now most often reserved for whites. Nikkei east of California—especially those beyond the mountain time zone—lived lives increasingly similar to those of other members of the eastern middle class, for whom exogamous marriage was already becoming more a norm than the exception it had been before the war.

Most of the descriptions of Japanese American life in the closing decades of the twentieth century are in reality descriptions of life in the West Coast states, above all, in California. Only in that state's larger cities, and to a lesser extent in Seattle, did anything like prewar Japantowns persist. In San Francisco, a much-reduced *nihonmachi* remained, but about half of its former space had become an African American neighborhood. In Los Angeles, remnants of the prewar concentrations in downtown Little Tokyo and the western neighborhood of Sawtelle were reestablished. But more characteristic of the era was that large numbers of Nikkei joined what was a predominantly white flight to the suburbs.

While not as dramatic as the wartime removal of some 94,000 California Nikkei and the subsequent return of some 85,000 Nikkei by 1950 was the migration of half a million African Americans to California during the same period. By 1960 the state's almost 900,000 African Americans clearly occupied the bottom step of California's ethnic escalator which had been occupied for most of a century by Chinese and Japanese. As noted, explicit anti-Asian statutes and ordinances were gone, but de facto discrimination continued.

California's Fair Employment Practices Commission in 1965 reported that persons of Chinese and Japanese ethnicity, almost all of whom except for very recent immigrants were now American citizens, surpassed the achievements of "white" Californians in education but received less income than members of that group. The disparities can be ascribed to both the glass ceiling—the reluctance to promote persons of color into positions in which they supervised whites—and the fact that most college-educated Nikkei were near the beginnings of their careers.

In terms of housing for postwar Nikkei whose empty wartime neighborhoods had been repopulated largely by in-migrating African Americans, a common reaction was a move to a single-family home in a suburb, such as Gardena in the South Bay region of Los Angeles County. Legal access to housing was increased after restrictive covenants were struck down by the Supreme Court in *Shelley v. Kraemer* (1948). Although fair housing advocates easily demonstrated that de facto discrimination against all people of color was widespread, it was less prevalent for Japanese and Chinese than for other persons of color.

In 1966 William Petersen, a skilled demographer with a deep-seated conservative ideology who taught at Berkeley, published in the *New York Times Magazine* the most discussed article ever written about an Asian American group, later expanded into a book. His thesis was that Japanese were a praiseworthy "model minority":

> The history of Japanese Americans challenges every . . . generalization about ethnic minorities. . . . Barely more than 20 years after the end of the wartime camps, this is a minority that has risen above even prejudiced criticism. By any criterion of good citizenship . . . the Japanese are better than any other group in our society, including native-born whites. They have established this remarkable record, moreover, by their own almost totally unaided effort. Every attempt to hamper their progress resulted in enhancing their determination to succeed. Even in a country whose patron saint is Horatio Alger, there is no parallel to this success story.

Petersen was hardly the first to praise Japanese Americans. Before World War I, the missionary and peace advocate Sidney Lewis Gulick championed Japan and its immigrants. During World War II, Carey McWilliams had, as a California official, proposed the establishment of camps for the Japanese Americans conveniently located in the Central Valley from which they could be sent forth daily to work in the state's "factories in the fields." He soon repented, became a champion of the Nisei, and published a courageous book defending them and attacking their incarceration in 1944. I myself had written in 1962, focusing on an earlier period of Japanese American history, that "the vast bulk of California's Issei and their descendants were superbly good citizens."

But Petersen, unlike most of those who praised the group, did so to support a reactionary ideology. There was nothing covert about this. The paragraph quoted here had been preceded by a negative assessment of African Americans' social progress since emancipation: "For all the well-meaning programs and countless scholarly studies now focused on the Negro, we hardly know how to repair the damage the slave traders started."

Petersen was using the word "model" in two quite different ways: to praise one group for what it had achieved, and to suggest that effective change would not result from government programs like those of Lyndon Johnson's Great Society. He argued that if positive change came at all, it would result from self-improvement by the oppressed. It resembled very much what passed for social thought in nineteenth-century America. Despite his reference to Horatio Alger, Petersen was not echoing Alger, whose young heroes depended on "pluck and luck" and such ploys as marrying the boss's daughter; his true exemplar was Yale sociologist William Graham Sumner, whose mantra—"stateways cannot change folkways"—was a classic denial of even the possibility of conscious social reform.

Nationally the model minority concept quickly developed legs: the mass media, led by *Newsweek*, soon transformed it into "model minorities," embracing other ethnicities, particularly Chinese Americans and Korean Americans, even though Petersen had insisted that the Japanese Americans were unique. Over time, it would be picked up and expanded by a small host of conservative publicists and theorists, most notably Thomas Sowell.

Within the Japanese American community the notion of being a model minority delighted many Nisei elders, including most JACL leaders, because it said what many of them had always believed but could not openly avow: that they were superior to any other group, including *hakujin*—a faintly derogatory Japanese American term for "white folks"—and that other American minority groups were less meritorious. But Sansei, third-generation activists—about whom more later—hated it as patronizing and immediately recognized it as a conservative concept. Half a century later, some of them and their successors still rage against any notion of a model minority.

The growing numbers of Nikkei college students began in the 1960s to learn in some detail about their collective history, in classes and from classmates, things that typically had never been discussed at home. Some of them, like other students, were influenced by the social and political factors that created student elements of the civil rights and antiwar movements on many campuses. A growing number of Nikkei students—but very much a small minority of them—began to think of themselves as Asian Americans; even smaller numbers began to speak of themselves as persons of color; a very few spoke of belonging to a Third World Liberation Front.

If the emblematic radical campuses were Berkeley, Columbia, and the University of Wisconsin, the undoubted center of Asian American student radicalism was San Francisco State College. While the school was best known for the student strike there at the end of the decade, a more enduring achievement was the first instruction in Asian American history taught in any university by what were then three part-time faculty members: James Hirabayashi (1926–2012), Gordon's cousin and the only one with a doctorate; Him Mark Lai (1925–2009), an engineer who became the undoubted dean of historians of Chinese America; and Edison Uno (1927–1976), an activist who also had a role in creating one of the first network television documentaries about the wartime incarceration, *Guilty by Reason of Race* (NBC, 1972). Their teaching not only helped to raise the consciousness of students in the Bay Area but also created demands, eventually successful, for similar classes and eventually departments of ethnic and Asian American studies elsewhere, first at the more prestigious California and West Coast institutions, and eventually in every part of the nation. This paralleled preexisting campaigns for recognition of black and African American studies departments. Not incidentally, the movement also refocused attention on the wrongs of the wartime incarceration.

This did not at all please many, perhaps most, of the leaders of the Japanese American community. In 1967, when Harry H. L. Kitano and I, both assistant professors at UCLA, organized the first academic conference devoted to the wartime incarceration, the JACL, after expressing an initial willingness to fund the publication of its proceedings, reneged with apologies. The stated reason was that it did not wish to reopen old wounds; some critics believed that what the organization really feared was a public reexamination of its accommodationist posture during the war.

In that year the Supreme Court helped to correct a postwar wrong inflicted by the executive branch. The Treasury had eventually agreed to pay the prewar rate on some funds that had been deposited in the seized branches of Japanese banks, but it did so in a way that denied adjustment to some 4,100 depositors or their heirs. A successful lawsuit in the Supreme Court, *Honda v. Clark* (1967), instituted by A. L. Wirin, eventually forced the government to pay them. Speaking of his victory, Wirin thought that the struggle for redress was over. "This result," he claimed, "brings to an end the last injustice visited by the U.S. government on Americans of Japanese descent during the war."

It is worth noting that national media had become aware of the wartime incarceration it had largely ignored in the immediate postwar era. In this instance *Time* magazine commented that the Court had, "as in all previous [decisions,] sidestepped the prickly problem of the government's 1942 action in interning U.S. citizens without benefit of charges or trial." In any event, it then seemed clear that there was no open path to redress or further mitigation of wartime wrongs through litigation, and that if meaningful redress were to come, it would arrive through political action. But before such action could be mounted with any likelihood of success, changes in community attitudes were a necessary precondition.

What can now be seen as an indicator of changes to come began at the end of the sixties in Los Angeles, when a small band of Nisei and Sansei activists organized the first symbolic group return to a place of wartime confinement: the Manzanar Pilgrimage on December 28 and 29, 1969. It was not that Japanese Americans had suppressed discussions of the camps; whenever postwar mainland Nisei met one another for the first time, an inevitable initial question had been, "What camp were you in?" The camps were part of the wallpaper of their lives, but few had spent much time or energy discussing them, and the all but universal testimony of Sansei is that they were never told anything about their family's incarceration.

The 1969 pilgrimage was a collective remembrance, one that had been preceded by years of discussions and debates. These did not immediately focus on redress but contributed to a heightened awareness among younger Nikkei, and, five years later the Tule Lake Pilgrimage began. A more general Day of Remembrance was first celebrated during Thanksgiving 1978 in Seattle and at the nearby state fairgrounds at Puyallup, site of an army-run temporary wartime camp. In later years the Day of Remembrance has come to be February 19, the date Roosevelt signed the fateful executive order. It is increasingly observed in various parts of the country, often by meetings in educational institutions.

Redress itself was first formally proposed by Edison Uno at the biennial JACL convention in 1970. He introduced a resolution committing the organization to work for federal legislation to provide tax-free "reparations" for Japanese Americans or their heirs who were incarcerated during World War II. No specific amount was mentioned. Uno's resolution also called on Congress to appropriate $400 million to fund community projects. To Uno's surprise the resolution passed, but he was not surprised that the JACL leadership did nothing to move the matter forward.

Although he and his allies were regarded as radicals—and so thought of themselves—by contemporary American standards in a period that saw the emergence of various Black Power movements and the Students for a Democratic Society, their views were well within the mainstream of American liberalism. And the redress proposal itself was no more than what the JACL had advocated in its first postwar convention in 1946, which had adopted a fourteen-item list of goals that included "reparations for discriminatory treatment during the war" and "a reexamination of the constitutionality of the evacuation." But those were never pursued as the organization concentrated on naturalization for Issei, challenging the alien land laws, and civil rights, goals that were compatible with those of national postwar liberalism. Yet it took eight years and four more biennial conventions before the organization was forced to act. As the notion of redress became more and more credible, various plans and approaches to redress began to proliferate. Most of the earlier ones were relatively modest in monetary demands. One limited total payments to $400 million, a widely used estimate of total property losses by Japanese Americans, falsely attributed to the Federal Reserve Bank of San Francisco, which had no real interest in such matters. Others proposed differential payments to individuals based on the length of their imprisonment. The first such proposed $5 a day, a formula that produced a maximum total individual payment of about $7,000; few who advocated it realized that such a formula would result in the largest payments going to Tule Lakers. The goofiest was carefully calibrated by two Nikkei systems engineers who worked for Boeing; they described their plan as "having Japanese Americans finance their own redress." What the plan actually called for was for Japanese Americans to be allowed to direct that their personal federal income tax payments be placed in a fund that would eventually contain enough money to make the redress payments. It borrowed the per diem approach of an earlier plan but doubled the ante to $10 a day. However logical such a scheme might seem, it was politically unimaginable and legally dubious.

During the next eight years these and other plans and the notion of redress itself were debated at great length throughout the entire Nikkei community. Growing differences about approaches to redress developed: some of them reflected long-standing community differences; others were created by disputes over the terms and methods of redress itself.

While this was going on, two events of national significance served to refocus some attention on the wartime injustices now more than thirty years in the past. Uno himself was deeply involved in the first of these, a campaign to get Congress to repeal Title II of the 1950 McCarran Act, which mandated standby concentration camps. A bill introduced by Hawaii's Daniel Inouye in the Senate, and cosponsored by his colleague in the House, Spark M. Matsunaga, got restrained support from the Department of Justice. Deputy Attorney General Richard Kleindienst wrote Congress that since "various groups, of which our Japanese Americans are most prominent, look upon the legislation as permitting a recurrence of the round-ups which resulted in the detention of Americans of Japanese ancestry during World War II," the department believed that the psychic benefit to be gained from "repeal of this legislation . . . outweighs the potential advantage which the act may provide in a time of internal security emergency." Congress repealed the measure with relative ease, and

President Richard Nixon in his September 26, 1971, signing statement gave it a more positive endorsement, noted fears that the law "might be used someday" in the manner of the World War II "detention of Americans of Japanese ancestry," and declared that he signed the repeal in order "to put an end to such suspicions. . . . I want to underscore this Nation's abiding respect for the liberty of the individual. Our democracy is built upon the constitutional guarantee that every citizen will be afforded due process of law. There is no place in American life for the kind of anxiety—however unwarranted—which the Emergency Detention Act has evidently engendered." The president went on to note that the powers available to the chief executive under the Constitution were adequate to meet any dangers. Many Japanese Americans pointed out, ruefully, that in 1942 no legislation had been necessary to build the camps and start the process of systematic wholesale incarceration.

While the repeal campaign had been planned and mounted for a considerable period, the second event came out of the blue. On February 19, 1976, the thirty-fourth anniversary of Roosevelt's executive order, President Gerald R. Ford, who as a naval lieutenant had served on an aircraft carrier in the Pacific during the war against Japan, issued a proclamation rescinding that order and offered a testimonial to the patriotism of Japanese Americans. Ford's proclamation, noting that it was the bicentennial year of the Declaration of Independence, insisted that an "honest reckoning . . . must include a recognition of our national mistakes." The key words of his proclamation were: "We now know what we should have known then—not only was that evacuation wrong but Japanese-Americans were and are loyal Americans."

One can only conjecture about what motivated Ford to speak out about injustices to Japanese Americans, with whom he seems to have had no previous or subsequent relationships. He makes no mention of either incident or any Japanese American in his memoir; a similar silence prevails in scholarly works focused on him. My notion is that Ford, in the wake of his shocking pardon of Richard Nixon, wanted to be remembered as a healer, and this was among a number of other actions designed for that purpose. This is not to suggest that Ford was not sincere; unlike the man he replaced, he was a decent person. Whatever his motives, his actions, which got little notice apart from the ethnic media, were indications of a changing if not yet transformed national mood.

In October 1977 the JACL Redress Committee got a new chair, Clifford I. Uyeda (1917–2004), whose life course set him off from most Nisei leaders. Raised in a family with an entrepreneurial involvement in the oyster business near Olympia, Washington, he had a characteristic Nisei boyhood. But for higher education he ventured first to the University of Wisconsin, earning a BA as an English major in 1940. He went on to medical school in New Orleans. Thus, he did not experience incarceration and would finish his MD there in 1945. He then completed a pediatric internship and gained further training at Harvard. After serving as a captain in the air force during the Korean War, he settled in San Francisco as a pediatrician at its Kaiser Permanente medical complex, where he practiced and directed clinics until his retirement in 1975. A student of Japanese American history, he was a cofounder of the Center for Japanese American Studies, which supported scholarship at San Francisco State and headed a JACL Issei history project. His profession, the breadth of his interests, and his personal ineligibility for redress differentiated him from almost all other JACL leaders who had been in camps and tended to be lawyers or businessmen. Uyeda gave the Redress Committee a new vigor; it carried on a growing campaign of information and advocacy, and in April 1978 he assembled a largish group drawn from each of the JACL's regional districts to develop the basic proposal to be presented to that year's convention. This group settled on a public apology coupled with monetary redress to those incarcerated or their heirs, and it stipulated $25,000 as the goal for individual payments. Statements were made to the effect that the amount could be adjusted later, but Uyeda understood that Congress was highly unlikely to agree to everything that was asked for, and that the final settlement, if there were one, would almost certainly be for less than $25,000.

At the July 1978 convention all went well. It marked the beginning of Uyeda's term as JACL president, which recognized his accomplishments with the Redress Committee. The main convention action was its unanimous adoption of the committee's plan with the $25,000 price tag. Uyeda quickly named John Y. Tateishi (b. 1939), who had been incarcerated at Manzanar as a three-year-old, as his replacement to head the committee. After a great deal of work aligning support from various groups within the community, which was far from united, the committee arranged to have a meeting with the Japanese American members of Congress. Tateishi led a group of his new colleagues to Washington to discuss the details of the bill that they wanted the Japanese American members of Congress to introduce.

There were five of them. Two Hawaiians, Senators Inouye and Matsunaga, were both 442nd veterans with prior service in the House. Two Californians in the House were relative newcomers: Norman Y. Mineta, an insurance executive and mayor of San Jose, had been first elected in 1974, and Robert T. Matsui, a lawyer and Sacramento politician, was in his first Congress. All were Democrats; all favored redress.

The fifth Japanese American national legislator, California Republican senator Samuel I. Hayakawa, opposed redress. Born and raised in western Canada, he came as a graduate student to the University of Wisconsin in the mid-1930s and remained to teach and write in the midwestern United States. A skilled writer but not an original thinker, he effectively popularized the new field of semantics. As an alien of an Allied nation he was not significantly restricted during World War II. Shortly after the McCarran-Walter Act made it possible, he became an American citizen. In 1955 he moved to California as a professor of English at San Francisco State College; during that school's turbulent period, after Hayakawa had opposed student and faculty members he regarded as radicals and denounced such innovations as ethnic studies, Ronald Reagan, then California's governor, appointed him as the college's president in 1968. He retired in 1973. His 1976 election victory resulted in a single six-year term in the Senate, where he produced no important legislation but gained attention with striking language, such as opposing a treaty returning the Panama Canal because "we stole it fair and square." As the featured speaker in the closing banquet at the JACL convention in 1978, he had not mentioned the just-approved redress resolution, but the delegates were shocked the following morning to read that Hayakawa had given an interview to local reporters denouncing the JACL's advocacy of redress, declaring that asking for payment was "merely the rekindling of resentment and racism that no longer exists." Even those in the JACL who had misgivings about redress were angry about his bad manners as an honored guest, but politeness was not Hayakawa's thing.

In a Washington meeting on February 1, 1979, with the four Nisei Democrats, the committee explained the kind of legislation it needed and was shocked to be told, primarily by Inouye in no uncertain terms, and with the explicit agreement of the other three, that there was no way that such legislation could pass and that they would not introduce any enabling measure. The JACLers were stunned. They had naively believed that whatever they wanted would be crafted into legislative form. They had not checked with any of the lawmakers and had spent most of the six months since the convention trying to paper over the serious differences that divided redress advocates.

Inouye, who felt a responsibility to the mainlanders even though they were not his constituents, threw them a lifeline and promised that if the JACLers were to come out for the creation of a presidential commission to deal with the matter, he and the three other Democrats would sponsor legislation to that effect. As the statute eventually phrased it, the commission would do the following:

1. Review the facts and circumstances surrounding Executive Order numbered 9066, issued February 19, 1942, and the impact of such Executive Order on American citizens and permanent resident aliens;
2. Review directives of United States military forces requiring the relocation and, in some cases detention in internment camps of American citizens, including Aleut civilians, and permanent residents of the Aleutians and Pribilof Islands; and
3. Recommend appropriate remedies.

As it turned out, even Hayakawa was willing to support such an inquiry, and his backing was useful in attracting other Republican support; his opposition at that point might have had serious consequences.

Presidential commissions are a standard way of gathering information for future legislation. Among the more prominent postwar examples were the President's Commission on Civil Rights (1946), the Commission on Intergovernmental Relations (1953), and the President's Commission on the Status of Women (1961), but the Redress Committee had never even considered asking for such a body. Meeting later in February 1979, the Redress Committee, using the authority that the convention had given it, and with the tacit support of Clifford Uyeda, voted 5–2 to take the advice of Inouye and his colleagues and actively support an effort to create a presidential commission. The two dissidents, associated with the militant Seattle group, resigned amid bitter claims that the committee's action was illegitimate and a betrayal of the previous commitment to a $25,000 individual redress award. This created a schism in the activist minority of the Japanese American community whose faint aftershocks can still be felt in the twenty-first century. A left opposition within the pro-redress movement soon coalesced and mounted other eventually unsuccessful approaches to redress.

With what passes for speed on Capitol Hill, Inouye, whose twenty years in Washington had enabled him to acquire both influence and power, dropped a bill into the hopper on August 29, 1979, creating the Commission on Wartime Relocation and Internment of Civilians (CWRIC) with more than an absolute majority of the Senate as cosponsors; two months later a companion measure was introduced in the House with 119 sponsors and cosponsors. The Seattle dissidents prevailed on Michael E. Lowry, a freshman House member from Seattle, to introduce a bill calling for the outright cash payment of $25,000 plus $5 for each day of incarceration for the victims of Executive Order 9066. In the face of the overwhelming support for the competing measure, the chances of its passage approached zero. It never came to a vote. The Senate bill passed overwhelmingly in late May 1980 after being amended to include provisions to examine the circumstances under which Aleut citizens had been moved from far northern islands in the wake of the invasion of two islands by Japan under authority of Executive Order 9066. The House followed suit in mid-July, and the bill creating the CWRIC was enacted on July 31, 1980. At the signing ceremony President Jimmy Carter congratulated "Danny Inouye" and other legislators present, expressed his pleasure in signing the measure, and concluded:

> This Commission study will be adequately funded. It's not designed as a witch hunt. It's designed to expose clearly what has happened in a period of war in our Nation when many loyal

American citizens of Japanese descent were embarrassed during that crucial time in our Nation's history. I don't believe anyone would doubt that injustices were done, and I don't think anyone would doubt that it is advisable now for us to have a clear understanding, as Americans, of this episode in the history of our country.

The commissioners were a distinguished group. Of the original appointed seven, three were chosen by President Carter, and two each by the Speaker of the House and the president pro tem of the Senate; all were Democrats, but only four of the seven appointees could be Democrats. The commission they appointed was essentially representative of the liberal establishment. The three Republicans were Arthur S. Fleming, a university president appointed to the Social Security Board by Roosevelt in 1936 who had served in Eisenhower's cabinet; Edward W. Brooke, the first African American elected to the Senate in the twentieth century, who had represented Massachusetts from 1967 to 1979; and Daniel E. Lungren, a sitting Republican member of the House from California. The four Democrats were former Supreme Court justice Arthur J. Goldberg; Hugh B. Mitchell, a former senator from Washington; and the commission chair, Joan Z. Bernstein, a capital insider who had been general counsel of the Department of Health and Human Services. The special role of the only Japanese American member of the commission, William J. Marutani, a judge on Philadelphia's Court of Common Pleas, who had been exiled and incarcerated in 1942, will be discussed in the next chapter.

An anecdote is associated with the appointment of two additional commission members in early 1981. The victory of Reagan over Carter in November 1980 was accompanied by the election of enough new Republican senators to give their party control of the Senate, while the House remained Democratic. Appointment of two commission members in 1981 came about because Alaska's senior senator, Republican Ted Stevens, belatedly realized that the Aleut people, his constituents, were not represented on the commission; he gained agreement from his colleagues that the Reverend Ishmael Y. Gromoff, an Aleut who had been evacuated, be appointed. Accordingly, the still Democratic House would have an additional appointment. Legend has it that House Speaker Tip O'Neill remarked, "If they name a priest, I'll name a priest." His man was Father Robert F. Drinan, S.J., who had just given up his seat in the House after ten years' service on orders from Pope John Paul II. The official appointment of this radical Democrat was one of the first documents signed by President Reagan.

That amusing story points up the important fact that the creation of the CWRIC came at the very end of a liberal period. It was not a measure that would have been likely to pass in the early days of what many call the Reagan Revolution, and even if it had, its appointees would have been more like the most conservative commission member, Daniel Lungren. Many of those within the broader redress movement who had opposed the commission approach as a "sellout" came to realize that it was a compromise vital to the ultimate success of the movement; others, like William Hohri (1927–2010), continued to denounce it.

The commission organized itself, put together a staff for administration and investigation, consulted a variety of scholars, and was aided by a number of volunteers, mostly Japanese Americans, some of whom performed vital tasks. The most important of these were the Nisei Aiko Herzig-Yoshinaga (b. 1924), who, with the assistance of her husband, Jack Herzig, acquired a good command of archival materials used in the commission's report. Its first key decision was to hold two different kinds of public hearings. Initial and closing hearings in the capital were largely to get the testimony of surviving wartime officials on record. As the commission's report states, "The account of decisions made by officials of the federal government is primarily drawn from contemporaneous memoranda, writings, and transcribed conversations with a lesser reliance on memoirs and testimony before the Commission." But the Washington hearings did have their moments of drama, and media coverage of them raised the public level of understanding of what had happened to Japanese Americans during World War II. The initial hearing in Washington opened on July 14, 1981. Its most important testimony came from the two ranking subcabinet-level survivors. Former Supreme Court justice Abe Fortas, who as Interior undersecretary had overseen the WRA after it had been shifted to Ickes's control, began by noting, "This is a sad and nationally humiliating day." He described some of the things that were inflicted on Japanese Americans by their government and concluded: "I believe that the mass evacuation . . . was a tragic error . . . I cannot escape the conclusion that racial prejudice was the basic ingredient. . . . I think that it is clear—perhaps it was always clear—that the mass exclusion order by General DeWitt was never justified."

Conversely, John McCloy, Stimson's point man for Japanese American matters and many other things, complained:

> There has been, in my judgment, . . . a spate of irresponsible comment to the effect that this wartime move was callous, shameful, and induced by racial or punitive motives. It was nothing of that sort. . . .
>
> I therefore believe in the interests of all concerned, the Commission would be well advised to conclude that President Roosevelt's wartime action in connection with the relocation of our Japanese-descended population at the outbreak of our war with Japan, was taken and carried out in accordance with the best interests of the country, considering the conditions, exigencies and considerations which then faced the nation.

McCloy insisted on being called back during the second Washington hearings in November, maintaining that the actions taken against the Japanese Americans were "reasonably undertaken and thoughtfully and humanely conducted." He also admonished the commissioners not to advocate policies that might someday prevent the forcible relocation of other American citizens because of ethnic background.

The second set of seven hearings in cities across the continent were designed to give Japanese Americans a chance to tell the commission—and the press and public—their individual stories. Some hard-boiled commission staffers thought them a waste of time. The hearings became, to a degree surprising even to those who had advocated them, a transforming event for the Japanese American community, especially its Nisei women. Their collective testimonies, often accompanied by tears and other evidence of stress, were both influential and shocking to a community that accorded few nonfamilial roles to women and frowned on any public shows of emotion. It was these hearings that created the conviction of many, perhaps most, Japanese Americans that meaningful redress was a real possibility and not some fairy tale. A decade later one Nisei woman explained to a meeting commemorating the wartime acceptance of Nisei college students from the camps that until she testified at the commission hearings, she had never spoken in public. "That loosened my tongue," she told the audience, "and I have been speaking out ever since."

After a concluding session back in Washington on December 9, 1981, the CWRIC staff continued its work out of the public eye for some fourteen months. On January 30, 1983, a second front in the campaign for redress of the wrongs done to Japanese Americans opened in federal district court in San Francisco. As will be related in detail in the next chapter, an ad hoc consortium of lawyers, predominantly young Nisei, filed the first of three extraordinary petitions to challenge the convictions of Gordon Hirabayashi, Min Yasui, and Fred Korematsu. From that point each campaign drew strength from the other and increased the media coverage and thus the public interest and understanding.

Less than a month later, on February 24, 1983, the commission issued its comprehensive report of more than 400 pages, *Personal Justice Denied*. Written largely by the CWRIC's special counsel, Angus Macbeth, it had the unanimous approval of the nine commissioners. A trenchant paragraph in the twenty-three-page summary that opened the report, said it all:

> The promulgation of Executive Order 9066 was not justified by military necessity, and the decisions which followed from it—detention, ending detention, and ending exclusion—were not driven by analysis of military conditions. The broad historical causes which shaped these decisions were race prejudice, war hysteria and a failure of political leadership. Widespread ignorance of Japanese Americans contributed to a policy conceived in haste and executed in an atmosphere of fear and anger at Japan. A grave injustice was done to American citizens and resident aliens of Japanese ancestry who, without individual review or any probative evidence against them, were excluded, removed and detained by the United States during World War II.

There was one calculated omission from the report. It deliberately failed to say anything about the "appropriate remedies" it had been instructed to recommend, but the commission let it be known that recommendations would be forthcoming before its dissolution at the end of the fiscal year. The initial reactions to the report were predictable. A JACL representative described the organization as "very pleased" with the substance of the report, but, of course advocates were nervous about the commission's silence about remedies. The spokesman for the die-hard and increasingly inconsequential Native Sons of the Golden West stressed to reporters that Japan bombed Pearl Harbor and added, "Who knows what would have happened if the government had not put the Japanese in camps." That McCloy could find nothing specific to complain about in the report is a compliment to its careful marshaling of the evidence. Admitting that "the report's conclusions are well and good in hindsight," he found it a "shocking outrage" that the report "assailed" the reputations of men "who could no longer defend themselves." The only defense he could offer for himself was that "none of us had [hindsight] at the time."

On June 16, 1983, commission chair Bernstein announced two packages of five recommendations, one for each ethnic group. For Japanese Americans the first four unanimous recommendations called for "a formal apology by Congress signed by the president; presidential pardons for those who ran afoul of laws and other restrictions based on ethnicity; that Congress direct Executive agencies 'to review . . . with liberality' applications from Japanese Americans for restoration of lost privileges; that Congress should 'establish a special foundation' to sponsor and disseminate research about the wartime incarceration in particular and civil liberties in general."

The fifth Japanese American recommendation was passed, 8–1, with Commissioner Lungren objecting. It called for the appropriation of $1.5 billion to fund the onetime tax-free payment of $20,000 to each of a presumed total of 60,000 survivors excluded by Executive Order 9066, with remaining funds used to finance the foundation prescribed in the fourth recommendation.

A somewhat parallel set of provisions existed for the "few hundred" surviving Aleuts. They had already received significant compensation, had been evacuated to get them out of harm's way but were not adequately cared for in captivity. The commission proposed a total appropriation of less than $10 million, including individual payments of $5,000. Commissioner Bernstein recused herself because the law firm she was associated with had Aleut clients, and Commissioner Lungren voted against two of the five Aleut recommendations that involved money. He gave a traditional modern Republican justification: "It is inappropriate that present day taxpayers should be held accountable for actions that occurred 40 years ago."

In the final analysis, the prolonged political postcommission struggle over redress was about the individual cash payments, which did not begin until 1990, seven years after the commission's recommendations. There were many persons, including more than a few Japanese American survivors, who had serious doubts about the appropriateness of cash settlements. Even Senator Inouye, who would eventually manage a parliamentary maneuver that expedited payment, had in November 1981 publicly opposed payment, arguing that "it would be almost impossible to place a price tag on reparations" and "insulting even to try to do so." Few put the positive case for redress better than his colleague in the House, Norman Mineta, who argued:

> I realize that there are some who say that payments are inappropriate. Liberty is priceless, they say, and you cannot put a price tag on freedom. That's an easy statement when you have your freedom. But to say that because constitutional rights are priceless they really have no value at all is to turn the argument on its head. Would I sell my constitutional and civil rights for $20,000? No. But having had those rights ripped away from me, do I think I am entitled to compensation? Absolutely. We are not talking about the wartime sacrifices that we all made to support and defend our nation. At issue here is the wholesale violation, based on race, of those very legal principles we were fighting to defend.

In the larger society some responsible voices were raised, suggesting that redress was not appropriate. Even before the CWRIC announced its proposed award, the *New York Times*, which during the war had not protested either the incarceration or the Supreme Court's sustaining of it, delivered a preemptive strike. In an editorial headlined "How to Atone for 'War Hysteria'" it concluded: "In our view, symbolic atonement would be most appropriate—like a scholarship fund for Japanese-American students."

A whole chorus of prominent voices made similar remarks, and a small group of critics, of whom John McCloy was the most visible, denounced the notion of payment as an outrage, a raid on the

Treasury, and a stain of the memory of Roosevelt and other wartime leaders. In addition, a considerable vocal minority of the general public continued to use the three-letter "J word" and make references to Pearl Harbor, with some suggesting that if any payments were to be made, they should come from Tokyo, not Washington.

But the idea of redress soon began to take hold in the public mind. Among the factors that made the idea of monetary compensation for the victims of governmental misconduct more acceptable were two very different precedents: the increasing attention paid to the Holocaust and the fact that representatives of the American Jewish Committee not only endorsed redress for Japanese Americans but referenced the precedent set by the West German laws of 1953, 1956, and 1965 that paid billions to Holocaust survivors and the Israeli government. Closer to home and more recently, its own courts had forced the United States to pay as much as $10,000 in damages to individual peaceful protesters who were improperly arrested by federal police at antiwar demonstrations at the Pentagon and elsewhere for incarcerations that were measured in hours and days, rather than weeks, months, and years.

Even more important in creating a public acceptance of the principle of redress was the growing awareness of what had been inflicted on Japanese Americans. Serious scholarship, beginning with the work of the army historian Stetson Conn in 1959, had long since demonstrated what the CWRIC would package and disseminate. After 1970, increasing numbers of college students were taught about the wartime incarceration and the relevant Supreme Court cases. Even more significant in terms of public awareness of what Japanese Americans had to put up with in the concentration camps was the role played by television. Even in the "vast wasteland" that the new medium had become by the 1960s, the two major networks each produced a single substantial documentary program—half an hour by CBS in 1965, and an hour from NBC in 1970, *Guilty by Reason of Race*, with Edison Uno as an on-camera guide. With the coming of public television, the networks largely ceased making such programs unless they were "news," but the new public television network of the seventies provided facilities that gave independent filmmakers access to American living rooms. Many documentaries with points of view about American minority groups were shown, and a number of them on aspects of the wartime ordeals of Japanese Americans were created and broadcast nationwide. Among the best were Loni Ding's *Nisei Soldier* (1983) and Steven Okazaki's *Unfinished Business* (1984), which examined the Supreme Court cases and their litigants.

Probably even more influential in changing public attitudes was a commercial television production of a dramatization of *Farewell to Manzanar*, a 1973 memoir of camp life by Jeanne Wakatsuki Houston and James D. Houston, shown on NBC in prime time in 1976. Audiences for PBS documentaries were "counted" in the single-digit millions; those for prime-time commercial successes such as *Farewell to Manzanar* are "measured" in the tens of millions.

On September 30, 1987, as the congressional struggle over redress was approaching a climax, a controversial exhibit opening at the National Museum of American History provided a stunning perspective on the Japanese American experience. The exhibit, A More Perfect Union: Japanese Americans and the U.S. Constitution, was created by staff members of the museum led by curators Tom D. Crouch and Edward C. Ezell. When word got out about its content, concerns were raised in many quarters. However, once the exhibit opened to critical and public acclaim, it was another factor in shaping public and congressional attitudes toward redress. Intended as a temporary exhibit, designed to stay up for a year or two, A More Perfect Union remained in place for sixteen years until it was dismantled in 2003.

A widely believed but possibly apocryphal tale has it that former chief justice Warren E. Burger, who was chairing the official arrangements for the forthcoming bicentennial celebration of the adoption of the Constitution, insisted to the museum's director, Roger G. Kennedy, who had played a key role in the project, that while "what happened to those people was unfortunate, it had nothing to do with the history of the Constitution." When asked if he could confirm the story, Kennedy smiled and said that he "could not possibly comment on such a matter."

Be that as it may, it is worth noting that in 1985, when as a scholarly part of the celebration of the Constitution's 150th year, the American Historical Association and the American Political Science Association commissioned twenty-two senior scholars to write essays to promote "public understanding and appraisal" of the Constitution, the Japanese American cases were still so far below the scholars' radar that even though one of them mentioned *Oyama v. California*, a 1948 Supreme Court case that impaired but did not void the state's alien land act, neither that nor any other essay mentioned either *Korematsu* or any of the other wartime cases. They, too, failed to see any connection between the cases and the Constitution. Years later curator Crouch reminisced: "I remember the day that President Reagan signed the redress bill. I don't think that I ever felt better about what I do for a living, or about the institution where I am employed than I did on that day."

Counting from the February 1983 publication of *Personal Justice Denied*, it took almost five and a half years to get a redress statute enacted; more than two more years passed before the initial payments were made; and Congress prolonged the process so that the final payments authorized were not made until early 1999.

The legislative process, which has been detailed in two scholarly volumes, need not detain us long. It soon became clear that the legislation, enacted as the Civil Liberties Act of 1988, would pass Congress. Its passage was aided by the fact that in the 1986 off-year election, control of the Senate was regained by the Democrats after six years of Republican control so they now controlled both bodies. The early versions of the bill had been introduced in the House by a Texas Democrat, majority leader James C. Wright, with the symbolic designation HR 442, and by Senator Matsunaga in October and November 1983. Although much of the Republican leadership was opposed, especially in the House, and the Reagan administration's Department of Justice opposed both statutory and judicial redress, legislative progress was positive but slow, particularly on the House side. While the Japanese American congressmen were active and effective, much of the heavy lifting was done by Massachusetts congressman Barney Frank, who as a key subcommittee chair made special efforts to move the legislation over the various hurdles on the path to final approval. CWRIC special counsel Macbeth made a point of Frank's importance in a 1997 oral history: "If there hadn't been someone like Frank who at some point said, 'I'm going to put it on the agenda, we're going to have a vote,' it could have gone on a long time without anything happening."

When the redress bill finally came before the House, an amendment by Commissioner/Congressman Dan Lungren to strike the per capita payments but retain the apology was defeated but garnered 161 votes; the House passed the full package recommended by the commission, 243–141, on September 17, 1987, the 200th anniversary of the Constitution. The Senate, with a conflict-filled calendar, did not vote until the following April 20. Minor differences between the House and Senate versions necessitated a conference report, which the Senate approved by unanimous consent on July 27, with the final vote by the House scheduled for August 4, 1988. Either of the two previous negative vote totals in the House—161 or 141—would be enough to sustain a presidential veto, which most observers expected and redress activists dreaded.

But President Reagan, who had kept his own counsel on the subject, stunned many of his supporters on August 2—and delighted redress advocates—with a brief letter to Congress endorsing the redress legislation as closing "a sad chapter in American history in a way that reaffirms America's commitment to the preservation of liberty and justice for all." He went on to urge the House "to act swiftly and favorably on the bill." His message did not change votes—156 House members voted no as the measure passed with 257 yes votes on August 4, 1988.

Six days later, in a signing ceremony in the Executive Office Building, Reagan, center stage, spoke his lines as if he had been a long-term supporter of redress. He even replayed—and rewrote—an old scene from the World War II era. He told his audience that a Japanese American woman had sent him a 1945 clipping describing a ceremony in California's Orange County in which General Joseph W. Stilwell pinned a posthumous Distinguished Service Cross on Mary Masuda, who had recently returned from a WRA camp. The medal had been awarded to her brother, Staff Sergeant Kazuo Masuda of the 442nd, for bravery that cost him his life. After naming several show business folks who were present, the president added:

And one young actor said: "Blood that has soaked into the sands of a beach is all of one color. America stands unique in the world: the only country not founded on race but on a way, an ideal. Not in spite of but because of our polyglot background, we have had all the strength in the world. That is the American way." The name of that young actor—I hope I pronounce this right—was Ronald

Reagan. And, yes, the ideal of liberty and justice for all—that is still the American way.

The president did not explain that it was not a young actor but thirty-four-year-old Captain Ronald Reagan, an Army Air Force public relations officer, or that his lines had been composed by an Office of War Information writer, and that the whole thing was part of the government program to make the return of Japanese American families like the Masudas easier.

Despite the low comedy at the ceremony, something important had been done. A victorious nation acknowledged that it had done wrong and paid a significant price for it. Eventually some 82,000 persons received payments totaling $1.6 billion.

And, in an echo effect, after Reagan's action on redress, the Canadian government concluded negotiations with the National Association of Japanese Canadians for similar payments, $21,000, to each of a smaller number of victims of its similar wartime incarceration policies, with an eventual cost of $188 million, which Prime Minister Brian Mulroney announced in Parliament on September 22, 1988.

In a 2010 oral history interview, Orest Kruhlak, who had been a senior civil servant involved in both the Canadian settlement with Japanese Canadians and its implementation, revealed that the Canadian government, assured by its contacts with the Reagan administration that the United States would not approve any legislation that provided for cash payments to individuals, and that only when it learned of Reagan's action did it reverse its policy. "In my judgment had [redress] not happened in the United States . . . there would have been no individual compensation in Canada, none whatsoever."

While human rights advocates had hoped that the principle of meaningful monetary redress for wartime actions against a nation's own citizens would be adopted elsewhere, it has had no tangible effect outside North America.

We simply do not know why Reagan decided to sign the bill after allowing members of his administration to oppose redress before Congress, in the courts, and in the media. It is merely one of many matters that his mini-memoir does not clarify. And, large as this event seems from a Japanese American point of view, Reagan's most convincing biographer does not mention the issue or Japanese Americans in a volume of nearly 900 pages on Reagan's presidential years.

If, in fact, Reagan did change his position on redress, there were a number of factors that might have caused him to do so. The 1988 election was just over three months away, and while redress was not a major issue nationally, it was popular in California, where Republican strength was weakening; the state and the city of Los Angeles had already enacted a limited form of redress for Japanese Americans who had been prewar state and city civil servants. In addition, once the episode with General Stilwell had been called to the attention of the president and some of his staff, concern for what redress advocates could say about him should he veto the measure might have been a factor. And, of course, having been reminded of the 1945 incident could have focused the president's attention on the rights and wrongs of the matter.

Reagan's signing of the act created an entitlement program for any Japanese American found to have suffered directly from Executive Order 9066 who was still alive on that date. But, as in most instances, separate legislation was necessary to create the appropriations necessary to make payments, and such was the case for the redress bill. Some fifteen months later, on November 21, 1989, President George H. W. Bush signed an appropriations bill that included funds to make redress payments during fiscal years 1991 through 1993.

Finally on October 9, 1990, in a ceremony in the Great Hall of the Department of Justice, Attorney General Richard Thornburgh presented checks for $20,000 and a letter from President Bush to each of nine elderly Nisei, some of them in wheelchairs, who ranged from 73 to 107 years of age. The oldest, Mamoru Eto, a former minister who had been incarcerated at Gila River, opened the meeting with an invocation in Japanese. As Thornburgh knelt beside Eto's wheelchair and handed him his check and letter, the attorney general remarked: "Even when the American system failed you, you never lost your faith in it. While finally admitting a wrong, a nation does not destroy its integrity, but, rather reinforces the sincerity of its commitment to the Constitution and hence to its people."

The letter that Eto and others received was neither a proper letter—it was not addressed to anyone—nor the presidential "apology" that almost all accounts describe. Documents at the Bush Presidential Library at Texas A&M University show a careful drafting of a text without a presidential apology, which the attorney general's draft of the document had included. Printed on a sheet headed by the presidential seal and the words "The White House" and "Washington" aligned beneath it were two bare paragraphs of text, a closing word, and a signature, its block, and October 1990:

> A monetary sum and words alone cannot restore lost years or erase painful memories; neither can they fully convey our Nation's resolve to rectify injustice and to uphold the rights of individuals. We can never fully right the wrongs of the past. But we can take a clear stand for justice and recognize that serious injustices were done to Japanese Americans during World War II.
>
> In enacting a law calling for restitution and offering a sincere apology, your fellow Americans have, in a very real sense, renewed their traditional commitment to the ideals of freedom, equality, and justice. You and your family now have our best wishes for the future.

There can be no doubt about what was intended; Bush staffers and partisans insisted that the payment was the apology, and the president need not make one. When the time came for another increment during President Bill Clinton's term, Attorney General Janet Reno also recommended that the president apologize, and he did so. His brief letter of October 11, 1994, was truly a presidential apology, although its format was the same as the Bush version:

> Over fifty years ago the United States Government unjustly interned, evacuated, or relocated many Japanese Americans. Today, on behalf of your fellow Americans, I offer a sincere apology to you for the actions that unfairly denied Japanese Americans and their families fundamental liberties during World War II.
>
> In enacting the Civil Liberties Act of 1988, we acknowledge the wrongs of the past and offered redress to those who endured such grave injustice. In retrospect, we understand that the Nation's actions were rooted deeply in racial prejudice, wartime hysteria, and a lack of political leadership. We must learn from the past and dedicate ourselves as a nation to the spirit of equality and the love

of freedom. Together, we can guarantee a future with liberty and justice for all. You and your family have my best wishes for the future.

By that time the scope of redress had been expanded by congressional, executive, and judicial amendment. The most important congressional expansion came, again, in a presidential election year. It had become apparent that the original estimate of 60,000 redress survivors significantly underestimated the number of survivors, and the monies previously appropriated were insufficient to pay all eligible survivors. The statute amending the 1988 act, passed by voice vote in both Houses, which meant unanimous consent, appropriated an additional $400 million and expanded the scope of redress to a few dozen persons who were not Japanese Americans but had voluntarily accompanied an incarcerated parent or spouse, and contained language saying that it was the intent of Congress that the determination of individual eligibility should be interpreted "liberally."

In his September 27, 1992, signing statement the first President Bush said:

> Today I am pleased to sign into law H.R. 4551, the Civil Liberties Act Amendments of 1992. This legislation fulfills the commitment that this country made in 1988 to individuals of Japanese ancestry who were interned or relocated during World War II, and to their families. . . . These payments are compelled by justice, and I am proud to sign this bill into law. . . . No monetary payments can ever fully compensate loyal Japanese Americans for one of the darkest incidents in American constitutional history. We must do everything possible to ensure that such a grave wrong is never repeated.

The eventual basic requirements for eligibility were as follows:

> An applicant had to have been alive on August 10, 1988; a U.S. citizen or permanent resident alien during the internment period (12/7/41–6/30/46); a person of Japanese ancestry, or the spouse or parent of a person of Japanese ancestry; and, evacuated, relocated, interned, or otherwise deprived of liberty or property as a result of federal government action during the internment period and based solely on their Japanese ancestry.

Shortly after the redress bill was signed, Attorney General Thornburgh, acting on a suggestion in the CWRIC recommendations, created the Office of Redress Administration (ORA) in the Civil Rights Division of the Justice Department. Its chief tasks were to find and verify everyone who was ever in a WRA camp and to administer the distribution of the checks. It even had staffers attached to the American embassy in Tokyo to track down eligible repatriates and renunciants. It also established a number of categories of persons, who, although they were never in a WRA camp, could, under the mandate of liberal interpretation of eligibility, be certified for redress. These included Japanese Americans who were post–Pearl Harbor "voluntary" resettlers who left the forbidden zone before DeWitt forbade further migration, farmers in Hawaii who were forced off farms and out of homes, and railroad workers fired from their jobs all over the trans-Mississippi West.

Just after the ORA closed its books, it reported on February 19, 1999, that it had paid more than $1.6 billion to more than 82,250 individuals. Among them were 189 Japanese Latin American claimants, some of them born in captivity, eligible for the full $20,000 in redress compensation under the revised redress statute, because they had the required permanent residency status or US citizenship during the defined period.

The fate of the remaining 2,000-plus Japanese Latin Americans who had been in DoJ camps was varied. In 1943, 476 of them went voluntarily to Japan on the second voyage of the exchange ship *Gripsholm*. By the time the war ended, it had become clear that most of the nations that had handed them over to the United States did not want them back. Peru, which had supplied some 80 percent of the Japanese, accepted only a hundred back. The Department of Justice planned to send all the rest to Japan, regardless of their wishes. A few, mostly formerly well-to-do persons with influential relatives and friends in the country they came from, managed to be readmitted. The remainder of those still in the United States were not compensated or accounted for by the Department of Justice. As will be discussed in the next chapter, there was a still further legal episode in their saga.

Attorney General Janet Reno, summing up for the Clinton administration, concluded: "This was a tragic chapter in the history of our nation. The U.S. Government recognized the injustice of its actions during the war and provided a presidential apology and compensation. It was a time when we took away the liberty of an entire community of Americans."

For the Civil Rights Division, Assistant Attorney General Bill Lann Lee called it "a great example of a program that worked." The ORA had "set out to locate every possible claimant" who had been in WRA custody, and "we have accounted for almost 99% of them. That's a remarkable accomplishment."

There is no gainsaying this claim. His department had finally provided a measure of justice to the Japanese American people. But a truly honest reckoning would have also acknowledged the often ignored redress compromise that placed the heirs of those who died before the enactment of the 1998 Civil Liberties Act—roughly a third of the WRA's victims—beyond the pale of even long-delayed redress.

CHAPTER SEVEN

Judicial Redress

Although Eugene Rostow's 1945 hope that the "basic issues" of the wartime Japanese American cases might "be presented to the Supreme Court again, in an effort to obtain [their] prompt reversal," has not materialized, a special set of circumstances did result in a significant reopening of the three wartime cases that the government won. Academic research conducted by Peter H. Irons, an attorney and a professor of political science at the University of California, San Diego, was instrumental in beginning an unusual legal procedure that reopened the wartime convictions of Gordon Hirabayashi, Min Yasui, and Fred Korematsu. Irons was following up his successful first book, *The New Deal Lawyers* (1982), with a similar archival study of Roosevelt's Justice Department in a period of national emergency and war. He tells us that while researching what became his second book, *Justice at War* (1983), he found archival evidence demonstrating that Solicitor General Charles Fahy had suppressed footnotes written for the government's briefs by Edward Ennis that cast doubt on some of the evidence used to convince the court of the military necessity that led the government to exile and incarcerate Japanese Americans.

While his research was still going on, Irons testified along with a number of other legal scholars at the final hearing held by the Commission on Wartime Relocation and Internment of Civilians in Cambridge, Massachusetts, on December 9, 1981. The commission chose to take no notice of Irons's damning evidence; neither he nor it is mentioned in the CWRIC's report, *Personal Justice Denied*. That document made the case it needed without reference to that potentially volatile material in a brief section, "The Supreme Court Rulings" (236–239).

But one member of the commission made a vital suggestion. Philadelphia Judge William J. Marutani had been exiled from his Kent,

Washington, home and incarcerated for some months in the camps at Pinedale, California, and Tule Lake, before being released to attend Dakota Wesleyan College in Mitchell, South Dakota. He left school to enter the army and, as a second lieutenant, served in postwar Japan. He returned to finish his degree and then earned a law degree at the University of Chicago in 1953. A legal activist in civil rights, he had been national legal counsel for the JACL (1960–1970), arguing against laws prohibiting interracial marriage in *Loving v. Virginia* and obtaining desegregation orders against Washington Parish, Louisiana. He was appointed to Philadelphia's Court of Common Pleas in 1975, and in 1977 was elected to a ten-year term, becoming the first Asian American judge in Pennsylvania. Marutani suggested to Irons that the somewhat obscure writ of coram nobis might be a device to force a reconsideration of the wartime convictions. When he joined the commission majority appointees, he recused himself from payment, the only eligible Nisei known to have done so.

At that time the best-known attempt to use a coram nobis writ to quash a federal conviction was Alger Hiss's unsuccessful effort to get his perjury conviction reversed in 1973 on the basis of new evidence and a claim of prosecutorial impropriety. The writ itself—the Latin may be translated as "the matter before us"—is an old common-law writ recognized in federal criminal statutes, which provide that a conviction may be vacated if new evidence, including evidence of prosecutorial misconduct, can be shown to cast doubt upon it. The Supreme Court had cautioned that coram nobis should be used "only under certain circumstances compelling such action to achieve justice" and to correct "errors of the most fundamental character." In addition, only a living defendant may use it, and the case should be brought in the court in which the defendant was originally convicted. In a successful case the initial court may order a new trial or simply vacate the conviction. The losing side may appeal.

Irons decided to try to put together three legal teams, one in each of the three cities—San Francisco, Portland, and Seattle—where district courts had convicted the Nisei who would again become litigants. But first he needed the agreement of the prospective litigants. He easily obtained the consent of Gordon Hirabayashi, by this time professor emeritus of sociology at the University of Alberta, and Min Yasui, a nonpracticing attorney and executive director of Denver's

Commission on Community Relations. Both were public figures in the Japanese American community and active participants in the redress movement. Both eagerly agreed to be litigants. But Fred Korematsu had never participated in any Japanese American community affairs except for his forced wartime confinement, and, as I personally learned through Ernest Besig in the 1950s and 1960s, he was unwilling to discuss his case with anyone, even a sympathetic scholar. Irons had written Korematsu but had received no reply. Overturning Gordon's and Min's convictions would result in little but personal vindication if the *Korematsu* decision remain unchallenged. As Justice Lewis F. Powell Jr., a 1971 Nixon appointee, wrote in 1980: "Under this Court's established doctrine, a racial classification is suspect and subject to strict scrutiny. . . . Only two of the Court's major cases [*Hirabayashi* and *Korematsu*] have held the use of racial classifications to be constitutional."

Therefore, getting Fred Korematsu's participation was vital. Irons relates that in January 1982 he had phoned Fred at his San Leandro home and persuaded him to agree to a meeting that Irons approached "with trepidation." At first both men were "formal and nervous." Irons asked Fred a number of questions about his trial and received detailed answers:

> After Korematsu finished his account, I handed him about twenty pages of Justice Department documents. He read through the entire batch . . . in silence, pausing only to fiddle with his pipe. After what seemed to me an eternity, he looked up. "They did me a great wrong," he said of the Justice Department officials who persuaded the Supreme Court to affirm his conviction. He then asked me an unexpected question. "Are you a lawyer?" when I answered that I was, Korematsu asked, "Would you be my lawyer?" I would be delighted to give him any help that I could, I responded.

That done, assured of the three necessary litigants, Irons needed to find lawyers. He had consulted Min Yasui, who sent him a list of ten Japanese American attorneys: only one of them lived in a city where a writ would be filed. Dale Minami, a Sansei whose parents had been incarcerated at Heart Mountain, and a 1971 JD from Berkeley's Boalt Hall, was a partner in a small Bay Area law firm and had been an active member of Bay Area Attorneys for Redress, which had filed a brief supporting monetary redress with the CWRIC. He and Irons had a meeting of minds, and it was Minami who played the key role in initiating the recruitment of lawyers, largely young Sansei, and overwhelmingly Asian American. Minami organized the San Francisco team to conduct the hearing for Korematsu, and he recruited Peggy Nagae, a JD from Lewis and Clark's Northwestern Law School and then a dean in the University of Oregon Law School, to organize and lead the Portland team that would prepare Yasui's case; Kathryn Bannai headed the Seattle team preparing Hirabayashi's case. Except for Minami, who had ten years' experience, most of the other key attorneys were very recent graduates. When it came time to appear in court, the Portland and Seattle teams co-opted a more senior lawyer with trial experience to share the presentation. One of the original 1942 attorneys, Seattle's Arthur Barnett, seventy-six, was the oldest team member and the only link to the wartime cases apart from the petitioners themselves.

All the attorneys were genuine pro bono volunteers receiving neither pay nor expenses; Minami told Densho interviewers in 2004 that some $150,000 in contributions helped defray expenses; the largest single gift was $5,000.

On January 19, 1983, a year after Irons first met with Fred Korematsu, a number of key attorneys gathered in the clerk's office in San Francisco's federal courthouse to file their first coram nobis petition. The clerk assigned it a number, punched a code into a machine, and announced, "You got Judge Patel." The legal team was delighted. Marilyn Hall Patel had earned a JD from Fordham Law School in 1963, and after four years of private practice in New York City, she became an attorney in the San Francisco office of the Immigration and Naturalization Service (1967–1971) and then went into private practice there. In 1976 she became a state judge, serving until 1980, when President Carter appointed her to a newly created federal district court seat in San Francisco. In less than three years she had established herself as one of the most liberal judges on what had become the nation's most liberal federal circuit. As will be shown, the three petitions alleging the same wrongs in similar cases achieved three very different results. Justice, usually depicted as blindfolded, was in this instance merely random. It was *lex ex machina*, law out of the machine.

The lawyers then went to the nearby San Francisco Press Club to join their three clients: Hirabayashi and Yasui had met the reclusive Korematsu for the first time the day before. Don Tamaki, a Boalt Hall JD of 1976 who was executive director of the Asian Law Caucus, a pro bono group of Bay Area ethnic lawyers founded in 1972 who handled media relations and fund-raising for the coram nobis team, had managed to attract more than a hundred journalists, including camera crews representing all the national TV networks, for the first public airing of the coram nobis lawsuits.

Both Irons and Minami spoke briefly about their objective, but the real news was the appearance of and remarks by the three war-time defendants. As had been the case with many of the coram nobis team members, an all-but-universal reaction was surprise: "Are these guys still alive?" The fact that the press conference was followed by the release of the CWRIC report just over a month later resulted in broader media coverage. By the end of the decade there would be a vastly greater public awareness of the wartime incarceration than had previously existed and an increasing conviction on the part of large numbers of Americans that Japanese Americans had been unjustly treated.

The *Petition for Writ of Error Coram Nobis*, first filed in Judge Patel's court on January 19, 1983, and refiled, with minor adjustments in similar courts in Portland and Seattle shortly thereafter, plus two appendices, takes up pages 125 through 209 in Peter Irons's 1989 documentary history. The government's "response," after three separate requested continuances, was finally filed on October 4, 1983, and requires only pages 210 through 212. It agreed with and cited President Ford's 1976 proclamation and mentioned the CWRIC report—but not its conclusions or recommendations—and argued that the "mass evacuation was part of an unfortunate episode in our nation's history." Therefore, it concluded, "without any intention to disparage those persons who made the decisions in question," that "the government hereby moves to vacate petitioner's conviction and dismiss the underlying indictment. . . . Thereupon, petitioner having reached all the relief which this Court can render, the petition should be dismissed." For the press, the government's lawyer Victor Stone spun his notion to make it appear that he supported Korematsu's petition: "I hope this does for them what they want. I think it's a big step on our part."

There were surely federal judges then sitting who would have acceded to such a notion; perhaps there was one in the Northern District of California, but it was certainly not the liberal activist Judge Patel. What the experienced Victor Stone, a 1971 Harvard Law school JD, can have been thinking is hard to imagine. He had been sent from Washington to dispose of all three coram nobis cases while the local federal attorneys sat as spectators. Judge Patel received the brief and set a hearing for November 10, 1983. Before that hearing opened, Stone asked the court for yet another delay, which Patel denied.

The transcript of that brief hearing takes up only pages 213 through 224 in Irons's book, which records the remarks of Dale Minami, Fred Korematsu, and Victor Stone. It also records the procedural remarks of Judge Patel but does not include her oft-quoted closing remarks. Judge Patel, who had ordered the hearing held in the courthouse's ceremonial courtroom, which was filled by some 300 persons, mostly Nisei, briefly explained in three paragraphs, for the audience rather than the lawyers, what it was all about:

> In January a petition for the writ of coram nobis was filed by Petitioner Korematsu in the Court . . . the Court in which he was convicted in September of 1942 [and] affirmed by the Supreme Court in 1944. . . . The petition was [about] misrepresentations made in the nature of supporting military necessity . . . as well as the arguments of military necessities supporting both the conviction and the affirmation of that conviction [and] alleged failure to provide certain information to the Supreme Court.

She then asked Minami to begin.

Minami's remarks, like the judge's, were directed at the audience. Minami and most of his colleagues not only were defending their three clients but also were defending the reputation of their parents and their parents' generation. He explicitly acknowledged that he was seeking "a measure of . . . justice" for Korematsu and his community in 1942. What the government called a "40-year-old misdemeanor," he saw as a "monumental precedent" in the lives of "a hundred thousand Japanese Americans." Calling the case "a great civil rights disaster," he insisted that the petition was "the last opportunity to finally achieve the justice denied 40 years ago."

Then Fred Korematsu, for the first time, was allowed to speak for himself in open court. "I still remember," he began,

> when I was arrested as a criminal here in San Francisco [and] escorted to [a] concentration camp. . . . The horse stalls that we stayed in were made for horses, not human beings. . . . As long as my record stands in federal court, any American citizen can be held in prison or concentration camps without a trial or a hearing. . . . I would like to see the government admit that they were wrong and do something about it so that this will never happen again to any American citizen of any race, creed, or color.

Victor Stone then stepped to the podium and insisted that the government also wanted the conviction vacated and that "the underlying information be dismissed." He then proceeded to relate all the gestures the government had made since the war, beginning with the Japanese American Claims Act. More than half his brief statement consisted in reading President Ford's 1976 proclamation. He also spoke of the CWRIC investigation but did not discuss its findings or mention its suggested remedies. In what may be described as a "dishonest reckoning," Stone concluded that President Ford had settled the matter. It was all a piece with what seemed to be the Reagan administration's inexorable opposition to any meaningful redress.

Minami and possibly other members of the legal team expected Judge Patel to end the hearing and perhaps indicate when she would rule on their petition. Instead she read a prepared statement in which she described the government's response as "tantamount to a confession of error," pointed out that she could not reverse a Supreme Court decision, and observed that the case "lies overruled in the court of history":

> Korematsu remains on the pages of our legal and political history. As a legal precedent it is now recognized as having very limited application. As historical precedent it stands as a constant caution that in times of war or declared military necessity our institutions must be vigilant in protecting constitutional guarantees. It stands

as a caution that in time of distress the government must not be used to protect governmental actions from close scrutiny and accountability. It stands as a caution that in times of international hostility our institutions, legislative, executive, and judicial, must be prepared to exercise the authority to protect all citizens from the petty fears and prejudices that are so easily aroused.

After a pause, she announced, before leaving the bench and ending the hearing: "The petition for a writ of coram nobis is granted."

Patel's opinion of April 19, 1984, some four months later, which occupies pages 225 through 249 in Irons's documentary volume, retained the passage she read at the hearing and included both extended argument and some wartime documents. She refuted the government's claims in some detail and supported the petition's claims of government misconduct, finding "substantial support" for its claim of governmental suppression of evidence. She took favorable notice of the CWRIC report and provided in appendices copies of wartime Justice Department internal correspondence that laid bare the suppression of evidence. She held that the petition demonstrated that "the government deliberately omitted relevant information and provided misleading information" to the Supreme Court and observed that the "judicial process is seriously impaired when the government's law enforcement officers violate the ethical obligations to the court." It was a splendid decision, greatly pleasing to the coram nobis teams and concerned observers, even if Judge Patel gently refrained from pointing out that suppression of evidence was more than an ethical failing. It was, and is, a criminal offense.

After the November hearing the delighted legal team again went to the Press Club for a news conference in which Korematsu told reporters: "I had to do some deep thinking to reopen this case again and I am certainly glad that I did."

Meanwhile, the work of the two legal teams in the Northwest went on. These cases had been filed shortly after Korematsu's. Yasui's case had been assigned to Judge Robert C. Belloni, a 1941 graduate of the University of Oregon who had served as an army lieutenant (1942–1946), earned a JD from his alma mater in 1951, and established a private practice in his hometown of Myrtle Point on Oregon's coast. Elected as a council member and mayor, he served as circuit judge for two rural counties for a decade before appointment to the federal bench by President Johnson in 1967. He had no history of involvement in civil rights cases but had distinguished himself in deciding a 1974 case that was the first of a series of cases in which the states of Oregon and Washington were forced to respect the treaty rights of Indian tribes to a share of the salmon runs, which those states had routinely violated.

Hirabayashi's case fell to Judge Donald S. Voorhees, a 1938 graduate of the University of Kansas who had served as a naval officer during World War II and, with the aid of the GI Bill of Rights, earned a JD from the Harvard Law School in 1946. He had practiced law in Seattle for almost thirty years when President Nixon made him a federal judge in 1974. The Seattle team noted with pleasure that he had ruled in that city's main school integration case that a voter-approved antibusing initiative was unconstitutional.

Neither of the northwest judges had even scheduled a hearing by the time of Judge Patel's ruling, and the teams came to believe that they were waiting to see how Korematsu's petition had been decided. It seems likely that the judges were responsive to requests from Stone, who was handling all three cases, that they be heard seriatim. Once Patel had announced her decision, the teams hoped that the other judges would take her path, but that was not to be. Each judge made a very different response, emphasizing again the often random nature of legal justice.

Judge Belloni acted first, setting an initial hearing on Min Yasui's petition for January 16, 1984, in his Portland courtroom, sixty-seven days after the final hearing in San Francisco. The essence of the Portland team's petition was the same as San Francisco's, and Stone's initial filing echoed his first effort. But just days before the hearing, he filed a lengthy memo Irons describes as claiming that the government had an inherent right to "dismiss criminal prosecutions after convictions had been entered." The team had to scramble to frame a response, which was filed just minutes before the hearing opened. Peggy Nagae had arranged for Don S. Willner, a Harvard Law School JD of 1951, an experienced Portland trial lawyer and supporter of most liberal causes, to appear for Yasui. Judge Belloni, although he knew that a similar case had been heard, opened with a traditional judge's question asking Willner what the case was about.

After Willner had explained, the judge then asked why, if the case was about misconduct before the Supreme Court, he had not gone there. Willner responded with a discussion of why it was appropriate to try the case in the court of original jurisdiction. Nagae, in Irons's phrase, then "tried to educate" the judge about the pervasive damage done to Japanese Americans because of incarceration by their own government, and their need for remedial justice. Min Yasui used his few minutes at the podium to talk about the need to restore faith in the fairness of the Constitution, which he said had been damaged but not destroyed by the government's actions. Victor Stone, as he had in San Francisco, spoke as if the government and Yasui's team were working toward the same end, which he said could be best achieved by vacating Yasui's conviction and rejecting his petition.

Judge Belloni then ended the hearing and made the kind of statement the San Francisco team had expected from Patel: that he would consider the motions and announce his decision at a later date. Just ten days later, on January 26, 1984, he issued a two-page opinion accepting Stone's contention that both sides had requested the "same relief" and accordingly vacated the conviction. He did not deny Yasui's claim the his constitutional rights had been violated because "the government knew about and withheld evidence refuting military necessity," but simply refused "forty years after the events took place" to make the finding requested in the petition. Deeming that he had been asked "to engage in fact finding that would have no legal consequences," he directed a philosophical slap at his San Francisco colleague without naming her: "Courts should not engage in that kind of activity."

Although disappointing, Belloni's refusal to consider the coram nobis petition did present an opportunity not provided by the victory in Patel's court. An appeal to the Ninth Circuit Court of Appeals was possible and seemed to offer three possible results: the higher court could refuse to hear it, could grant it, or could reject it. And if it rejected or refused to hear the appeal, there was the possibility of an ultimate appeal to the Supreme Court. An appeal was mounted. At the Ninth Circuit the vexed question of what lawyers call "laches"—were necessary procedures done at the proper time?—was raised about Yasui's 1983 filing, and that question was sent back to Judge Belloni, who ruled that it had been timely and sent it back to the

Ninth Circuit. All this had proceeded at a leisurely pace. Min Yasui's death at age seventy on November 12, 1986, almost three years after his initial filing, effectively ended his appeal, although the legal team tried to get the Ninth Circuit to consider it postmortem.

Meanwhile, in Seattle the *Hirabayashi* case was still going on forty-two years after his arrest and trial. By the time of Judge Voorhees's initial Seattle hearing on May 18, 1984, almost four months after Judge Belloni filed his opinion, he had both that opinion and Patel's forty-one-page opinion in hand. Kathryn Bannai's team filed the now familiar petition for a writ of coram nobis, but Stone, anxious to achieve a victory, completely changed his approach. He filed a greatly expanded brief praising Judge Belloni's ruling as "correctly decided" and raised the timeliness question, again pretending that the government and Hirabayashi were seeking the same ends, and that the petitioner had not suffered any continuing injury from his conviction. Stone also threw in the fact that the day before, in a federal court in what Seattleites call "the "other Washington," a judge had thrown out a class action suit against the government—the so-called NCJAR suit, which will be treated later in this chapter—because of timeliness and urged a similar fate for Hirabayashi's petition. Voorhees said that he would read that case when he got it but noted that the class action was a civil case, and different rules applied to a criminal conviction such as Hirabayashi's.

As the Portland team had done, the Seattle team chose to co-opt an experienced local trial counsel from a prominent firm to present its case in court. Camden Hall, who had a 1965 JD from his alma mater, the University of Washington, led off for the team. Like Willner in Portland, he had considerable court experience and had often appeared before Judge Voorhees. He reminded the judge that the government had not raised the issue of timeliness in either of its two previous briefs, while its present brief raised a variety of issues. He also made the point that Hirabayashi's case had "a fair amount of symbolic importance."

Hirabayashi then spoke for himself, focusing initially on his postwar experience teaching in the Middle East. He noted his difficulties in explaining to students aware of the wartime incarceration of Japanese Americans why the American democracy had confined its own citizens on the basis of their ancestry. Then, in speaking of his 1942 trial, he told how the government had unnecessarily brought his aging parents back to Seattle from the concentration camp where they were being held and then housed them in the cockroach-infested county jail before bringing them into the court for no discernible legal purpose. "I'll never forgive the government for that," he stated.

At that point Judge Voorhees began to wind up the proceedings and make his initial judgment. Like Patel, he spoke to the large audience as well as to the participants. He denied the government's motion to dismiss and told the audience of his admiration of Hirabayashi's courage: "What he really is seeking now is vindication of his honor, and I feel that he has that right."

Just how Voorhees proposed to do that was revealed a week later when he announced that he would hold a full evidentiary hearing. It was not quite the "trial" that the press described, as there would be no jury, although each side could cross-examine the hostile witnesses. Judge Voorhees alone would decide the results. In his written order he observed that Hirabayashi "had made a prima facie showing that evidence essential to his defense . . . may have been knowingly suppressed by the government." The government would be able to file motions about timeliness and to counter the suppression charges. Voorhees also announced that he did *not* "intend to reexamine nor to rule upon the wisdom of the exclusion or curfew orders" that had been the basis for Hirabayashi's protest, arrest, and trial. Finally, he set the hearing for June 17, 1985, one day short of thirteen months away.

Both sides prepared briefs, marshaled evidence, arranged for witnesses, and planned strategy and tactics. The defense let it be known that it would call Edward Ennis, and it was bruited that the government would call the two surviving figures who had largely shaped and planned the wartime incarceration: former assistant secretary of war John J. McCloy, who since the war had had a spectacular career in government and business, leading one admiring journalist to dub him the chairman of the mythical American Establishment; and retired colonel Karl Bendetsen, General DeWitt's main man in running the army's roundup of Nisei. All three men had testified before the CWRIC, and McCloy led a media blitz against both the commission's reports as they appeared. Both McCloy and Bendetsen had been accused by Ennis of concealing information from the Justice Department. That neither of the two accused men appeared for the government suggests that they were unwilling to deny Ennis's charges in court under oath. In any event, Stone's potential important witnesses were never called.

Possibly because of the uncertainty about the putative witnesses, Stone supplied no list of witnesses or exhibits by the December deadline and filed them only in March. In addition, he arrived at the opening day of the hearings with seventeen boxes of documents, which he tried to introduce, and made a motion to restrict the scope of the hearing, which was denied. Camden Hall, leading for Hirabayashi that day, objected to the late admission of evidence and moved to exclude from the trial documents that Stone had sent to him belatedly. When Voorhees asked if he had a list, Stone promised to have a handwritten one later that day. The judge shook his head, replying, "Too late."

After the preliminaries were over and the hearing adjourned for the day, Stone complained bitterly to reporters about his inability to use about a thousand wartime documents, most of them only recently declassified. The Associated Press reported him as saying, "I don't know how much is left of the case."

After two days of motions and countermotions and a good deal of bickering, the third day, Wednesday July 19, 1985, began with opening motions from each side. Rod Kawakami, a 1986 JD from the University of Washington, began for Hirabayashi:

> This is not just Gordon Hirabayashi's case, and this is more than just a Japanese American case. . . . This is a case where an American citizen with a deep and abiding faith in American principles stood up and was one of the few voices to proclaim that as an American, evacuation and incarceration based solely on ancestry was contrary to the most fundamental concept of what being an American is all about.

He was calm in manner and spelled out all the charges of governmental misconduct, eventually charging that the government in 1942 and 1943 was so intent on defending the evacuation decision and winning at all costs that it "fixed" the cases against Hirabayashi, Yasui, and Korematsu.

Opening for the government, Victor Stone insisted, like a Gilbert and Sullivan prosecutor, that any improprieties by Justice Department lawyers "has nothing to do with the subject matter of the prosecution," and that "if mistakes were made it was due to the pressure of the war." Pressed by Judge Voorhees to state what the government intended to show, Stone's final response was as follows:

> Our evidence will show it has to do with whether the prosecutors, in one of many cases that they prosecuted, acted properly, and whether or not we can show that at this late date, is something that is very difficult, thirty years after all the events have been made a part of the public record. . . . we will try to show you that this case is not—what is before you right now, this hearing, has nothing to do with Japanese-American rights. It has nothing to do with the Commission on Wartime Relocation and Internment of Civilians. . . . It has nothing to do with the Japanese American Claims Act. . . . Our evidence will show that it has to do with whether the prosecutors in one of many cases they prosecuted, acted properly, and whether or not we can show that at this late date is something that's very difficult, thirty years after all the events have been made a part of the public record.

Hirabayashi's team led off its evidentiary presentation with the only wartime official to testify, Edward Ennis, now seventy-seven years old and described by Peter Irons as "white-haired and chipper." He related Solicitor General Fahy's insistence in 1943 that he remove from the government's brief references to reports from the FBI, the Federal Communications Commission, and the Office of Naval Intelligence that were at variance with what was alleged in General DeWitt's *Final Report.* He also testified that General DeWitt feared that Japan would land troops in Mexico wearing civilian clothes and melt into the Japanese American community. Ennis stated that as head of the Justice Department's Alien Enemy Control Unit, "I did not believe there was any evidence authorizing the holding of U.S. citizens."

Stone spent the better part of two days cross-examining Ennis in an attempt to minimize the effect of his testimony. He went to great lengths to establish what Ennis readily acknowledged: that he had not been aware of once top secret "Magic" intercepts that American code breakers had been able to glean from radio messages sent by Japan's military and diplomatic officials. Although the existence of the intercepts had been revealed in postwar congressional investigations, this was the first time they had been referred to in the second round of the wartime Japanese American cases.

The second week of the hearing began with the testimony of Gordon Hirabayashi, now a sixty-seven-year-old professor emeritus returning to sue the government that had convicted him forty-three years earlier. He explained that, in 1942, "I felt that the Constitution, as I understood it, gave me certain protections as a citizen." He said that he had decided if he was going "to consider himself as an American," he would have to disregard the wartime orders issued to restrict people of Japanese American ancestry. And Aiko Herzig-Yoshinaga testified about her discovery that revealed previously unknown federal suppression of evidence.

Stone began his cross-examination of Hirabayashi by declaring, "It is an honor and a privilege to have this conversation." His questions aimed to establish what was patent: that Gordon had deliberately violated governmental regulations. When he asked if the government had ever charged him with disloyalty, the response was, "They put me in jail." When Stone rephrased his question to ask, "Had the government ever accused him of espionage or sabotage?" the response was, "If I were given that charge I would have had a chance to defend myself."

After his cross-examination of Hirabayashi, Stone called five witnesses, none of whom had anything relevant to impart. One has to wonder what Stone thought he could accomplish with their testimony. The first, who had served during wartime in coastal Oregon and at the Presidio, told of hearing about radio transmissions and coastal lights, which the wartime papers had been full of, but acknowledged under cross-examination that he had no personal knowledge of any improper act by any Nikkei. Neither could a second army officer or two former FBI agents. All four thought it was likely or probable that some Nikkei had helped or would have helped Japan if an opportunity arose to do so, but they had no direct knowledge of any such espionage.

Stone's fifth witness, David A. Lowman, was a retired Cold War employee of the hush-hush National Security Agency, who had supervised the declassification of the so-called Magic documents, which the Department of Defense had published in 1977. Lowman had thrust himself into the limelight, in May 1983 as a critic of the

CWRIC, telling the *New York Times* that the diplomatic cables intercepted and decoded by American cryptanalysts in 1941 might have justified the relocation and internment of Japanese Americans and was quoted as saying, "I doubt that it does justify it." A handful of the thousands of messages in 1941 discussed getting intelligence from Nisei and Issei, as well as from black and white informants. The suggestion that President Roosevelt and Secretary Stimson, the only two persons who were both involved with the decision to incarcerate the Japanese Americans and were on the tiny "subscription list" to receive selected excerpts from the Magic intercepts, had been sent any of the handful of meaningless messages exhorting diplomats to recruit agents is far-fetched. The documents revealed what any politically sophisticated person would have expected. But the CWRIC leaders were embarrassed that their research had ignored the Magic documents. The commission's chairman, Bernstein, its counsel, Angus MacBeth, and member Father Drinnon, interviewed for the same story, admitted that they had not been aware of the messages and found them "historically interesting." Why Lowman had not asked to appear before the commission is unknown, and no one asked him.

A possible clue to what Lowman's intervention was really about was that the *Times*'s reporter also conducted a telephone interview with John McCloy, who told him that the commission should have called members of the intelligence community—something McCloy, the commission's chief public critic, had not previously mentioned. Also significant was the timing of Lowman's attack: the second part of the commission's report, the one that recommended the level and variety of redress, was due in the following month. Lowman subsequently told his story to a House subcommittee hearing in June 1984 that was considering redress legislation. By that time the commission's volunteers Aiko Herzig-Yoshinaga and Jack Herzig had gone through the published and unpublished intercepts, and Jack, an attorney and a retired lieutenant colonel who had served as an intelligence officer, presented a forceful rebuttal before the same subcommittee. After Stone had revealed in March 1985 that he might play the Magic card, the Hirabayashi team arranged to have Herzig on hand to counter Lowman's testimony.

Lowman's testimony before Judge Voorhees on June 27, 1985, the last day of the hearing, was of a piece with his previous performances: it was overheated and lacking in any direct evidence. Camden Hall cross-examined him vigorously, and Herzig's forceful rebuttal stressed that Lowman's testimony was hypothetical and that the handful of Magic intercepts that dealt with espionage contained no direct evidence of espionage by any Japanese American.

As Judge Voorhees was winding up the hearing and preparing to give guidelines to the attorneys about the posthearing briefs he wanted them to present, Stone again urged the judge to accept a batch of Magic documents as evidence of espionage by Japanese Americans. Voorhees again refused to consider them, but then, for whatever reason, according to Peter Irons's account, told Stone: "'I'll take a look at your best one.' Stone rifled through his notes and handed one to the bench. After a quick glance, Judge Voorhees burst into laughter and told the audience, 'I'll have to read it into the record. "The intelligence net operating in England is made up of eight Welshmen, two Irishmen, eleven Scotsmen and two Spaniards."'"

Voorhees then instructed counsel to prepare and submit posthearing briefs summarizing the evidence, testimony, and legal issues by October 4, 1985, just over three months away. As the parties left the court, Hirabayashi, questioned by reporters, delivered one of his aphoristic gems: "Ancestry is not a crime." The posthearing briefs were filed by the petitioner and the government, in July and September, and on October 4, the petitioner filed a reply brief.

Judge Voorhees issued his memorandum opinion on February 10, 1986, more than three years after the case had been assigned to him, and twenty-one months after his initial hearing. It was a split decision. The initial element held that the "petitioner was in fact very seriously prejudiced" by nondisclosure of information in possession of the government about the real reasons for General DeWitt's basic decision. In consequence, Hirabayashi's conviction for "failure to report" was vacated. The second element of Voorhees's opinion upheld Gordon's conviction for curfew violation.

The latter was not a unique distinction. In his dissent in *Korematsu*, Justice Roberts had rationalized his previous vote to convict Gordon Hirabayashi by calling curfew "a case of keeping people off the streets at night." Both Roberts and Voorhees failed to note that the travel restrictions in the curfew order made it all but impossible for most Nikkei to leave the forbidden zone to avoid incarceration. Using that as a rationale for not reversing Hirabayashi's conviction for curfew violation produced a paradoxical result. Voorhees, in effect, reversed a conviction for failing to report, which the Supreme Court had not directly reviewed, and sustained the conviction that the court had explicitly reviewed and upheld. In the process Voorhees rapped the knuckles of the War Department. It is noteworthy, I think, that the example of suppression of evidence that Voorhees chose to support his vacation of Hirabayashi's conviction for failing to report for incarceration, largely cherry-picked from the petitioner's brief, was one in which the army, in the person of McCloy, deliberately withheld from the Justice Department, while Voorhees ignored flagrant examples in which the Justice Department withheld evidence from the Supreme Court. The crux of Voorhees's opinion was clear:

> The Court finds that the failure of the government to disclose to petitioner, to petitioner's counsel, and to the Supreme Court the reason stated by General DeWitt for his deciding that military necessity required the exclusion of all those of Japanese ancestry from the West Coast was an error of the most fundamental character and that petitioner was in fact very seriously prejudiced by that non-disclosure in his appeal from his conviction of failing to report. In consequence, petitioner's conviction on the failure to report count must be vacated.

Voorhees expressed his confidence that, had the justices, or at least five of them, known the real basis of DeWitt's 1942 decision, they would not have sustained Hirabayashi's conviction for failure to report.

Without questioning the justice and propriety of Judge Voorhees's decision, a historian must doubt the validity of his speculation about what the justices, or most of them, might have ruled had they known the truth about the original basis of General DeWitt's decision in 1943. I am convinced that there was no way that Chief Justice Stone and a majority of his colleagues were going to overrule or call into question a major decision affecting a war directive of the commander in chief in mid-1943.

In the immediate aftermath of Voorhees's decision, Gordon in a telephone interview told the *New York Times:* "Although this has been a 40-year crusade, I have never lost faith in the legal system. I feel today that justice has been served. The court has recognized the injustice committed against Japanese Americans during World War II."

He also told the *Times* that he was not going to appeal the conviction on the curfew count because the vacation of the more serious count "erases the factual underpinning from the curfew charge." In the event, each side filed a brief asking Voorhees to reconsider different parts of his opinions. He rejected both motions in a memorandum opinion on April 26, 1986, which closed with his verdict not on the *Hirabayashi* case but on the man, placing him in the tradition of English Members of Parliament who went to jail in Stuart England for refusing to grant that the king had any power to imprison them: "[Hirabayashi's] steadfastness, like theirs, has earned him a place in the pantheon of those who have sacrificed themselves in order to further the common good." As for the wartime policy of Roosevelt's government, he argued that "almost everyone" now felt that what was done to "Japanese Americans was simply a tragic mistake for which American society as a whole must accept responsibility."

Hirabayashi either changed his mind about the appeal or was persuaded to do so, and each side appealed the result it found unsatisfactory: the government opposed the vacating of the count on failure to report, while the petitioner appealed the failure to vacate his conviction on the curfew account.

The Ninth Circuit Court of Appeals, sitting in San Francisco, agreed to hear both appeals. Oral arguments were heard by a three-judge panel, Alfred T. Goodwin, a 1969 Nixon appointee, Mary M. Schroeder, and Joseph J. Farris, both Carter appointees of 1979 (a white man, a white woman, and a black man), on March 2, 1987. More than six months later, on September 24, 1987, Judge Schroeder delivered her opinion for a unanimous panel, which sustained Judge Voorhees's decision striking down Hirabayashi's conviction for failure to report, while overruling his decision upholding the conviction for curfew violation.

After a paragraph in which she summarized the wartime judicial history of both *Hirabayashi* and *Korematsu*, she bluntly demolished the wartime jurisprudence:

The Hirabayashi and Korematsu decisions have never occupied an honored place in our history. In the ensuing four and a half decades, journalists and researchers have stocked library shelves with studies of the cases and surrounding events. These materials document historical judgments that the convictions were unjust. They demonstrate that there could have been no reasonable military assessment of an emergency at the time, that the orders were based upon racial stereotypes, and that the orders caused needless suffering and shame for thousands of American citizens. The legal judgments of the courts reflecting that Hirabayashi and Korematsu had been properly convicted of violating the laws of the United States, however, remained on their records. Petitioner filed this lawsuit in 1983 to obtain a writ of error coram nobis to vacate his convictions and thus to make the judgments of the courts conform to the judgments of history. . . . In his coram nobis petition Hirabayashi contended that the original report, the circumstances surrounding its alteration, and recently discovered related documents provided the proof, unavailable at the time of his conviction, that the curfew and exclusion orders were in fact based upon racial prejudice rather than military exigency. Hirabayashi further alleged that the government concealed these matters from his counsel and the Supreme Court, and that had the Supreme Court known the true basis for the orders, the ultimate decision in the case would probably have been different.

Judge Schroeder summarized the "full evidentiary proceeding" in the Seattle court, emphasizing the testimony of Edward Ennis and Aiko Herzig-Yoshinaga, and noted that its "careful opinion . . . confirmed Hirabayashi's . . . contentions in virtually every factual respect" while rejecting the several government arguments as "factually and legally unsupported." She pointed out that the district court had ruled that Hirabayashi's conviction for violating the exclusion order was "a violation of due process" and ordered it vacated. In addition, another district court had made a similar decision in *Korematsu* in 1984 that had not been appealed. Judge Schroeder concluded her summary of Voorhees's decision by reporting:

> The district court in this case, however, concluded, as a matter of law that the curfew conviction should not be vacated. It ruled that because the curfew order less significantly infringed Hirabayashi's freedom, the Supreme Court would have distinguished it from the

exclusion order and would have affirmed the conviction even if it had known the racial basis of the order.

Faced with appeals from both Hirabayashi and the government, Schroeder pointed out:

> We must uphold the findings of fact unless they are clearly erroneous, and review the legal issues de novo. We agree with the district court's factual and legal analysis leading to its vacation of the exclusion conviction. We disagree with the court's conclusion that the curfew conviction rests upon a legal foundation different from the exclusion conviction. We therefore hold that both convictions should be vacated.

Hirabayashi, interviewed by the Associated Press, was naturally gratified by the result, saying that although it was "very good news," he would be disappointed if the government "suddenly lost its appetite" and did not appeal. That is exactly what happened. The entire coram nobis proceedings, which began on January 19, 1984, were essentially over on September 27, 1987, but the Justice Department asked the Ninth Circuit to reconsider, which it denied in an order on December 24, 1987. Judge Voorhees thereupon, on January 12, 1988, issued the obligatory order for the vacation of Hirabayashi's conviction for curfew violation. The Supreme Court's rules provided that the government had sixty days to appeal the appellate court's decision. On the sixtieth day Peter Irons, as Hirabayashi's counsel, telephoned the Justice Department and was told that the solicitor general Charles Fried, a Harvard Law School professor who had been in charge since mid-1984, had decided not to appeal. Whether that switch in prosecutorial tactics had anything to do with the impending switch on the question of redress by the Reagan administration is unclear. Queried about the prosecutorial switch in November 2012, Fried answered: "Sorry, I have nothing to tell you unless I did a lot of research."

A parallel effort for a different kind of legal redress had been mounted by an ad hoc group, the National Council for Japanese American Redress (NCJAR). Led by the Nisei William Hohri, it raised money to finance a group of midwestern lawyers to prepare a class action suit on behalf of all those incarcerated pursuant to Executive Order 9066. They developed twenty-two separate counts and asked for $10,000 on each count, for each litigant; that was a total potential cost to the government of $220,000 per litigant. Multiplied by 120,000 possible litigants, it represented a potential cost to the government of $26.4 billion. The chance of such a suit being approved by the Supreme Court was absolutely zero. Even had all the justices in the 1980s been liberals, the problem of sovereign immunity, the inability to sue the United States without its permission, was a fatal impediment. In the final analysis, apart from the false hopes that the suits raised in its supporters, the main political effect of the suit was to make the relatively modest proposals of the CWRIC and its adherents seem less outlandish than they would have otherwise.

The five-year course of the NCJAR suit, which reached the Supreme Court, can be briefly traced. It was first heard in the Federal Court of the District of Columbia by Louis F. Oberdorfer, a 1977 appointee of President Carter, who clearly felt that the government had been in the wrong during World War II. Oberdorfer denied the petition, ruling on May 17, 1984, that a six-year statute of limitations was an insuperable barrier to its success, and also noted sovereign immunity. An appeal to the large DC Circuit Court of Appeals produced a variety of opinions. Of the fourteen judges who participated, eight voted to deny the petition, and six did not; most of the latter wanted it heard en banc. The majority opinion upheld Judge Oberdorfer's opinion on May 30, 1986.

On a petition from the government the Supreme Court ruled that the appeal of Judge Oberdorfer's ruling had been heard in the wrong court and was thus invalid. Oberdorfer's original ruling was thus reinstated on June 1, 1987.

But before that ruling, Solicitor General Fried made a trenchant and remarkable oral argument about the substance of the case, doubly remarkable when one considers that Justice Department attorney Victor Stone was continuing the government's persistent attack on every aspect of the coram nobis cases. Fried began:

> This case arises out of a deplorable episode from what was surely the greatest cataclysm in modern times, the Second World War, in which over 60,000,000 people lost their lives and whole populations were herded from their homes and cruelly massacred.

The allies did not always adhere to the standards and the values for which they were fighting. The British for instance, after a debate which is eerily foreshadowing of the same debate that we had in this country, interned in 1940, indiscriminately German and Austrian Nationals in Great Britain, even though the largest number of them were known to be Jewish refugees.

The Japanese internment was surely our greatest departure from the values for which we are fighting. Not so much because of the suffering which was inflicted on these Japanese American, many people suffered during that war, but because of the basis on which that suffering was inflicted, the basis which was urged publicly and before this Court. The basis that was urged was a political judgment reached at the highest levels.

That and more said, the solicitor general went on to note that it was all overt, made no mention of military necessity and other lies, and explained the technical reasons for the government's claim that the case had been tried in the wrong court. The justices all agreed, although Justice Thurgood Marshall gave him a thorough barracking and Justice John Paul Stevens undertook a gentler reproach.

The NCJAR then appealed to the indicated court, the Court of Appeals, Federal Circuit, which also sat in Washington. A three-judge panel of that court heard the appeal and in a perfunctory per curiam opinion on May 11, 1988, upheld the negative judgment of the district court.

On October 31, 1988, as Linda Greenhouse wrote in the *New York Times*, the Supreme Court "shut the door on a five-year effort to reopen the legal issues posed by the wartime detention of 120,000 Japanese Americans in prison camps." The court let stand the Oberdorfer decision as endorsed by the Federal Circuit. But the judicial struggle for redress was not quite over.

A class action suit on behalf of uncompensated Latin Americans who had been rendered into the United States during World War II, *Mochizuki et al. v. US*, was filed in August 1996. It sought to have its members included in and to receive all the benefits that had been authorized by the Civil Liberties Act of 1988, as amended. The suit seemed to face insuperable obstacles, including timeliness, sovereignty, and the previously established redress guidelines. But unlike previous legal redress actions, it challenged an administration and a Department of Justice firmly committed to the belief that the government's wartime actions toward Nikkei had been unjust and its postwar actions largely inappropriate. The result was a judicially monitored mediation.

On June 11, 1998, Chief Judge Loran A. Smith of the US Court of Federal Claims announced his court's preliminary approval of a negotiated mediation of the lawsuit; the final approval was on November 17, 1998. The plaintiffs, represented by attorneys from Southern California ACLU, the JACL, and their support group, the National Coalition for Redress/Reparations, received an apology and a tax-free award of $5,000 per eligible member, a quarter of the sum provided in the original legislation. The funds used were those remaining from previous appropriations; in the event, more applicants qualified than could be fully compensated. The Office of Redress Administration (ORA) thought that there were sufficient funds for 880 awards of $5,000 each, and supporters believed there might be as many as 1,200 applicants. The settlement defined the class as previously uncompensated persons: "(a) Persons of Japanese ancestry who were living in Latin America before World War II and were interned in the United States at any time during the period from December 7, 1941, to June 30, 1946; OR (b) persons who are the spouses, children, or parents of persons who died after August 10, 1988, and who met the qualifications of (a) above."

It turned out, as the ORA reported in February 1999, it received "approximately 710 claims" stemming from the *Mochizuki* settlement and "successfully resolved" almost 600 of them; however, funds were available to pay only 145 of the claims. It expressed the hope that Congress would provided the necessary funds to pay the remaining claims, which would have cost less than $3 million, but no further funds have been appropriated. In 2006 and 2007, Senator Inouye and Representative Xavier Becerra, a California Democrat, introduced identical bills to establish a Commission on Wartime Relocation and Internment of Latin Americans of Japanese Descent, but none even reached a congressional floor. In seems unlikely that any further World War II redress will occur.

The lead plaintiff, Carmen Mochizuki, told a Los Angeles press conference that although she was "disappointed" at not receiving the full amount specified in the original legislation, "I feel that we are victorious for making the United States government finally accept responsibility for its actions against us." Not all class members agreed. The negotiated settlement provided that those plaintiffs who were not satisfied with the result could opt out and file lawsuits. Several did. Their suits were unsuccessful, and so far they have received nothing.

After Redress

The redress movement, like no other event since their wartime ordeal, involved, eventually, almost all Japanese Americans in one way or another. More important than the tangible rewards, the psychological impact of redress was transforming. Even in Hawaii, where only a tiny fraction of the Nikkei population received direct benefit, an increased sense of identity with mainlanders developed. There was a positive change not only in the group's self-image but also in the way in which it was viewed by other Americans. Judge Voorhees's comment that Gordon Hirabayashi's case was really about honor drew little public attention, but when Presidential Medals of Freedom were awarded to Fred Korematsu and Gordon Hirabayashi in 1998 and 2012, respectively, a general public approval and no significant public disapproval followed.

The community itself, of course, had changed. By the year 2000, the Issei generation, those who had come before 1925, was all but gone. Their Nisei children, mostly born before the war, were of retirement age, and increasingly positions of community leadership were in the hands of Sansei, while many of their children, the fourth-generation Yonsei, were in college, starting their careers, and beginning families of their own. Even more than was the case in the nation at large, leadership in the Japanese American community remained in the hands of men. Slowly those leaders had come to understand that they were also Asian Americans, a term the federal government began to use in the mid-1970s. As the concept spread, they easily assumed the informal leadership of that newly conceived grouping, most obviously in terms of civil rights unconnected with their wartime experience. In 1960, as the broader civil rights issues were emerging, Japanese Americans were the largest Asian American group. The census that year tallied 464,000 Japanese Americans, a little more than half of all Asian Americans, but also the only Asian American group in which most of the members were citizens.

Nowhere has this leadership role been more pronounced than on college campuses, particularly elite ones. Allan W. Austin, the historian of the wartime Nisei college experience, has observed that their college experiences east of California made Japanese Americans "forerunners for the relatively large numbers of native and foreign-born Asian American and Asian students who play such a prominent role on many American campuses."

The leadership role of Japanese Americans within what came to be styled the Asian Pacific group endured even as their numerical superiority vanished. The 1952 McCarran-Walter Act and the broader 1965 immigration law pushed through by President Lyndon Johnson enabled the great surge in Asian immigration that followed, which included only a very few immigrants from prosperous postwar Japan. Thus by 2000 the Census Bureau reported an Asian American population of 10.2 million, of which only 8 percent were Japanese Americans. Their numbers were surpassed by five other ethnic groups of Asian origin—Chinese, Indians, Filipinos, Vietnamese, and Koreans—each of which was tallied at more than a million and increasing at a rate above the figure for the nation. But the Japanese American total of 797,000 represented a 6 percent dip from the 1990 figure, a decline that the 2010 census reported as continuing. The reduction, little noted in the ethnic media, was a result of a low rate of immigration, a diminution of the once robust Japanese American birthrate, and decades of a high level of exogamous marriage. The last was difficult for many Nisei to get used to. One mother, each of whose four daughters was married to white men, told a *New York Times* reporter in 1995: "Because we are not living in Japan, because we are living in America, we have accepted that our children will not marry Japanese. . . . As the second generation, being Japanese was the thing that held us together. Perhaps now there's nothing cohesive to hold us together any longer."

Unlike the other Asian American groups, which contained large numbers of poor people, end-of-century Japanese Americans were overwhelmingly middle-class, with a higher incidence of college graduates and advanced degrees than the population classified as white. They were well represented among the learned professions, in the US Army's officer corps, and in federal, state, and local civil service positions.

Redress affected government actions as well. In the aftermath of redress and the refocused national attention on the wartime incarceration, the federal government began to respond favorably to long-standing efforts by a few handfuls of Japanese American activists who had been calling for memorial attention to their wartime experience and its sites. The first positive results of some two decades of such efforts came when the camp site at Manzanar, which had been a National Historic Site since 1976, was made a National Historic Monument by Public Law 102-248, signed by the first President Bush on March 2, 1992. It provided for "the protection and interpretation of the historical, cultural, and natural resources associated with the relocation of Japanese Americans during World War II" by the National Park Service (NPS). That designation presupposed further development, which its presence on the National Register of Historic Places did not. In the mid-1980s, anticipating eventual action, an NPS historian assigned to survey all ten of the major WRA camp sites had found that Manzanar was "the best preserved and [had] the greatest potential as a national park unit." Located in the California desert some 220 miles east of Los Angeles, it was a logical first choice, since Southern California contained the largest concentration of mainland Nikkei.

On November 12, 1996, near the end of the first Clinton administration, an Omnibus Public Land Act included an appropriation to build a facility at Manzanar to explain the site to visitors. The president made no reference to Manzanar in his signing statement. Such matters do not move rapidly. The site was turned over to the NPS in 1997, and a growing stream of visitors continued before the "preserved site" was officially opened on April 24, 2004. That year the camp had more than 70,000 visitors. Construction and other improvements continue, and the historical interpretation provided is increasingly sophisticated.

On November 9, 2000, President Clinton sent a three-paragraph memo to the Interior secretary headed "Preservation of Japanese American Internment Sites." It praised a recently published NPS report, *Confinement and Ethnicity: An Overview of World War II Japanese American Relocation Sites*, and directed the secretary during "the next

60 days" and in consultation with other federal agencies "to develop recommendations to preserve the existing Japanese American internment sites and to provide more opportunities for the public to learn about the internment." He added:

I also direct you to consult with Members of Congress, States, tribes, local officials, and other interested parties as you develop these recommendations. You should also consider expanding partnerships with private organizations and landowners and explore the creation of an interagency team to coordinate the work of Federal agencies. Your recommendations should include proposals for administrative and legislative action to help preserve these sites, within existing budget resources.

That report by Interior secretary Bruce Babbitt on January 9, 2001, described the current status of each of the ten WRA camps, noted other incarceration sites, and laid out a kind of agenda for future preservation and educational projects.

On January 17, 2001, three days before his presidency came to an end, President Clinton issued seven proclamations establishing new national monuments. One of them created the Minidoka Internment National Monument. In each instance Clinton invoked a provision of the Antiquities Act of 1906, which enabled him to bypass Congress and proclaim it by fiat. That act had been crafted imperfectly in Congress for a specific purpose: the protection of pre-Columbian Native American sites such as Mesa Verde. President Theodore Roosevelt and his chief forester Gifford Pinchot saw the loose language of the statute as a way to bypass a poky or unwilling Congress and used it to create national monuments unrelated to pre-Columbian sites. Since 1906, fourteen other presidents have used the act to create more than a hundred national monuments, almost none of which were related to pre-Columbian sites. In his several actions Clinton was setting an agenda for the NPS in a number of areas that is still being implemented a dozen years and two administrations later.

Minidoka had been a natural choice to become the second camp to be developed as a cultural resource because it was the camp where the vast majority of the state of Washington's Nikkei had been incarcerated. Located in southern Idaho, some 500 miles from the Puget Sound region where most Washington Nikkei lived, it had been placed on the National Register in 1979. The establishment of the Minidoka Monument intensified existing private efforts to establish a memorial on Bainbridge Island to commemorate the first Nikkei group to suffer mass expulsion and incarceration subsequent to General DeWitt's Exclusion Order 1. In November 2002 Congress approved and funded the Bainbridge Island Japanese American Memorial Study Act, which directed the NPS to investigate the feasibility of such a memorial. Six years later Congress approved the creation of the Nidoto Nai Yoni (let it not happen again) Memorial on an eight-acre site on the spot where, on May 30, 1942, a total of 257 island Nikkei had been herded by armed soldiers onto a ferry that took them to Seattle, where they were crammed into a train that took them to Manzanar. (Most accounts, including those of the NPS, report that the number of Nikkei was 227, but DeWitt's final report lists 257.) The memorial's cost was partially borne by private contributions, which the government matched. The site was made a part of the renamed Minidoka National Historic Site 500 miles away. This was not only convenient for the NPS but also logical, since most of the Bainbridge Islanders had been sent to the Idaho camp from Manzanar. The park was opened in a festive, well-attended ceremony on July 30, 2011. At Minidoka itself, by 2013 a Minidoka support group had designed, erected, and paid for a large billboard-type honor roll listing the names of the soldiers who had entered the army from that camp, and other improvements, including the reconstruction of a guard tower and creation of an interpretive center, were afoot.

Although a number of congressional Republicans had criticized Clinton for his Antiquities Act monument creation, no such criticism resulted when President George W. Bush did the same thing toward the end of his second term. His Antiquities Act Proclamation 8327 of December 5, 2008, created the World War II Valor in the Pacific National Monument, which included nine separate sites in three states. Five were in or adjacent to Pearl Harbor's Battleship Row: the USS *Arizona* Memorial and Visitor Center, the USS *Utah* Memorial, the USS *Oklahoma* Memorial, the six chief petty officer bungalows on Ford Island, and mooring quays F6, F7, and F8. Three sites were on Alaska's Aleutian Islands, which were invaded by Japanese forces in 1942: a Liberator bomber crash site on Atka, the remains of Japanese military installations on Kiska, and a still littered battlefield on Attu. The last marks the only land battle in World War II fought in North America, although it is seven degrees west of the 180th meridian. The ninth site was in California: it includes both the Tule Lake Segregation Center National Historic Landmark and nearby Camp Tulelake. The latter was a former CCC camp used to house the strikebreakers brought in from other camps in 1944; later it housed German prisoners of war until 1946. Although there is no interpretation now on the site, the NPS says that "the Tule Lake Unit of the World War II Valor in the Pacific National Monument will bring increased understanding of the high price paid by some Americans on the home front." It's about time.

As far as future NPS public interpretation of the camps is concerned, that probably means that in the next decade or so there will be full-scale public interpretations present at both the Minidoka and Tule Lake sites, as well as continuing expanded treatment at Manzanar and on Bainbridge Island. In addition, as a result of a recent congressional enactment, a possible further expansion of the NPS interpretive program in Hawaii is being studied. The Honouliuli Special Resource Study was authorized in Public Law 111-88, enacted by President Barack Obama on October 30, 2009. The study, still in process in mid-2013, has identified thirteen incarceration sites on six Hawaiian Islands. Because Hawaii was under martial law throughout the war, all incarceration was internment. All told there were some 2,000 prisoners, largely persons of Japanese descent, both citizen and alien, and about a hundred German and Italian nationals, and, in the closing months of the war, Japanese prisoners of war. The only purpose-built site in Hawaii, the Honouliuli camp in central Oahu, opened on March 1943 with a capacity of 3,000 but never had more than 320 prisoners. Prior to its opening, prisoners from Oahu had been kept in the existing immigration station and in a makeshift camp on Sand Island, Honolulu. Among its American citizen prisoners were two former members of the Hawaii Territorial Legislature who were of Japanese ancestry.

Although there is no federal memorial of the wartime incarceration in the national capital where it was planned, both Democratic and Republican administrations hastened to endorse a private memorial, authorized by a 1992 statute but privately financed. The National Japanese American Memorial sits in a small triangular park about 600 yards north of the Capitol. Its most striking feature is a fourteen-foot sculpture of two cranes, one struggling to fly free of strands of barbed wire, the other already free, rising above it. It is framed by a low, semicircular wall of ten granite slabs, each bearing the name of a WRA camp and the number of persons incarcerated in it. There are also a bell tower, a rock garden, and cherry trees. The names of Japanese American combat dead in World War II are inscribed, but they are not the central focus, as in Maya Lin's Vietnam Memorial. A statement by Senator Daniel Inouye—"The lessons learned must remain as a grave reminder of what we must not allow to happen again to any group"—is sited to be seen as one leaves the central grouping. The cranes' sculptor was Oklahoma-born Nina Akatsu, whose grandfather was one of the few Issei interned in Hawaii after Pearl Harbor and who died in captivity three months later.

Attorney General Janet Reno, the ranking speaker at the dedication on November 9, 2000, quoted a letter from President Clinton: "We are diminished when any American is targeted unfairly because of his or her heritage. This memorial and the internment sites are powerful reminders that stereotyping, discrimination, hatred and racism have no place in this country."

At the memorial's formal opening on June 29, 2001, the two speakers, Norman Mineta and Daniel Inouye, each personified one of the two groups the memorial honors and demonstrated how far some Japanese Americans had come. Mineta, a ten-year-old Californian when war came, spent most of the war in WRA custody, and the Hawaiian Inouye, who won glory and lost an arm in Italy, were living representatives of the incarcerated and the World War II veterans. Mineta, who had been elected to Congress in 1974 and reelected ten times, gave up his seat in the House in 1995 after the Democrats lost control, and he had to give up his two committee chairs. He became a vice president of Lockheed Martin, a major defense contractor. He left that post in July 2000 when Bill Clinton appointed him secretary of commerce, making him the first Asian American member of the cabinet. It was assumed by many that if Al Gore won the 2000 election, Mineta would become the housing secretary. Although Republican George W. Bush became the president, Mineta stayed in the cabinet. Bush's campaign pledges included having a Democrat in his cabinet and "diversity" among his high-level appointments, and Mineta lobbied to be that Democrat. Mineta's appointment as secretary of transportation fulfilled the first pledge. In postappointment interviews Mineta stressed that he was a "Democrat with both a small 'd' and a large one," and that there were "no Democratic or Republican highways" or partisan "traffic congestion." He joined a cabinet that included an African American secretary of state, two Mexican Americans, and an Arab American. Except among Japanese Americans and his former constituents, Mineta was little known.

Inouye was the best-known Japanese American political figure. After he left a military hospital, he returned to Hawaii, earned a degree at the University of Hawaii, and went on to George Washington University for a law degree in 1952. Back in the islands, he began a law practice and served in the territorial legislature. In the election held immediately after Hawaii achieved statehood in 1959, he was elected to the House of Representatives, where he served until 1963; he had been elected to the Senate in 1962 and was reelected in 1968, 1974, 1980, 1986, 1992, and 1998. By 2001 Inouye had long been a Senate oligarch. Although he preferred to work behind the scenes, he drew national attention as the keynote speaker at the 1968 Democratic National Convention and as a participant in the two most gripping televised Senate committee hearings of the later twentieth century, the investigations into Watergate and the Iran-Contra affair. After Watergate the Gallup poll reported that the low-key and precise Inouye received an 84 percent approval rating, even higher than that of the committee's chair, the flamboyant North Carolina Democrat Sam Ervin.

In the immediate aftermath of the terrorist atrocity that we have learned to call 9/11, speculation about whether "it could happen again" became observation. A tentative analysis of the results, in terms of national security reactions, a dozen years after the events, were much worse than the optimists had hoped for, but not as devastating as the pessimists had feared. As had been the case in 1942, Congress panicked, and with much less cause. On October 26, 2011, just forty-five days after hijacked airliners destroyed the twin towers of New York City's World Trade Center, seriously damaged the Pentagon in Washington, and killed more than 3,000 Americans, President George W. Bush signed the USA Patriot Act, which was designed to override most of the inhibitions provided by the Constitution against overly intrusive government procedures and techniques. Unlike the unanimity of 1942, there was some opposition. It had passed the House by a vote of 357–66, while in the Senate it was 98–1, with only Wisconsin Democrat Russell D. Feingold in lonely opposition. He insisted, vainly, that it was "crucial that civil liberties in this country be preserved, otherwise I'm afraid that terror will win this battle without a shot."

President Bush spoke of the blessings of the new law in a signing statement of some 1,200 words in which a form of the word "terror" occurs twenty times; he closed with an imprecation of "the evil ones." "The law," he said, provided "new tools to fight a present danger." He described the law as preemptive, enabling the government "to identify, to dismantle, to disrupt, and to punish terrorists before they strike." He boasted that the new law makes warrants "valid across all districts and across all States" and asserted, "We're making it easier to seize the assets of groups and individuals involved in terrorism. The Government will have wider latitude in deporting known terrorists and their supporters. The statute of limitations on terrorist acts will be lengthened, as will prison sentences for terrorists." The president's closing claim was that "this Government will enforce this law with all the urgency of a nation at war." In other words, the net effect of the Patriot Act was to give the government war powers without actually going to war.

The government had not waited in many instances for the Patriot Act to be crafted and enacted. By the day before the law was effected, the Justice Department later reported, 360 suspects were in custody, and that number was doubled in less than a month. By that time, however, the Bush administration had developed new fears that focused not on what terrorists might do but on how liberal American judges might rule about the legality of the methods by which the suspects were being seized, both at home and abroad.

On November 13, 2001, President Bush took another soiled leaf from the wartime record of Franklin Roosevelt and issued a military order—"Detention, Treatment, and Trial of Certain Non-Citizens in the War against Terrorism"—which decreed that all such persons, if tried, would be tried by military commissions appointed by him. During World War II, Roosevelt had issued two such military orders pertaining only to two sets of Nazi saboteurs who had landed in the United States by submarine and were quickly captured. The two groups were quickly disposed of in secret military trials; the Supreme Court, in the *Quirin* case in 1942, ruled unanimously that such a trial for unlawful military belligerents in wartime was permissible.

The announcement of Bush's tribunals set off more controversy and drew opposition from some conservatives as well as many liberals. Journalist William Safire criticized them as "Kangaroo Courts." The whole issue of what to do with the hundreds of imprisoned but untried terrorists is, as I write, an unsolved one and a constant affront to anyone who believes in equal justice under law. But as far as the subject of this book is concerned, the term "Non-Citizen" in the title of Bush's order, although it calls to mind the term "Non-Alien" in General DeWitt's notices, is not a euphemism but a distinction.

The focus of the post-9/11 government efforts to uproot domestic terrorism was almost totally directed against aliens, and at the higher levels of the executive branch there have been regular warnings not to make assumptions about guilt based on race or religion. Yet it is clear that, as far as the national mood was concerned, prodded by much of the media, many members of Congress, and large numbers of state and local officials, the CWRIC's description of causes—"race prejudice, war hysteria, and a failure of political leadership"—can be applied to the post-2001 public as well, although religious prejudice, largely absent in 1942, was central in the 9/11 aftermath. The repeated calls for tolerance from the top were not followed up by stern insistence on appropriate behavior by public servants in law enforcement and the various agencies of the Department of Homeland Security. In the 1980s Congressman Norman Mineta, campaigning for redress, touched listeners by describing how as a ten-year-old he had reported for shipment to an assembly center wearing his Cub Scout uniform. In 2001 Secretary of Transportation Norman Mineta took no public action against airlines and their pilots who refused to carry "middle eastern looking" men on certain of their airplanes and gained praise from right-wing journalists for doing so.

A fair reckoning must also note that, as opposed to the general acquiescence in 1942, there was considerable protest. The ACLU acted appropriately, as did a considerable number of members of the public who spoke out against the government's program after 9/11; a surprising number of those who did so used what had been done to the Japanese Americans as a negative reference point. It was clear that the wartime events that had been almost forgotten by press and public in the postwar decades were much more widely known almost six decades after their occurrence. A few years later, after military expeditions in Iraq and Afghanistan had further stoked anti-Muslim rhetoric and activities, some ethnic institutions, like the Japanese American National Museum in Los Angeles, evinced solidarity with the local Muslim community by hosting a joint event in which the events triggered by Pearl Harbor and 9/11 were compared and contrasted. Of course, the scale of the two events was quite different, and, at first glance, what happened to those under suspicion—a thousand or so confined, an uncounted number deported for technical violations usually ignored—cannot compare to the almost total ethnic cleansing and mass incarceration suffered by Japanese Americans. Some have argued that it is not fitting to mention the two events in one breath and continue to insist that the relative mildness of domestic measures taken by the government after 9/11 are clear evidence that a mass incarceration of Americans of whatever ethnicity cannot recur in our multicultural society.

Reflection on the American past suggests to me that such a reaction is far too sanguine. We all speak of Pearl Harbor, but it was just the first of many hammer blows delivered by the Imperial Japanese forces in the weeks and months that followed that attack. Executive Order 9066 was issued on the seventy-second day after the December 7 attack. Had there been further attacks in 2001 or later, would the response have been so relatively mild? And if further attacks were to occur, we can be sure that there would be those in the bloated national security organizations who would put part of the blame on the lack of draconian measures at home.

———

What may turn out to be last significant public reaction stemming from the Japanese Americans cases themselves came on May 24, 2011, when Neal K. Katyal, the acting solicitor general, delivered a lecture in the Great Hall of the Department of Justice on Pennsylvania Avenue in which he discussed, decried, and apologized for the misbehavior of his wartime predecessor, Charles Fahy, in his presentations to the Supreme Court in 1943 and 1944. It was the first public acknowledgment by any sitting Justice Department official, and long overdue.

He had given notice of what he was going to say in a Department of Justice blog, so Attorney General Eric Holder, who gave him a glowing introduction, apparently knew what Katyal was going to say although he made no mention of it. Katyal has said that he had no written text of his eighteen-minute talk, but the gist of it can be reconstructed from press accounts and the blog of the *Legal Times*. After explaining what Edward Ennis and John Burling had told Fahy, without naming them, Katyal asked: "What does Fahy do? Nothing! He decides not to alert the Court."

Katyal went on to assess the consequences of Fahy's decision: "I think it did harm the Court. But it obviously harmed others as well. It harmed approximately 120,000 Japanese Americans. It harmed the department, which led the Court, in part, to the results that it reached. It harmed our reputation as lawyers. Ultimately it harmed our commitment to those magnificent words carved on the front of the Supreme Court, at the top: Equal Justice Under Law."

CHRONOLOGY

1941

December 7—Japanese naval aircraft attack Hawaii; other attacks in Asia and Pacific islands.

December 7–8—United States begins roundup of alien enemies aged fourteen and older.

December 8—United States declares war on Japan—"Date of Infamy" speech.

Late December—Draft boards told to stop calling up Japanese Americans for military service.

1942

February 19—FDR signs Executive Order 9066.

February 25—US Navy ousts all Nikkei from Terminal Island, California.

March 2—General DeWitt issues order establishing military areas.

March 18—Executive Order 9102 establishes War Relocation Authority (WRA).

March 21—Public Law 503 makes violating a military order a crime.

March 24—Curfew established for alien enemies and Nisei.

March 24–31—Civilian Exclusion Order 1 expels all Nikkei from Bainbridge Island, Washington, and sends them to Manzanar, California.

March 28—Min Yasui turns himself in to Portland, Oregon, police for curfew violation.

May 16—Gordon Hirabayashi turns himself in to FBI in Seattle.

May 22—American Civil Liberties Union decides not to contest the constitutionality of incarcerating Japanese American citizens.

May 30—Fred Korematsu, arrested by San Leandro, California, police.

July 12—Mitsuye Endo files habeas corpus petition from Tule Lake Relocation Center.

September 8—Korematsu convicted in San Francisco Federal District Court.

October 20—Hirabayashi convicted in Seattle Federal District Court.

November 16—Yasui found guilty in Portland Federal District Court.

December 6—Manzanar riot; troops fire into unarmed crowd, killing two and wounding at least eleven others, including one GI.

1943

January 29—Secretary of War Stimson announces plan to form Japanese American combat team.

February 8—Loyalty questionnaire program begins in WRA camps.

February 19—Appeals in *Hirabayashi*, *Yasui*, and *Korematsu* come before Ninth Circuit, Federal Court of Appeals in San Francisco, which asks the Supreme Court about procedure.

April 3—Supreme Court agrees to hear *Hirabayashi* and *Yasui*; sends *Korematsu* back to Ninth Circuit for decision.

June 23—Supreme Court upholds Hirabayashi, 9–0; sends Yasui back to Ninth Circuit.

July 3—Judge Roche denies Endo's habeas corpus petition; his decision is appealed to the Ninth Circuit.

July 15—Tule Lake Relocation Center becomes Tule Lake Segregation Center, beginning the most infamous chapters of its history.

November 1–4—A strike and other disturbances at Tule Lake lead to its takeover by an army Military Police battalion, resulting in many gross violations of human rights in an occupation that lasts until January 15, 1944.

December 2—Ninth Circuit sustains Korematsu, 6–1.

1944

January 20—Secretary Stimson announces the reestablishment of the draft for Nisei, in and out of camp.

April/May—Supreme Court agrees to hear *Endo* appeal and schedules it and *Korematsu* for the fall 1944 term.

July 1—Roosevelt signs law making renunciation of US citizenship while in the United States legal in wartime.

December 18—Supreme Court announces decisions upholding *Korematsu*, 6–3, and granting Endo's petition unanimously.

December 18—WRA announces that all its camps will be closed by the end of 1945.

1945

August 14—Japan surrenders; peace treaty signed September 2.

October/November—All WRA camps but Tule Lake closed.

November/December—Wayne Collins's filings for petitions of habeas corpus effectively block further shipping of unwilling renunciants to Japan.

1946–1952

March 20, 1946—Tule Lake Segregation Center closed.

July 15, 1946—President Harry Truman convokes a review honoring the 442nd Regimental Combat Team at the White House.

December 27, 1947—President Truman includes Nisei draft resisters in his pardon of some 1,500 draft resisters of conscience.

July 2, 1948—President Truman signs Japanese American Claims Act.

September 23, 1950—Congress passes Emergency Detention Act over Truman's veto.

June 27, 1952—McCarran-Walter Act abolishes all purely racial or ethnic bars to naturalized citizenship; Issei are the chief immediate beneficiaries.

Since 1953

January 6, 1966—William Petersen's *New York Times Magazine* article initiates national media use of "model minority" stereotype.

December 28–29, 1969—Manzanar Pilgrimage becomes exemplar for refocusing community attention on the wartime camps.

September 26, 1971—President Richard Nixon signs bill repealing 1950 Emergency Detention Act in response to a campaign instituted by Nikkei activists.

February 19, 1976—President Gerald Ford issues Proclamation 4417, "An American Promise," revoking Executive Order 9066.

January 19, 1977—President Ford pardons Iva Ikuko Toguri, who had been convicted of treason in San Francisco in 1949 and was identified as the mythical Tokyo Rose, who had broadcast morale-damaging words directed at American troops in wartime.

July 25–27, 1978—The 1978 JACL biennial convention, meeting in Salt Lake City, endorses a redress proposal eight years after it was first introduced.

July 31, 1980—President Jimmy Carter signs bill creating the Commission on Wartime Relocation and Internment of Civilians (CWRIC).

April 1983—Publication of Peter Irons's book *Justice at War* provides evidence that makes a coram nobis petition feasible. (Irons had discussed his findings with the CWRIC in late 1981.)

November 10, 1983—San Francisco federal district judge Marilyn Hall Patel grants Fred Korematsu's coram nobis petition vacating his 1942 conviction.

September 24, 1987—In the last major action on the coram nobis cases, Ninth Circuit Court of Appeals judge Mary M. Schroeder rules that both counts of Gordon Hirabayashi's 1942 conviction were invalid.

August 10, 1988—President Ronald Reagan signs Civil Rights Act of 1988, which passed a restricted measure for "redress" of the wartime incarceration and expressed a congressional apology.

March 2, 1992—President George H. W. Bush signs bill making Manzanar a National Historic Monument.

January 17, 2001—President Bill Clinton creates the Minidoka National Historic Monument by proclamation.

December 5, 2008—President George W. Bush creates the World War II Valor in the Pacific National Monument by proclamation. It includes sites in the Aleutian Islands, Hawaii, and two sites in California, the Tule Lake Segregation Center and nearby Camp Tulelake.

October 30, 2009—President Barack Obama signs Public Law 111-88 authorizing the Honouliuli Special Resource Study, which has identified thirteen incarceration sites on six of Hawaii's islands.

BIBLIOGRAPHIC ESSAY

Note from the Series Editors: The following bibliographic essay contains the major primary and secondary sources the author consulted for this volume. We have asked all authors in the series to omit formal citations in order to make our volumes more readable, inexpensive, and appealing for students and general readers. In adopting this format, Landmark Law Cases and American Society follows the precedent of a number of highly regarded and widely consulted series.

For general histories of the Japanese Americans and of their wartime incarceration, see my own work: *The Politics of Prejudice* (1962), *Concentration Camps, USA* (1970), *Concentration Camps, North America* (1981), *Asian America* (1988), *Prisoners Without Trial* (2nd ed., 2004), and the edited anthology with Sandra C. Taylor and Harry H. L. Kitano, *Japanese Americans: From Relocation to Redress* (2nd ed., 1991), and *American Concentration Camps: A Documentary History*, 9 vols. (1989); Michi Weglyn, *Years of Infamy* (2nd ed., 1996); and Arthur A. Hansen, ed., *Japanese American World War II Oral History Project*, 6 vols. (1991–1992). For a reference work that approaches comprehensiveness, see Brian Niiya, ed., *Encyclopedia of Japanese American History* (updated ed., 2001), and its continuation and expansion online as the Densho Encyclopedia.

For chapter 1, which presents the facts behind the cases, Akira Iriye, *Pearl Harbor and the Coming of the Pacific War* (1999), is a good introduction to a large literature. The outstanding work on the ACLU is Judy Kutulas, *The American Civil Liberties Union and the Making of Modern Liberalism* (2006). There is no good history of the JACL; Bill Hosokawa, *JACL: In Quest of Justice* (rev. ed., 1992), is an eloquent apology. For the government's list, see John J. Culley, "Enemy Alien Control in the United States during World War II," pp. 128–151, in Kay Saunders and Roger Daniels, eds., *Alien Justice* (2000). I have also learned much from an unpublished manuscript by Culley. Max Paul Friedman, *Nazis and Good Neighbors* (2003), and C. Harvey Gardiner, *Pawns in a Triangle of Hate* (1981), analyze the State Department program. Tetsuden Kashima, *Judgment Without Trial* (2003), and Louis Fiset, *Imprisoned Apart* (1997), focus on Issei internment. The pioneering and still authoritative accounts of army plotting are Stetson Conn's essays "Japanese Evacuation from the West Coast" and "The Hawaiian Defenses after Pearl Harbor," in Conn et al., *Guarding the United States and Its Outposts* (1962). Francis Biddle, *In Brief Authority* (1962), apparently frank, conceals much and sometimes misleads. For Bendetsen, see Klancy de Nevers, *The Colonel and the Pacifist* (2004). Dillon S. Myer, *Uprooted Americans* (1971), is self-serving; Richard Drinnon, *Keeper of*

Concentration Camps (1997), is harsh but telling. US War Department, *Final Report: Japanese Evacuation from the West Coast, 1942* (1943), although "doctored," is an important collection of documents.

For chapter 2, the indispensable book for understanding the Japanese American cases is Peter Irons, *Justice at War* (1983), a work about legal history that made history. Also useful is his edited volume *Justice Delayed* (1989), which includes the coram nobis cases. Oral histories of the three male litigants are online in Densho. Ennis has an enlightening oral history online in the Bancroft Library's Earl Warren Project. See also Gordon K. Hirabayashi, with James A. and Lane Ryo Hirabayashi, *The Story of Hirabayashi v. United States* (2013). I hope to publish a brief biography of Gordon soon.

For chapter 3, the in-house history Samuel Walker, *In Defense of American Liberties* (1990), should be supplemented by the Kutulas book cited above and Dwight Macdonald, "In Defense of Everybody," *New Yorker,* July 11, 18, 1953. Del Dickson, ed., *The Supreme Court in Conference (1940–1983)* (2001), has a few passages about the cases.

For chapter 4, Linda Tamura, *Nisei Soldiers Break Their Silence* (2013), and Shirley Castelnuovo, *Soldiers of Conscience* (2008), are important accounts of discrimination against Nisei soldiers after they were in the army. US War Relocation Authority, *The Evacuated People* (1946), contains useful statistical data. US Selective Service System, *Special Groups* (1953), explains official discrimination. James McNaughton, *Nisei Linguists* (2007), is an army history. Arthur A. Hansen and David A. Hacker, "The Manzanar Riot: An Ethnic Perspective," *Amerasia Journal* 2 (Fall 1974): 112–157, was a milestone article. Eileen Tamura's biography of the Manzanar militant Joseph Kurihara, *In Search of Justice* (2013), is a most effective account of a citizen who voluntarily expatriated. For college students and others who went east of California, see Allan W. Austin, *From Concentration Camp to Campus* (2004); "Eastward Pioneers: Japanese American Resettlement during World War II and the Contested Meaning of Exile and Incarceration," *Journal of American Ethnic History* 26 (2007): 58–84; and *Quaker Brotherhood* (2012). Barbara Takei, "Legalizing Detention: Segregated Japanese Americans and the Justice Department's Renunciation Program," *Journal of the Shaw Historical Library* 19 (2005): 75–105, is the best existing study of Tule Lake. Douglas W. Nelson, *Heart Mountain* (1976), is the best account of the Wyoming camp; Eric W. Muller, *Free to Die for Their Country* (2001), and *American Inquisition* (2007), are major contributions to the literature.

A useful source for chapter 5 is US War Relocation Authority, *The Wartime Handling of Evacuee Property* (1946). John Dower, *War without Mercy* (1986), is a stunning study of wartime attitudes. The annual reports for the Department of Justice for the years 1945 through 1947 fail to account adequately for its export of persons to Japan. P. Scott Corbett, *Quiet Passages* (1987), treats the voyages of the *Gripsholm.* Donald E. Collins, *Native American Aliens* (1985), recounts

Wayne Collins's epic legal struggle for the renunciants. Gladys Ishida, "The Japanese American Renunciants of Okayama Prefecture: Their Accommodation and Assimilation to Japanese Culture" (PhD diss., University of Michigan, 1956), and Eileen Tamura, *In Search of Justice* (2013), present glimpses of renunciant life in Japan. Works that illuminate Truman's actions concerning Japanese Americans include Steve Neal, ed., *Eleanor and Harry* (2002); Donald R. McCoy and Richard T. Ruetten, *Quest and Response* (1973); Roger Daniels, ed., *Immigration and the Legacy of Harry S. Truman* (2010); President's Commission on Civil Rights, *To Secure These Rights* (1947); and Nancy Nakasone-Huey, "In Simple Justice: The Japanese-American Evacuation Claims Act of 1948" (PhD diss., University of Southern California, 1986). For the "standby" concentration camps, see Allan W. Austin, "Loyalty and Concentration Camps in America: The Japanese American Precedent and the Internal Security Act of 1950," in Erica Harth, ed., *Last Witnesses* (2001). Llyn De Danaan, "Mountain of Shell," *Columbia: The Magazine of Northwest History* 25 (Winter 2011–2012): 3–8, sketches a renunciant life.

For chapter 6, the most comprehensive account of redress is Mitchell T. Maki, Harry H. L. Kitano, and S. Megan Berthold, *Achieving the Impossible Dream: How Japanese Americans Obtained Redress* (1999). The general text referred to is Richard Hofstadter, William Miller, and Daniel Aaron, *The United States* (1957). For the "model minority," see William Petersen, *Japanese Americans* (1971), and Daniels, *Asian America* (1988). Carey McWilliams, *Prejudice: Japanese-Americans, Symbol of Racial Intolerance* (1944), was the only book denouncing the treatment of Nikkei issued by an established publisher during the war. For the development of Asian American courses, see Sucheng Chan, *In Defense of Asian American Studies* (2005). For the wartime role of the Fed, see Sandra C. Taylor, "The Federal Reserve Bank and the Relocation of the Japanese in 1942," *Public Historian* 5 (1983): 9–30. Clifford I. Uyeda's autobiography, *Suspended: Growing Up Asian in America* (2000), goes only to the 1950s; see also his "The Pardoning of 'Tokyo Rose,'" *Amerasia Journal* 5 (Fall 1978): 69–84. The most complete version of the CWRIC's final report, *Personal Justice Denied*, was published by the University of Washington Press in 1997. William M. Hohri, *Repairing America* (1988), is a memoir by a redress outlier. For the Smithsonian and the JANM exhibitions, see Tom D. Crouch. "Some Thoughts on Public History and Social Responsibility," *Illinois Historical Journal* 82 (1989): 196–200; and Karen Ishizuka, *Lost and Found* (2006). Angus MacBeth and Orest Kruhlak, oral history interviews by Densho, illuminate American and Canadian redress.

As noted in chapter 7, Peter Irons, ed., *Justice Delayed* (1989), is particularly valuable for the coram nobis cases. The *Seattle Journal for Social Justice* 11:1 (2012) is largely devoted to the *Hirabayashi* coram nobis case, with an introduction by Lorraine Bannai, and essays by Irons, Lane Ryo Hirabayashi, Kathryn

A. Bannai, Karen K. Narasaki, Judge Mary M. Schroeder, Eric K. Yamamoto, Natsu Taylor Saito, and Michael W. McCann. Again, see CWRIC, *Personal Justice Denied* (1997), and Dale Minami's Densho interview.

For chapter 8, see Allan W. Austin, *From Concentration Camp to Campus* (2004), and "Eastward Pioneers: Japanese American Resettlement during World War II and the Contested Meaning of Exile and Incarceration," *Journal of American Ethnic History* 26 (2007): 58–84. For attitudes toward exogamous marriage, see Norimitsu Onishi, "Japanese in America Looking Beyond Past to Shape Future," *New York Times*, December 25, 1995, 1; Jeffery M. Burton, Mary M. Farrell, Florence B. Lord, and Richard W. Lord, *Confinement and Ethnicity* (2000). The changing status of National Parks Service facilities can be traced on the NPS website. For Bainbridge Island, see Mary Woodward, *In Defense of Our Neighbors* (2006). There are accounts of the Japanese American Memorial in the capital in Elaine Sciolino, "Fighting for Space in Memorial Heaven," *New York Times*, June 28, 2001, A24, and on the sculptor Nina Akatsu's website. For *Quirin*, see Louis Fisher, *Military Tribunals and Federal Power* (2005). William Safire, "Kangaroo Courts," *New York Times*, November 26, 2001, A17, skewers contemporary military tribunals; for a scholarly analysis, see David D. Cole, *Enemy Aliens* (2005).

INDEX

National Council for Japanese American Redress (NCJAR), 176, 186–190
national defense migration, 20
National Historic Monuments, 193
National Japanese American Memorial, 196–197
National Museum of American History, 157
National Park Service, 193–194, 196
National Register of Historic Places, 193
Native Sons of the Golden West, 43, 154
naturalization, 3–4, 133
Navy, US, 26
NCJAR (National Council for Japanese American Redress), 176, 186–190
Nevada, 25
New Deal, 47
New Deal Lawyers (Irons), 166
Nidoto Nai Yoni Memorial, 195
nihonmachi. See Japantowns
Nikkei, 137, 189, 194, 195
    as college students, 141
    farm ownership, 116
    internal migration after war ends, 114
    living east of California, 138
    population in Hawaii by 1960, 137–138
    postwar housing, 139
    and renunciants, 133
    return to Japan, 117–118
    return to West Coast after war, 114–115
    unemployment, 117
9/11. *See* September 11 terrorist attacks
Ninth Circuit Court of Appeals, 42, 61, 126, 175–176, 184

Nisei, 1–2, 5–6, 13, 16, 19, 87–88, 107, 130, 191
    allowed to attend college, 94
    American Legion post removes names from honor roll, 81
    apprehended for curfew violation, 35
    citizenship restored to, 125
    deported to Japan, 120
    and draft, 31, 41, 108–109, 132
    442nd Regimental Combat Team, 84, 85
    loyalty of, 90
    and Manzanar Pilgrimage, 142–143
    as "model minority," 140
    as Seattle public employees, 18
    supported by JACL, 51
    at Tule Lake WRA Relocation Center (CA), 85
    veterans' groups, 133
    women, 152–153
Nisei Soldier (documentary), 157
Nixon, Richard, 145
non-aliens, 200
non-citizens, 199–200

Oahu, 14, 196
Obama, Barack, 196
Oberdorfer, Louis F., 187
Office of Redress Administration (ORA), 164, 165, 189
Office of War Mobilization, 70
Okada, Hito, 20
Okazaki, Steven, 157
Olson, Culbert L., 94
Omnibus Public Land Act, 193
Omura, James, 110
100th Battalion, 88–89
O'Neill, Tip, 150–151
Open Door policy, 2
Opler, Morris E., 51